YOU KNOW
YOUR
WAY HOME

You Know Your Way Home
by Suzanne Jauchius

www.YouKnowYourWayHome.com

Published by Bree Noa Publishing Company
P.O. Box 204, West Linn, Oregon 97068
Email: Info@BreeNoa.com · Phone: (503) 655-2386

Cover Art Painting: Steve Hanks
"Like Diamonds in the Sun"
ShanksArt@aol.com

Cover Design: Alina Blankenship
Author Photos: Tais Kulish
Set in Book Antiqua · Designed by Kathleen Krushas

Triskelion stone is a Trademark of Bree Noa Publishing Company

ISBN-13: 978-0-9840892-0-8
ISBN-10: 0-9840892-0-9
Printed in Canada

You Know Your Way Home

A Modern Initiation Journey

Doreen
Best to you on your
way Home!

Suzanne Jauchius
10/29/16

Suzanne Jauchius

"THERE ARE NO MORE
MYSTERY SCHOOLS.
THE ENTIRE WORLD IS A
MYSTERY SCHOOL."

– Rudolf Steiner

For Conner and Kaylyn

*My Lakota friends say that all of our ancestors line up
behind us to extend through us. If we come into this world
with an appropriate alignment of genetics and heritage, we
might be honored to carry "the medicine."
Ho, mitákuye oyás'n!*

One

"My God! Follow that car!" I shouted, pointing emphatically beyond the gravel parking lot to the road ahead.

My friend Debbi shook her head. "Uh, excuse me. You're the only one who can see it," she said with a bemused smile as she turned the car onto the deserted road.

It was October, 1989.

I'd been asked by Debbi, who worked with a local search and rescue team, to assist with the search for a little boy who had been abducted. Debbi and I had been friends since grade school. Our history together had familiarized her with my special way of *seeing* the unseeable. Having never worked on a missing person case before, I was reluctant but willing to give it a try.

The little boy, four-year-old Lee Iseli, disappeared from a southeast Portland playground after walking to the store with his older brother. As Debbi presented me with the facts of the case, I *saw* the boy in a blue house. I felt certain he was still alive. At this point I remained hopeful because it felt like whoever had him loved him. On the third day of my involvement, I awoke with a heavy heart and phoned

Debbi. I knew Lee was dead. A day later the news reported that his body had been found near a parking lot at Vancouver Lake in Vancouver, Washington. Shortly after she
heard the news, Debbi called and asked if I'd accompany
her to the crime scene. The FBI hadn't yet concluded its investigation and she had obtained permission to bring me
to the "dump site," as the search and rescue team referred
to it, before the park was reopened to the public.

"The FBI? You've got to be kidding. They don't work
with psychics," I protested, feeling more than just a little
intimidated.

"Who cares?" was her glib response. "They said you
could come. Let's go." She was eager for the opportunity.
I was not.

Later, as we pulled into the lake's parking lot, continuing past the yellow crime-scene tape, I *saw* close to the
tree line a parked car which appeared to me to be made of
Plexiglas. I suspected Debbi couldn't see it, but I pointed
anyway and excitedly asked if she saw it too.

"No," she confirmed.

I told her I needed to walk over to the *car* alone and
asked her not to be concerned about what she might see
me doing. Getting out of her car, we were approached
by two men wearing hats and jackets emblazoned with
FBI insignia. We introduced ourselves; they seemed more
amused than impressed. I excused myself and approached
this mysterious vehicle.

I soon identified the phantom car as either a Vega or
Pinto, possibly blue, with wood-paneled sides. It was a
hatchback. Stepping around to the back of the car, I found
myself lifting the hatchback.

*I looked down and noticed I seemed to be wearing steel toe
work boots. I heard the word "Freightliner." I lifted a large gar-*

bage bag from the trunk which I knew held the little boy's body. Turning, I carried the bag down a short path into the woods. After walking a few feet, I stopped and lay the body bag down among the dried leaves and pine needles. I brandished a scalpel-type knife and...

Horrified, I jumped back and the *seeing* stopped.

Turning to Debbi and the agents, who had quietly followed me, I described what I'd *seen*. The agents exchanged glances, but offered no comment.

I had been told previously by search and rescue that authorities were looking for a camper pickup. The car I had seen was unmistakably a hatchback, a Vega or Pinto, with wood-paneled sides. I insisted that was the vehicle they needed to search for. The agents thanked me and told me it had been "interesting." It was Debbi's and my turn to exchange glances.

I only shrugged. "Let's go."

We returned to Debbi's vehicle and as we buckled our seat belts, I *saw* the car again pulling out of the parking lot in front of us.

"Follow that car!" I shouted, pointing emphatically beyond the gravel parking lot to the road ahead.

We tailed the *car* for several miles, twisting and turning through downtown Vancouver. As we merged onto the highway leading to Camas, the *car* began to fade.

"Oh no," I groaned.

"What's wrong?" Debbi asked.

"We lost it," I announced.

She pulled over to the side of the road and turned to face me. "What do you think? Does the guy live in Camas?"

"No."

I sank back in my seat and closed my eyes. I *saw* him abducting another child.

"I believe that he's going to abduct another child soon. Most likely within the next 10 days. I think he'll strike in Camas!"

We sat quietly, staring at the cars zipping by on the highway next to us.

"A Vega or Pinto," Debbi mused.

I nodded. "He'll get caught this time. He'll make a mistake and get messy. They will catch him in Camas." I had no idea where these words were coming from.

"Great," Debbi said unenthusiastically. "We need to go back to the lake and give this information to the FBI."

"Are you kidding?" I asked incredulously. "They don't care about what a psychic sees."

"It doesn't matter," she said, turning the car around. "We're going back!"

That afternoon after she dropped me off at home, I excitedly shared with my husband T.J. what I'd seen. He was watching TV. As I finished my strange tale, he looked at me and said, "Great, so what's for dinner?"

One morning, two weeks later, as I made coffee and my husband left for work, life provided me with what I've come to refer to as a cosmic nudge toward my true destiny. T.J.'s morning ritual consisted of the drive down our long gravel driveway, opening the gate, stopping to grab the daily paper from the paper box and continuing on to work. This particular morning, however, I heard him turn around and head back up the driveway. Thinking he must have forgotten something, I greeted him at the door. He clutched the newspaper in his hand. He wasn't smiling. As he brushed past me, I followed him into the kitchen.

Turning to me, he threw the paper down on the countertop and spoke, carefully enunciating each word. "I want to know how the hell you do this!"

He slammed his fist down on the front page.

The bold headline across the top of *The Oregonian* blared "Police Arrest Suspect in Iseli, Neer Killings" above a color photo of a yellow Pinto hatchback with wood-paneled sides!

My mouth fell open. "Oh my God," I whispered as I picked up the paper. Westley Allan Dodd had been apprehended within blocks of a theater in Camas, Washington after attempting to abduct a young boy. The boy's screams had alerted nearby adults who then pursued Dodd. They were able to apprehend him because his car wouldn't start.

"My God," I whispered again.

The media swarmed the blue house where Dodd lived and had held Lee Iseli captive before killing him. Dodd had taken photos of Lee and kept a journal. In it he referred to his love for the boy. Scalpels were found. Dodd had at one time worked at a place called Fruitlander – not "Freightliner." It was all here: the blue house, the feeling of love, the scalpel, the employer. Everything I had *seen*.

I looked up at my husband, who was staring at me expectantly.

"Well, how did you do that?"

I said softly, "I just saw it."

We stared at each other, tensions mounting. Inside I quaked, trembling with excitement, knowing my *seeing* had been true.

"I don't like it," he said. Simultaneously, an old, deep fear was screaming at me as time collapsed. "And I don't want it in my life!" he continued, shouting now. "It's not normal!"

Two

"It's not normal."

I was eight years old, dressed up, gift in hand, ready to go to my friend's birthday party. At eight, I'd begun a round of birthday parties. They were fun and I loved the games.

"Suzanne, are you listening?" My mother's terse voice broke the spell of excitement I'd been feeling all morning in anticipation of the afternoon festivities with my school friends. "Suzanne!" she said again. My mother now had me by the shoulders, leaning over to look me in the eyes.

"Did you hear what I said? You can only go to this party if you promise not to bring home all the prizes." Her voice was loud and clear.

"But I can see…." I began.

She cut me off with a shake. "It's not normal!" she said dismissively. "I mean it. No prizes or there won't be any more parties."

I nodded reluctantly, struggling with the lump that had suddenly formed in my throat. Apparently I was a source of embarrassment for her. When playing party games, even with my eyes blindfolded, I could *see* where the tail went on the donkey, who was holding the thimble, etc. I thought I was just smart and clever.

I began to withdraw. Something in me was wrong.

I just wanted to fit in, to be normal. I nearly died trying.

On reflection, it's hard to recall any one incident as the single moment when the disconnect began. It probably occurred around the age of five or six. My night dreams were so vivid, so real, that I struggled with knowing when I was awake. With all of a child's innocence, I remember frequently asking my mother upon awakening which dream I was in now. It wasn't that question that made me feel different, but the look on her face as she attempted to respond to me.

When I was young, we rented a house in North Portland. It was a big old stone house, as cold inside as it looked outside. I began first grade at Peninsula Grade School. My best memory of that year was walking to school every day under the fir and chestnut trees that lined the streets. On windy days, an old fir along the way would creak and groan in the wind. I was scared to walk under it. So I ran.

During this time, I shared a bedroom with my younger brother and sister. Shortly after being tucked in for the night, I had my first *memory* of a future event. I remembered a bed catching on fire. I could see the smoke. Innocently, I discussed this at breakfast the next morning.

"Remember when Sally's bed caught on fire?"

Everyone looked at me with confounded expressions.

"Sally's bed never was on fire," my parents assured me. I was confused but accepting; they knew best.

A few weeks later the blanket on my sister's bed began smoldering from an electrical short. It happened just as I had *remembered*.

After this incident, I became more aware and cautious of the thoughts that visited my mind. I remember sitting on the front steps of that old stone house attempting to make my thoughts go away. I believed I made events occur by thinking about them. If I hadn't thought it, it would never have happened, right? In my magical child mind, I would try to hold only a white triangle, an innocuous image. If I could only do that, I believed all would be well in the world.

The next year, as I began second grade, school testing indicated I should be advanced to third grade. I am grateful that my parents decided against it. When asked a question on a test, I could *hear* or *see* the answer, rather than have a genuine understanding of the information. I was unable to demonstrate the process I used to arrive at my answers. It seemed that I had an inner informant.

At the beginning of my third grade year, we moved to a tiny white house in a big field next to a grade school in Southeast Portland. It had three rooms: a living room, kitchen and one huge bedroom that my parents partitioned off with a sheet to make two bedrooms.

It was at this house my life took a dramatic change through an unsettling series of events. My mother began providing daycare for some neighbor kids, two girls, ages three and five, and their brother, who was in my class. The three-year-old was not potty trained. Every time she wet her pants, my mom would scold and smack her. She sat on the toilet a lot. I'd seen Mom hysterical before, but she had never been physically hurtful. It scared me. If I cried, she'd turn on me and tell me that she would give me something to cry about. She had become really quick with her hands. I tried to stay out of the way. She'd make us sit quietly on chairs for hours, threatening to tie us up if we moved. She left some old white clothesline in sight in case we doubted her.

I found comfort where I could. The neighbor boy had a red pony named, aptly, Red. I spent hours out by his pasture, pulling clover and vetch and feeding it to him. Comfort came on the scent of the sweet grass released when he chewed, and in the sound of the occasional snort and stomp of hoof when a fly would bite.

I was in love. I dreamed about horses. I dreamed I was a horse.

My father sold insurance and was frequently transferred. I went to eight different schools between kindergarten and fifth grade. I became an expert on Alaska and the Yukon Territory; it was what each new class was studying. With each move, I became quieter and more withdrawn, fearful to make friends. At each new house, I would explore the yard while my parents unpacked. I would get to know every flower, shrub and tree. I especially loved the trees. They were stalwart and dependable; they had deep roots, which I longed for. I envied their long lives and nobility. I would pretend that I was one of them. Often we talked, as they seemed, somehow, to care about me.

I had two schools and two teachers in Salem and then we moved to Vancouver, Washington. On our last move from Salem I didn't even know we were moving. My folks just showed up at school with a moving van. I couldn't finish the clay caterpillar I was making or my recorder lessons. I remember crying about that, but mostly I remember the sympathetic look in the teacher's eyes as she explained how I could finish it at home. I threw it away a few days later.

Somewhere, among all the moves, I began to see lights in my room at night. I would call out to my dad for comfort when the orbs would appear.

"There is nothing. See, there's nothing there," he insisted.

I knew they were there: three orbs, two large and one small, but after my initial surprise, they did not seem at all threatening. Over time I began thinking of them as "my light family." I would also awaken during the night to what appeared as illuminated cobwebs spanning my room. Frequently, large spiderlike forms moved through the dewy webs. Eventually I would no longer be startled by their appearance either.

My brother Russ had not yet entered school at eight years old. Russ had been slow to walk and slow to talk. He managed okay; he was just slow. He talked funny. We couldn't always understand what he was saying which often made him frustrated, but he was just one of us kids. His tortoiseshell glasses, at least, made him look smart. When Russ was eight, Mom enrolled him in school. My father and maternal grandmother attempted to persuade her to defer for another year and to at least have him evaluated first. Her decision was immutable.

Russ was so proud to be going to school. We had gone clothing shopping the week before, so we were confidently well turned out. We walked excitedly hand in hand to school that first day. I made sure that he arrived safely at his classroom, shiny new lunch pail and school supplies in hand.

At the end of the first week, after I had picked Russ up from his classroom, the principal called us into his office as we walked by. Handing me a note for my parents, he told me, "Your brother may not return here."

With much dread, I delivered the note and predictably, all hell broke loose. Mom became hysterical. As Dad attempted to reason with her, it escalated. We three children hid in the bedroom. I heard one of them reading portions of the note aloud. The words "Russ can't learn his colors" stuck with me.

I felt certain I could remedy the situation. A few days later, out on the front porch I set up a classroom. I had paper and colors. I would teach Russ so that he could return to school. Mom interrupted our "class" and asked accusingly what I thought I was doing. She snatched up the colors and paper and demanded that I never, ever do that again. I sat stunned. Russ appeared divided and confused, unable to reconcile his eagerness to learn with Mom's angry demands.

This new awareness about my brother pushed our mother over whatever edge she had been teetering on. Our world as children became full of inconsistency. One minute it was okay to be playing. The next we had to sit in our chairs without making a sound. It was Russ who took the brunt of it. At the least thing, he would get a whipping. It killed me to watch and be so helpless. The neighborhood kids soon found if they accused Russ of anything, Mom would come blasting out of the house and strike him. I couldn't convince her that they were lying without her turning on me.

One day, I was helping a neighbor bake cookies. Her kitchen window looked out on our backyard. Suddenly she gasped and with tears in her eyes, more to herself than to me asked, "Why does she do that to him?" I looked out the window. My crazed mother was whipping on my brother. I had no answer for her.

Why did no one intervene?

Back then, you minded your own business. Today, we children would have been removed from our parents' custody. On more than one occasion when Dad arrived home, I would "tell" on Mom. If he would only see Mom's handprint on Russ' bottom or the belt mark on his legs. I desperately wanted my dad to come home, scoop us kids up and take us away. He never did. He couldn't. He made excuses for her. "Your mom really loves you, she's just confused."

When I was in seventh or eighth grade, the school added a class for children with special needs. Russ could go back to school. He was 10 or 11 years old. Mom, however, had difficulty letting him be with other kids in the Special Ed class. She maintained that he was not "like them." But Dad insisted he go, and the Special Ed teacher knew how to work with mom. Russ was back in school.

Our tenth and final move came in the middle of my fifth grade year. I was so happy to be moving back into the old neighborhood in Southeast Portland returning to the school I'd left at the beginning of fourth grade. My old friends and familiar faces were such a comfort to me.

A curious thing happened at this time. In that year our class went through a series of physical tests, such as eye tests and hearing tests. It was during the hearing test that I was singled out. Being 5'8" in the sixth grade and the new kid again, this was not enviable when all you want is to fit in.

I was in the library with all my classmates for our hearing test. We were asked to put on cold, metal headphones then lay our heads down on the table so we couldn't see each other. The test givers, a man and a woman, were in the back of the room. We were to raise our hands each time that we heard the sound that they were dialing in. At the conclusion of the test we were instructed to raise our heads. Everyone then was dismissed, except for me. Concerned that I had been cheating, they insisted on retesting me. I was instructed to lay my head down and once again was administered the high frequency tones. With each tone I raised my hand. When the test was finally completed, one of the facilitators approached me, informing me I could raise my head and remove the ear phones. As I handed them back to her, she looked at me with one hand on her hip, the ear phones in her other hand.

"You couldn't possibly hear those last few tones," she said accusingly. Her tone frightened me.

She continued derisively, "Only dogs hear those sounds. You're not a dog are you?"

Returning to my classroom, I took my seat among the stares and gawks of my friends.

In bed that night I had a new awareness of my hearing. I realized there was a constant tone in my room when the house got quiet at night, a sort of hissing. It seemed to be coming from the walls. What was I hearing?

Today, I believe that what I heard was the movement of electricity through the wires in the wallboard.

That same year, my mom had a full hysterectomy. My grandparents came to stay while she was in the hospital. All I recall about that time is Mom coming home and going straight to bed. She went into her room, closed the door and didn't come out for months. When she finally emerged and my grandparents left, I took over Mom's parental responsibilities. Each day when I arrived home from school, she'd be in the darkened living room on the sofa watching soaps. I'd have a list of chores: cleaning, mopping and cooking. If I didn't do a chore right, I'd have to do it again. No one noticed or cared that I'd become a star athlete, student body vice president or rally girl. I noticed my mom's growing collection of prescription drugs she kept on the windowsill above the kitchen sink.

My sister Sally and I were five years apart. She was, without doubt, Mom's favorite. She started first grade the year Mom had her hysterectomy. I was responsible for getting her off to school. How different her school experience was from mine. Because we never moved during her school years, Sally was able to develop real friendships. She was well liked, cute and sweet. Mostly I loved her and felt responsible and protective of her. Sometimes I hated her.

She told me once how hard it was following me at school. I was an honor roll student most of the time and active in sports. She hated sports and PE and cared even less about her grades. She was, however, social, funny and unafraid. She thought nothing of cutting class or sneaking a smoke. I envied her ability to laugh in the face of the authorities. There seemed to be no real consequences for her behavior, unlike I who would get grounded if I was late getting home from school. The more I did right, the more that was expected of me. Sally got by with a laugh and a shrug. Because I knew what punishments Mom was capable of, I would cover for Sally. I couldn't protect Russ, but I could protect her.

Fortunately for me, I had a refuge, a friend's farm I visited at every opportunity. During summers, it would offer sanctuary for a week or more. My love for horses grew as did my relationship with nature. After those extended visits I would cry all the way home. It felt like I'd been born into the wrong family.

Sometimes on visits to the farm, we slept outside. Lying under the stars was one of the most awe-inspiring events of my young life. I remember staring up into that darkness and sort of falling into it. It was in one of those moments the notion of infinity occurred to me. Sometimes I could feel myself hovering on the edge of forever, stretching out into the stars, beguiled by something deep inside that wanted to join them out there. Back in those days, there were only stars up there. A shooting star could quickly become a UFO.

The arrival of Sputnik had been quite an event. Everyone stared into the night to watch the Russian satellite pass overhead. I felt the excitement too, but also a quiet sadness. It didn't seem right to me. Man's presence seemed intrusive in the heavens.

The last house we'd moved into sat on about an acre of land. It was fenced and boasted a small ramshackle barn. I became determined to have my own horse. I babysat in the summers and on occasional weekends. Mostly I used the money for school clothes, but I also kept a stash for a horse. Every Sunday for months, I pored over the classified ads, hoping to find "the one." It didn't matter that both parents said no; I was determined. I'd found an old postcard some years back, which I tacked on the back of my bedroom door. It was a photo of a house on a hill with land sloping gently to a pond below. On the hillside several horses grazed. With each move, that postcard came along to each new bedroom door. This was my dream.

I had saved $90. Perhaps not believing it could happen, my dad told me that if I could find a horse for $90 I could get it. I shifted into high gear. In all my spare moments, I was out back repairing the fence and cutting the blackberries that had grown over the old barn. I worked tirelessly preparing for that inevitable day.

One brisk Sunday morning in the fall, I found the ad! A nine-month-old colt for sale: $90. It mattered not that he wasn't gelded or that he couldn't be broke for at least two years. This was my horse. A cowboy friend from the farm drove me to see him. It was, of course, love at first sight. He was bay, with Appaloosa in his breeding but no spots. His shaggy winter coat was caked in mud. He was not a pretty picture but I loved him.

I christened him Banner for the way he held his tail so high when he ran. He was wonderful. He was mine. The most important part for me as a tall, awkward pre-teen was that Banner became my confidante. I told him everything. When I was sad and crying his soft nuzzle on my arm reassured me. I could lie with him on his bed of straw and feel safe. I think he saved my life.

Three

Just as life began feeling stable after our many moves, change intruded again. Dad had begun driving cabs, working mostly nights. One morning he came home in a very good mood. He'd had a fare to Seattle and back. His pockets were full. While waiting for his fare to complete his business in Seattle, Dad had gone into a club and met a man who was singing there. He told Mom that the man sang and looked just like Harry Belafonte. His name was James. Mom was in love with Belafonte's music, so it didn't take much for Dad to persuade her to go on a rare weekend away to see James perform in Seattle. This was the first of several trips they would take to see him. He became a frequent topic of conversation.

Mom seemed to undergo a metamorphosis. She often seemed intoxicated; inconsistent with the prudish behavior we had always known from her. Before these club visits, she didn't smoke, didn't drink, never wore make-up and dressed very old fashioned. Suddenly she dressed differently and wore lipstick and mascara.

This happened about the time I had been desperately wanting to wear make-up and nylons to school, pleas which had always been met with a firm "No." Now, *Mom* suggested that I wear a little lipstick. I took her change of heart as a sign from God and ran with it. I got to stand and gaze in front of the Maybelline counter, brow furrowed with decisions, just as I'd so often envied other girls doing.

Mom and I were pals! Warily. I knew she could still turn on me.

I came home from school one day to a surprise, an attractive black man sitting at our kitchen table. I was about 14, and it was the early 1960s, when American society was coming of age with respect to people of other cultures and color. Thanks to events in Birmingham and Vietnam, the times they were a-changin'.

Nevertheless, I was still taken aback to see a black man in our home. James had moved to Portland. He would be staying with us for a few days. The days stretched into weeks.

With James around, it was party time at the Murphy house. We had a star living with us. For the first time, hard liquor was consumed in the house: bourbon, vodka and Scotch. Friends would come over and James would sing and people drank. A few friends fell away. Some of my school friends told me "If that black man is there, I can't come over." I felt scared and put off by my parents' new behavior. I spent a lot of time with Banner or in my room reading. I was accused of being a prude by my own mom. Had we traded places?

I liked James. He and I would sit and talk for as long as Mom would allow. We talked philosophy. He'd help me with my homework. Dad was still working nights. What was Dad thinking? Never once did I feel uneasy with James, unlike some of my parents' other male friends who had begun to notice me in ways that frightened me and made me feel uncomfortable. But James was safe. He was fond of Sally, who would sit and listen to him sing.

One morning as we three kids waited for the school bus, Mom and James came outside and stood with us.

It was bad enough I had to be seen with my little sister and brother, but my mom and a black man? I wanted to die! When the bus came, every face in every window was gawking. I was so embarrassed, as only a teenager can be. At the same time, I loathed myself for feeling bad.

My tolerance for this entire guest-in-the house experience ended when I came home from school one day to find Mom lying, fully clothed, on Russ's bed next to James, who had been staying in his bedroom. She laughed at my discomfort. I shut down. I knew this was not okay. It felt like I was a stranger in my own home. I fled to the barn, tears burning my face. I never told Dad. Where was he? Didn't this other man in the house bother him?

A few days later James moved out. He had gotten a job singing at a nightclub across town and would live in a motel a few blocks from the club. We could be a family again. But something had forever changed.

Mom's behavior was either manic or depressed. She and Dad fought a lot. She blamed and loathed Dad's family and reminded me often that I was just like "those Murphys." A dark yearning began forming, a longing to know my paternal grandparents. I resolved to someday meet them.

Sometimes during our parents' raging battles, we children huddled on the stairs, Sally and Russ crying, my arms around them, trying to be strong. If we appeared too soon in Mom's line of vision after one of these bouts, we too caught her wrath. Usually I would just start cleaning house. If I looked like I was taking care of her, she'd leave me alone.

Ah—so many seeds of codependency.

Four

Around this time, some peculiar events began to occur. Suddenly the old house we had lived in for years seemed to be haunted. Things definitely started going bump in the night. At first it was things that might be explained away. Cupboard doors would open by themselves. Lights that were turned off would be on. Missing items would show up in different parts of the house. Then it accelerated. We would be awakened in the night to pounding on the roof and along the walls. After one event, my mom and I watched the door handles turning on two of our outside doors. No one was there.

We called the police on one such terrifying occasion. After a cursory investigation, the police dismissed the incident with a meaningful glance at each other.

The most mystifying incidents seemed to occur in my bedroom, which was situated in a corner directly above my parents' bedroom. My mom would frequently hear me get up and walk across my room and down the stairs. She thought I might be sleepwalking, and determined that the next time she would try to catch me. The following night, she heard footsteps across my bedroom floor, along the hall and down the stairs. Aha! This is what she had been waiting for. She flung the stairway door open. To her horror, no one was there. This continued, along with other bumps and rappings. Soon the unexplainable became commonplace.

I, however, was not convinced of the footsteps, thinking it could be attributed to Mom's hysteria, until friends came to stay with us while Mom had a simple surgery. Dad was working nights, so Jim and Jane slept in Mom and Dad's bedroom. The morning after their first (and last) night, Jane, wide-eyed, said she wouldn't stay another moment. She'd heard the footsteps from my room come down the stairs and stop at the foot of their bed. Sitting up, expecting to see me standing there, she was horrified to see nothing. They fled.

Years later after study and research, I would come to understand that the old house had not become suddenly haunted. It was me, poltergeisting.

Another odd phenomenon began occurring. I would "wake up" hearing voices and movement in the other room. Sometimes I felt a cat jump on the bed with me. During these sensations, I couldn't move; it was as if I were paralyzed. I would struggle to wake up, but usually just fall back to sleep and awaken naturally. If I were successful in waking myself during this occurrence, it would feel like a thousand volts of electricity passing through me and I would be drenched in sweat. It was not a pleasant experience.

Psychiatrists refer to this phenomenon as "the hag experience," in which a person experiences sleep paralysis, sometimes affecting breathing and the ability to respond to one's surroundings. Raymond A. Moody, Jr., M. D., author of *Life after Life*, explained to me that the hag experience is not uncommon or unnatural. Usually caused by stress or irregular sleep patterns, it is a phenomena in which the lack of muscle tone which is part of REM sleep intrudes into other stages of sleep. It generally occurs during the hypnopompic state, the state of sleep prior to waking. For the longest time I feared it was a paranormal experience, as though something were trying to possess me. I do so love how once we understand something we no longer need fear it. It was indeed this need to understand that set me on my mystical path.

After Jim and Jane stayed with us, the word was out about our "haunted house." One day a family friend came by with her Ouija board. She had the bright idea the Ouija would tell us who was haunting us. We had some fun and scary times with that board. For me it confirmed my own abilities with telepathy. I always "knew" what the answers would be whether I was the one playing the board or not.

Through the years our family had gone to church off and on. The old church on Main Street was the one we called home. I became active in the teen youth group there, mostly because the teen advisors were such a hoot. However, sitting and listening to Sunday services always brought up more questions than answers. It seemed to me that the preacher didn't know what he was talking about, but I liked him just the same. That is, until the day he made a house call.

I can't recall where I'd gotten the little ceramic statue of St. Francis, but I loved it. Here was a man who not only loved and communicated with the birds but who had also been witnessed, on more than one occasion, levitating. I liked him.

In my many hours riding or walking, objects would often catch my eye. A leaf, a rock, a feather, a twig; I would pocket it and add it to my collection of special things kept in a shoe box under my bed.

One day, for no particular reason, I got out my St. Francis statue and placed him on a table in the living room. I surrounded him with objects from my collection. A few crystals my uncle had given me (he did demolitions for the highway department and often brought me amazing quartz crystals) and a candle completed the display.

It remained there for weeks, seemingly unnoticed, until the day the pastor came to call. As soon as he entered the living room, his eyes fell upon St. Francis. He exploded, quizzing my mother, wanting to know "the meaning of this." It was "blasphemy" he said, to have a display of saints in the house. Our church did not recognize saints.

"We are not Catholics," he reminded her. She turned an accusing look at me and I fled. Later, after he left, I was reminded what a source of embarrassment I was to my mom. "What's wrong with you?" she asked me, the shameful words sticking to me like a neon sign for the world to see. She told me to remove my display immediately.

That room was never again the same to me. A certain sweetness was missing. My silences grew deeper. It began to occur to me that I did not know how to behave in the world and I had no one to take my cues from. Maybe I could be invisible.

Five

By the end of sophomore year, it seemed I was the only girl in school interested in horses. The topic of all conversations among my friends was boys. Even my friend Claire, who did have her own horse, had a series of crushes. Boys.

It was hard to imagine a boy being attracted to me. I was at least a foot taller than most. I had acne. My clothes didn't even come close to the latest styles. Because I was so tall, nothing stylish fit me, making clothes shopping traumatic. It also gave my mom an opportunity to remind me of all my misproportions. My legs and arms were too long, my feet were too big. It costs so much more to find clothes for me, etc. My comfort clothes at home were jeans and sweatshirts, but at school girls were required to wear dresses. I thought I must look ridiculous most of the time. I pretty much hated high school. I didn't turn out for any clubs or sports as I had in grade school. In my desire to become invisible, I had become a wallflower.

At home I was reassured by Mom that I would have a hard time ever "finding a husband." Maybe that's why she became my scout, pointing out nice-looking guys or commenting loudly when she thought someone was no-ticing me. I hated it. I was, however, aware of older men noticing me.

In high school, I studied languages in hopes of becom-ing an interpreter, completing four years of Latin and three of French. I was fascinated by how people form thoughts differently from culture to culture. I didn't do well in science and math, although I excelled in and loved geometry. I also loved English literature and writing. During junior and senior years, I was on the school paper staff. I saw myself going to college.

Excited about a future immersed in foreign languages, I eagerly anticipated the upcoming senior counseling session with Mr. Decourcy, the school's guidance counselor, whom I had never met. After scanning my aspirations for college, he peered at me over my transcript with a condescending smile. My excitement deflated to embarrassment as he queried why I would even consider a course of study in languages. When I described my goal of becoming an interpreter, his stunned look said it all. He assured me there was no future for me in that field. He wanted to know why there were no office skills classes in my transcript. A girl of my "obvious" intelligence should have amassed the skills of stenography, typing, bookkeeping and shorthand by now.

He presented as an example one of my female classmates who already had secured a job after school working in a law office as a secretary. I felt like I'd been kicked in the stomach. Numb now, I dutifully signed up for a typing class. I felt the fool, believing I could have been a foreign interpreter. His parting shot was to remind me that girls went to college only to find a husband anyway. The defeat I felt leaving his office changed the course of my life.

With a last ember of hope, I took home applications for grants and scholarships. Surely, Dad and Mom would get behind my college plans. Mom ignored me, bemused. I optimistically approached my dad. Dad believed in me.

He had supported my efforts in school, always the one to sign my report cards and comment on my fine efforts. I held out the applications. He looked stunned, almost panicky. He explained that we couldn't afford college. He wasn't even interested in looking over the paperwork for the grants. He pushed the forms back across the table to me. He reminded me that girls went to college only to find husbands.

I can't begin to describe my feelings of futility, realizing I would not be going to college. What had all this school stuff been about anyway? What was the point? My grades began to slip. Only my geometry and Latin teachers noticed. They both inquired if everything was okay with me. I only shrugged. What could I say? What did it matter now? In a year I would graduate, turn 18 and be able to go out on my own. I no longer had a picture of my future. I was scared and cried a lot. Mom couldn't relate since she and Dad had dated since she was 15 and married at the end of her senior year. So maybe I should at least start thinking of dating. Right?

So she arranged it. She set up my first date, a young man two or three years older than I who attended our church. His name was Danny and he was creepy. Slightly overweight, hair greased back, he looked a bit like Jonathan Winters. He drove a hot car and he had a crush on me, said my mom.

I told her he repulsed me, and Mom replied, "But he's such a nice guy. You can't afford to be a snob." When Danny called to invite me on a double date she handed the phone over with a "you-better-say-yes" look.

It was the date from hell. We went to a drive-in movie with a couple from church who had been dating several years. They were all older than I was and talked among themselves. What do you say to a horse-crazy teen? I was so uncomfortable. Much to Danny's disappointment, I remained on my side of the car all evening, sometimes even clutching the door handle. After the movie, we went for a hamburger and then, to my horror, he drove to a lovers' lane. The couple in the back seat immediately started necking. I stayed on my side of the car terrified beyond belief. He put his arm around me to coax me towards him. I knew what was expected, but there was no way. No way. I sat frozen.

Finally, Danny asked, "You're a virgin, aren't you?"

I was not real clear exactly what that meant. My sex education up to that point had been a movie in seventh grade PE class. I was certain, however, the correct answer was yes. He let out a disgusted snort and with Danny it was a snort! Even the amorous couple in the back seat was jolted into stunned silence. The ticking of the dashboard clock was the only sound in the deafening silence. Apparently the ticking exacerbated his frustration. Danny abruptly yanked the clock out of the dashboard and threw it out the open window. I grabbed the door handle to make my own hasty retreat when the girl in the back seat sagely suggested it was time to go home. We drove in silence back to my house. Instead of getting out to open my door, Danny reached across me, grabbed the handle and popped the door open. I ran to our back door only to be greeted by my mom, who coyly suggested I was sure late getting home.

Collapsing onto the sofa, I felt beyond confused. The tenuous foundation beneath me was crumbling. I trembled from all that had taken place that evening. Dating was not for me if that's what dating was all about. Mom positioned herself across from me expectantly, eagerly awaiting details. Desperately wanting, needing, to be comforted, I stammered that he had demanded to know if I was a virgin. Her response was that she supposed I'd told him yes. The look on my face gave me away. Shaking her head in frustration, as if I had somehow disappointed her, she went to bed.

On the other hand, my sister Sally had discovered boys. And the Beatles, the Stones and the Doors. When she was around, the house was electric. She was always on the go, always had friends around, and was always laughing. I envied her carefree ways. I couldn't relate to her. We were five years and worlds apart. She made fun of my interests, or lack of them and I found her annoying. It didn't help that she chided me for not having boyfriends. She was able to tolerate Mom in a way that I never could. She'd just laugh her off. While it seemed much was expected of me, not much was expected of her.

There I stood, on the edge of 18, feeling lost and hopeless. I was failing everyone's expectations. I wanted out of my mother's house and was certain she wanted me out. In the days that followed my first date, I cried a lot. Not even my horse or time spent in nature could quiet the despair of my soul.

Meanwhile, life continued to deteriorate in our household. Despair seemed to be a family trait, like a crooked nose or blue eyes. Some time earlier, 14-year-old Russ had achieved something beyond what most thought him capable of. One day, after school, he had asked Dad for toothpicks and glue, settled down at the kitchen table and began assembling something. For days he toiled with focus and determination. Friends stopped in and brought Russ more boxes of toothpicks. The days stretched into weeks and finally he was finished. He had assembled, with no help or guidance, a three foot by one and a half foot sailboat. I was profoundly moved and felt it was a statement from him. We were amazed. The ship was placed on the kitchen buffet table, a prominent place of show and tell. I saw Russ differently from that time on. I knew he was capable of more.

I came home from school a few weeks later to the sound of Russ's angry voice. Following it to the kitchen I was just in time to see him smashing his toothpick ship to bits. Mom was watching from the doorway. With a shrug, she said they'd told Russ it was his last year of school. He had gone as far as he could go in grade school. The high school did have a Special Ed class, but Mom feared for him among high schoolers. Dad must have agreed. Russ's school days were done.

While my heart broke for Russ, I also felt admiration for him. At least he had something to smash. As I turned to go upstairs, I heard Mom follow Russ to his room. Judging by the tone of his voice there would be no reasoning with him. I wished she would just leave him alone. Later, when the house got quiet I tapped on his door.

"Go away," was his response. I opened it anyway. He was sitting on the edge of his bed, eyes red and swollen behind his thick dark-rimmed glasses. I sat next to him and took his hand. That's all it took. Uncontrollable sobs rose from his soul. Between tears, he kept saying "What can I do, what will I do?"

I could only hold him and cry with him. I had no answers for either of us.

Six

By the mid-1960s, the Vietnam War dominated our world. We watched it every night on TV. American men were dying there every day. Country Joe McDonald sang about it, Joan Baez protested about it and I felt it as some former classmates left home only to "come home in a box." The futility of those days enhanced my own inner futility. Maybe that's why I became attracted to Tom the summer between junior and senior year. He'd been to Vietnam. He served on a Navy destroyer in the Da Nang Delta. I'd known Tom and his family years before.

My friend Terri's backyard swimming pool was the place to be on a hot summer day. One day I went to swim and there was Tom. He'd grown up in that sailor's uniform. From the look on his face when he saw me, I must have grown up too. I was fascinated with his stories of Vietnam.

While Tom was home, we all hung out together, enjoying movies, midnight swims and music. I experienced for the first time the impulsive freedom of being a teenager. Tom was five years older than I with dark hair and a physical presence heightened by his time in the military. It never occurred that there might be any attraction between us. At the end of his leave, Tom surprised me when he asked me to write. He was scheduled to be discharged the following spring and hoped to see me then. The seeds of love had taken root. When I received my first letter from him I was pleasantly surprised. Mom was ecstatic. At Christmas, he sent me exotic gifts from Hong Kong. Corresponding with Tom brightened my senior year and made me feel special.

Tom was discharged spring of 1967. We'd gotten to know each other well through our letters. We started dating. At first I reveled in his attentiveness, but then I realized his attention had shifted into possessiveness. He wanted to be with me all the time. I quit seeing my friends. I missed out on many senior activities because he'd have other plans for us. I began to feel scared. He criticized me for everything. I wanted to flee. The answer presented itself after graduation. It was the summer of '67, the summer of LOVE. My aunt and uncle (Dad's brother) lived in San Francisco. I confessed to my aunt how unhappy I was and scared because Tom and I fought a lot. She invited me to live with them and arranged a job interview at the investment brokerage Dean Witter where she worked. In August, I mustered the courage to leave. Tom didn't appear upset, unusual for one so possessive. Within two weeks, I started getting sick every morning and so I returned home. We married a month later. My life careened again. I felt like its helpless passenger.

After we were married, we moved to Seattle to be close to Tom's family. He secured an assembly line job at Boeing. He hated the monotony and I couldn't blame him. He yearned to be a professional golfer.

Our son was born the following spring and I became a doting mother. Our small apartment in South Seattle was not inspiring. I took in ironing to help with the bills. We lived meagerly and unhappily. I sought refuge in any novel I could find. Little did I know a book I would read during these days was to have a huge impact on the rest of my life.

The book was *The Boston Strangler,* a true story detailing a murder investigation that had taken place a few years earlier. I was intrigued by a Dutch psychic, Peter Hurkos, whom the Boston police employed during the investigation. He would hold shoes that belonged to the deceased and *see* pictures. Psychometry! Something in me stirred. I knew that I could do that too. I began to do readings to test myself by persuading friends to let me hold something of theirs, a piece of jewelry or car keys for example. I would then close my eyes and allow pictures to form in my mind, sharing with them what I *saw*. As what I reported often would come to pass, my friends began bringing their friends to me. I sought out more books about psychics, although not much was available in those days.

In the winter of 1969, we decided to move back to Portland. I was relieved to be moving home. We lived with my family for two or three months while Tom looked for work. When I had lived in Seattle, my parents looked after my horse Banner. Upon my return, it became painfully clear that it was time to let him go. I could no longer care for him and he deserved more. I placed an ad in the paper. The following week a woman and her young daughter bought Banner sight unseen. I'll never forget the picture, forged in my mind, of holding my infant son in my arms as I tearfully watched my beloved Banner disappear from my life.

My dad was still in the cab business and one day he came home with an object in his hand. He passed it to me, saying he felt that it might have been left in his cab for me. It was a book wrapped in a brown paper cover. The name of the book was *Venture Inward*. Written by Hugh Lynn Cayce, it described the psychic experiences of his father, Edgar Cayce, the "Sleeping Prophet." I was thrilled and read nonstop. He would fall into a sleeplike state and do readings for strangers. His accuracy was amazing. I felt like I'd found kin; like I'd found home. I hungered for more information. In the late 1960s, there were no metaphysical bookstores in Portland. It was hard to find anything written by or about psychics. All I knew about psychics was what I'd heard about the gypsy fortune tellers on 82nd Avenue and that wasn't good. But this book set me on a course, and occasionally I would find information about other psychics like Jeane Dixon or Ruth Montgomery. They were the forerunners of today's popular psychics.

Once Tom found work, we rented a cute house not far from my parents. Soon our weekly routine included a bowling league, where we met Jack and Bonnie. They became our good friends. Jack had recently returned from Vietnam and was excited about taking flying lessons for his fixed wing and instrument rating. One evening after bowling he suggested we join him and Bonnie for a flight to Reno, Nevada. He needed to practice touch-and-go landings, in which the pilot repeatedly lands and takes off again without coming to a complete stop. Tom was enthusiastic. I was reluctant. The trip was scheduled for the following Saturday, June 20, 1970. All week long, I dreamed about falling out of the sky. Tom assured me it was just anxiety. Jack had offered his own measure of reassurance, that he would be flying the highways so that if anything bad occurred, he could just set the plane down on the highway. I knew he was trying to allay my fear, but his words only induced a sick feeling in my stomach.

The day arrived. We met at the Hillsboro airport on a beautiful morning. I was buzzing with excitement and trepidation. Bonnie reassured me with a smile as the plane took off, banking over Beaverton. The four-seater Cessna 182 was a tight fit. Bonnie and I shared the two back seats. The touch-and-go's were fun, like playing leap frog across the state. Other than the ups and downs, it was a calm and uneventful flight. But as we began our approach to Reno, the little aircraft coughed. I shot an anxious look at Bonnie who smiled comfortingly. It coughed again, and then began to sputter. Jack's hands deftly moved about the controls as he radioed the Reno tower while pumping something with his free hand. Just as he was confirmed emergency clearance, the engine began to purr. We relaxed, sort of. Jack assured us it must have been an air pocket in the gas line. He radioed the Reno tower, cancelling the mayday. Reno asked us to drop to a lower elevation, allowing a United Airlines DC-10 to land. As we did, the engine died. There was no sound. Nothing. We were falling from the sky. Jack continued moving at the controls, calmly and quietly. But we continued falling.

"Mayday, mayday!" Jack urgently addressed the tower. We were now within sight of the airport. He began porpoising the little plane, hoping to gain some lift. As we flew (or fell) over a train yard, I was sure I could have reached out and touched the top of the trains. Then, seconds before we crashed, a sudden peaceful calm overcame the panic we felt. Bonnie and I held hands and exchanged glances. There was a fifth presence among us. I realized then that we wouldn't die. As we hit, landing in a field inches from the runway lights and mere feet from a deep ravine, the plane leaned over on its right wing, snapping it before settling back down. Bonnie and I were out of the fuselage before the two men whose seated positions blocked the exits. To this day, I don't know how that was possible. Emergency crews arrived minutes later, grabbing us away for fear of fire. Fire wasn't an issue, however; we were out of gas. Later at the terminal we waited as Jack spoke with FAA officials.

"You the folks from the crashed aircraft?" a raspy-voiced older woman with bright red hair asked. She held a bottle of Wild Turkey in one hand and a stack of shot glasses in the other. We nodded, still dazed.

"You know, any landing you can walk away from is a good landing," she chuckled, pouring us each a shot of the gold liquid. "Here," she said, "bottoms up."

I held the shot glass, watching Bonnie take a sip, not wanting to confess I'd never had a drink. I tipped the glass back; it was only a few ounces, how bad could it be? It burned all the way down.

As I coughed and choked, the woman said, "Here, better have some more." I held up my hand, shaking my head, but she poured another shot anyway. As she poured she explained there had been a fly-in that day. "You know, like a car rally, only from the sky," she said in response to our quizzical looks.

"I was in charge of the hospitality table," she said, gesturing to the liquor. "Not for the pilots of course, that's illegal," she exclaimed. "It's for the guests. I'm packin' it up and see you all come in ridin' in that fire truck, nobody hurt, huh? Boy you gave us a scare. Lots of activity there for a few minutes."

Bonnie and I burst out laughing. The woman stood staring at us, then turned away.

"Bet you can see yourselves on the six o'clock news," she said over her shoulder.

She was right. A few hours later, as we sat in the Mapes Hotel bar, the news came on the TV. There we were. Remembering that we still had to fly home, I groaned. Fortunately the commercial flight was uneventful.

Seven

It never occurred to me to go to work. I was a mother and our son needed me. He was the light of my life; apparently, too much so for Tom. He became jealous and abusive. The first time he hit me, I took our son and fled to my parents. Dad was livid with Tom. Mom, however, wanted to know what I had done to deserve it. Her message: go back and don't do it again. I did go back but felt trapped. When the abuse escalated and I realized that he would hurt our son, I left for good. With no alternative, I reluctantly retreated to my parents. Lacking a job or work skills, I put an ad in the paper to clean houses and took my son with me to work.

During this time I relished the opportunity to become reacquainted with my sister Sally. She was a wild thing. Still a teen, she was nevertheless pretty worldly. She had become in every sense of the word a flower child: a groupie for a local band and a hitchhiker convinced that the world was safe and loving. Once I drove her to Eugene to see a friend. On the way home we stopped for gas. At the next pump was a Porsche with two guys in it. She got out to talk to them, came back, got her purse and told me she'd see me later. She was going to San Francisco. Off she went with the two strangers, scoffing at my concern. Sally was always confident that she'd be fine. A few days later she'd phone Mom and Dad for airfare, they'd send it and she'd be home.

Sally showed up one Sunday evening at dinnertime with a great-looking guy named Ted. He had picked her up hitchhiking on her way home from Eugene. She wanted me to see how she had to ride in his car, a VW Bug. It had no passenger seat or back seat. She had ridden to Portland on an apple box with pillows on top. She thought it was funny and adventuresome. He had told her the upholstery was being repaired. Mom invited him for dinner, but he quietly declined; he was a law student and was heading back to Seattle for school. After Ted left we commented on what a well-mannered and nice-looking guy he was. Sally shrugged it off, saying he wasn't her type. I commented that it was probably because he was too clean-cut for her and that she could have at least set him up with me.

Years later, while reading Ann Rule's book, *The Stranger Beside Me*, about serial killer Ted Bundy, I was stunned by the eerie resemblance of Sally's chauffeur to the good-looking young law student from Seattle that Rule described.

Romance found me soon after. One day, a cute little sports car, a Healey, pulled into my parents' driveway as I was unloading groceries. The man greeted me and claimed to just be passing by. I recognized him as Steve, a neighbor who'd gone to the same high school a few years before me. A few weeks later motorcycles in front of the house got my attention. Opening the door, I was greeted by the smiles of Steve and his friend, Mike. These guys had been the popular ones in high school. What were they doing here? Mom ran out greeting them with an invitation to come in for a beer. They passed on the offer, but Steve suggested I hop on back and go for a ride. What a ride it was! I had so much fun. When he dropped me off a few hours later he asked if he could call some time. Three or four days later he did call and we started going out.

We dated all winter. The following spring, he graduated from Portland State University and a few days later suggested we get married. For a wedding gift his folks gave us a piece of property right behind them. We bought a house and had it moved onto the property. It wasn't exactly the house on the hill of my childhood dream, but that dream now seemed inaccessible. I could feel it slipping away. Instead of horses, we had cars, motorcycles and skis. I found myself fitting into this new life, but only halfheartedly. The life I was leading wasn't really me and somewhere deep inside, I knew.

Often in the evenings, we visited Steve's family for dinner and television. They enjoyed spending time with us and I didn't have to cook! One summer evening I'd become absorbed in a movie on TV, so Steve took my son home for bed. When the movie was over, I bid my in-laws good-night and began walking home.

It was clear, the air still warm from the beautiful day. As I searched the starry sky, a glow caught my attention. The entire top of a big fir tree between our two houses was on fire. Fearing it had been hit by lightening, I rushed back to the house and urged my mother-in-law to call the fire department. She followed me out onto the porch. We both looked at the fir tree, silhouetted perfectly against the quiet, night sky. Nothing unusual was to be seen. I was baffled. With concern etched in her face, Steve's mom asked if perhaps I was coming down with something. I shook my head and assured her that I was fine.

As her door closed, I resumed my walk home. Cautiously I turned my gaze upward, looking at the big fir. It was again aglow, just the top half. Keeping my eyes trained on the fir aflame, I continued home and watched the tree from my porch, fearful that it would disappear if I took my eyes off of it. Finally, I went inside and pulled back the drapes to be certain. The fire remained, glowing bright. Mystified, I finally went to bed. What was the meaning of this glow that only I could see?

A few nights later I awoke suddenly. I was startled to see the orange glow of a fire reflecting on our window curtains. Certain the house behind us was on fire, I yelled for my husband as I bounded out of bed. Tearing open the blinds, expecting to see a house fire, I was dumbfounded to see only the quiet dark of the night.

Shaken I returned to bed as my husband mumbled, "What's wrong?"

"Nothing," I replied, seeking comfort under the bedcovers. Timidly, I rolled over to face the window and my uncertainty. I continued to watch the glow of the fire on the curtains as I drifted off to sleep.

The next day I mentioned it to Steve, who shrugged it off. The only reference I had to "fire that doesn't burn" was Moses and the burning bush. I certainly wasn't receiving any commandments or voices from God here. It didn't frighten me, strangely enough. I had instead felt comforted in its presence. Was this perhaps somehow an encounter with the Divine?

I turned to the church for explanations. There, I was reminded and assured that such an experience was reserved only for Jesus' holy disciples, the twelve.

"But what about the Holy Spirit descending on them as tongues of flames?" I persisted.

Looking over the top of his glasses, the minister reminded me we are simply not that holy or deserving of such attention from God. It is our job to find our way back to Him with a life of penance and forgiveness in Jesus... blah blah blah. I mentally checked out as he finished his sermon to me. I had had a genuine experience. As I turned to leave, the minister admonished me to beware the seduction of the devil. I shook my head at that; when all else fails, bring out the bogeyman.

Moving with the times, two bookstores that carried small selections of metaphysical books had crept into Portland. One was the Vortex, downtown across from the main library. The other was a hippie store called Atlantis Rising. I began frequenting both. Not much was available about contemporary psychics, so I took what I could find: lots of old school philosophy by the likes of Alice Bailey and Annie Besant. Much of the text was difficult and incomprehensible to me, but I persisted.

As my husband watched the strange assortment of books coming home, he began to be disturbed, at one point collecting them all and throwing them away. I got the "Why do you care about this stuff?" lecture and suggestion to go back to school to learn some secretarial skills.

I felt like I was pretending in my life: pretending to be happy, pretending to love my husband and marriage. The only genuine love I felt was for my son.

Whenever I thought of leaving this marriage all of my inadequacies came up. How would I support myself and my son? I signed up for the stenography class.

About this time my parents met a couple who captured their interest and attention. He was a pilot and hypnotist. She was a psychic. They lived out of town, but planned to visit soon. I begged my parents to introduce us. After much anticipation, Steve and I were invited to join them at dinner at my parents' house. As we entered the front room I saw this couple, named Charles and Sharon, sitting on the sofa. He stood to meet us and I was aware of something familiar in him. Maybe it was the way he looked right into me. She smiled at me in a knowing sort of way. I was hooked.

Our conversations that evening were like nourishment to me. I couldn't get enough. She did most of the talking. He seemed quiet in a mysterious way. Her expertise was in psychometry, a huge delight for me, having already begun doing that myself after reading about Peter Hurkos. They owned a small café in Montana. He was a pilot for the FBI, he said. He also spoke about spending time in a monastery in Tibet, but when pushed about where and how, he would only smile. He'd learned hypnosis to overcome some of his own fears, he said, and to practice mind-over-matter control. To me, it felt like God had answered my prayers and sent me not one, but two teachers.

On the drive home I was elated. They had given me their address and phone number. I was to call, to write, to come visit anytime. While I chatted excitedly, my husband was quiet. His only comment was that there was something not quite right about them. I thought he was jealous. Little did I know his cautious remark was well-founded. I was so hungry for soul food, for someone who understood me that I was incapable of recognizing the danger that lurked.

Over the next few months I wrote or phoned them weekly. My hope was to persuade Charles to be my teacher. Sharon, however, did all the communicating. Whenever I directed any thoughts or questions towards Charles he was vague; his mysterious tone drew me in even more.

In the meantime they suggested books for me to read. In *The Search for the Girl with the Blue Eyes* author Jess Stearn investigated hypnosis-regression as a means of verifying past lives. They also recommended Stearn's book *The Miracle Workers: America's Psychic Consultants* as well as *Life and Teaching of the Masters of the Far East* by Baird Spalding. Those, along with *Linda Goodman's Sun Signs* formed the bulk of my reading. Reincarnation and karma were new concepts to me, but these books resonated. I was desperate to learn more and hoped that Charles could hypnotize me so I might remember past lives.

With my new-found teachers my life felt suddenly alive. It was like finding home after wandering lost for years. I was no longer alone. I felt a new vitality and was intoxicated with spirit. A few months after meeting Charles and Sharon, my husband and I drove to Montana to visit them. We stayed a few days and when it was time to leave I cried. Actually, I cried off and on all the way home. It felt like they were home and I was going back to my pretend life. Needless to say this was taking a toll on my marriage.

I began meditating daily. Perhaps because of my early childhood practice of holding an image of a white triangle in my mind, achieving "no mind" was relatively easy for me. It was during one of these meditative moments I *heard* a voice, not outside of me but inside. It was a male voice simply saluting and welcoming me. I began eagerly looking forward to my days, planning everything around that daily hour of meditation. A new feeling of confidence and happiness began to emerge from that inner time I spent with myself, a new sense of guidance at the possibility of having access to God's voice or at least one of His angels or emissaries.

One day it occurred to me to ask of that voice, "Who are you?"

The response didn't surprise me. "An angel, your angel." What did surprise me was the idea I could ask a question of that inner voice and receive a response. We could have dialogue! And so it began, slowly and cautiously, until one day I brought pen and paper to my meditation time. If I wrote down a question prior to "no mind," perhaps I could write the response as it came to me. It worked. Not only did it work, but in forming the dialogue I began to be aware of the ability to access it during nonmeditative times as well. The voice was never authoritative, but rather, informing. I also noticed as long as my questions were of a philosophical or universal nature, there was plenty of dialogue. As soon as I attempted personal questions of a day-to-day nature, there was silence. Disappointment accompanied this silence. That was fine with me. I got it that I was on my own. Something to do with free will, I supposed.

For months I kept a journal of my dialogues from within and kept it hidden away. This journal was too sacred to share with anyone. I certainly didn't want someone's opinion or criticism of my new inner awareness.

Then one day, I returned from the grocery store and found Steve was home early. Fearing something was wrong at work or maybe he was ill, I rushed in. He was sitting at the kitchen table, my journal open in front of him. I saw horror in his eyes. Or was it fear?

"Are you out of your mind?" His voice grew louder with each word. I was mortified. I felt violated and betrayed. My world was spinning. He stood up, waving the journal in my face, as he demanded an explanation. Speechless, I let the groceries fall as I lunged, trying to recover my pages from his moving hands.

"Let me have it! How dare you!" I shouted.

"I'll give it to you," he threatened with a malicious grin.

Who was this man? He seemed transformed into a hateful monster. I knew Steve had a temper; I'd seen it flare. But this was unreal, surreal. As Steve spoke he moved to the sliding door off the dining room. Opening the door, he reached in his pocket and pulled out his lighter. Holding my journal an arm's length away from me, he took his lighter and set it aflame.

"No!" I shrieked.

By now my son, who'd followed me in from the car, spoke. "Mommy, what's wrong?" His voice brought me back.

I grabbed my keys and purse, took his hand and said, "We're leaving."

As we drove away, tears streaming down my face, my six-year-old son said "Mommy, this isn't love is it?"

Shaking my head, I patted his leg. "No, it isn't love," I said.

"Then we need to leave, don't we?"

"Yes, yes, we do," I responded as I signaled to turn onto the main street that led back to my parents' house.

Eight

It was midsummer in 1974. My sister had recently moved back home and was living with Mom and Dad. She was happy to share the huge basement rooms of that old farm house with me and my son. As each day passed I realized that I could not return to my own home. It was not safe. My son, too, was happier with Gramma and Gramps. Curiously no one pressed me for a decision. Maybe they knew my marriage was over. Steve made a few attempts to talk. He even tried to convince my parents I was crazy, involved with wacky occult stuff. But we knew whatever had taken place that day sealed the fate of our marriage. It was over. I felt broken. Several weeks later, I was served with divorce papers.

My faith, too, was shaken. Whatever this was in me, this need to know and understand more about my psychic and spiritual nature, seemed to bring only grief and pain to others in my life. It was curious to me how something so extraordinary could be so feared and misunderstood. I vowed to again be silent. I would endeavor to be normal and not so distressing to the people I loved.

One morning the phone rang with an early call from Montana. I was surprised to hear Charles's voice. In the chaos of the last few weeks I hadn't thought about him and Sharon much. With equal surprise, he asked why I was answering my folks' phone. I briefly explained what had happened. With a wry chuckle, he responded that the same thing had happened to him. Only his wife had taken off with another man. The reason for his call was to alert my parents of his impending visit to Portland to assess aircraft for possible purchase. He said he'd call on us when he arrived. Dad was enthusiastic at the thought of checking out airplanes with Charles.

A week later, Charles arrived. Although our house was clearly crowded, my parents eagerly offered him a spare room while he was in town. So for the next few weeks, he and I spent long hours talking. Charles perceived that I was despondent over the way things were going in my life and urged me not to give up on my metaphysical studies. In the evenings he entertained my parents and their friends with his hypnotic parlor games.

I became fascinated by what the mind appeared capable of believing upon receiving a mere suggestion. One evening Charles told one of my dad's friends that an onion was a Red Delicious apple and he should eat a few bites. Much to my surprise, he did and wanted more. I watched as Charles stuck a pin in a woman's arm, telling her she'd feel no pain; she didn't flinch. The pièce de rèsistance was to convince a teenage girl that she was as stiff as a board and balance her by her neck and ankles over the slender backs of two kitchen chairs. The feat became more astonishing when a 250 pound man stood steadily on her stomach. The evening crowds at my parents' house grew. Charles was acquiring a devoted following. Who was this man? Each time I pushed him to talk about his spiritual training or his supposed time in Tibet, his response was a silent smile.

One afternoon he rallied my father, "Come on, Dave. Let's go flying."

He'd bought a plane. Or more exactly, the Beverly Hills attorney who employed him had bought a plane. He indicated that his employer didn't care where he lived as long as he was where they needed him when they needed him. The following week he made a business trip to the south.

Upon return, he said to my sister and me, "I've got money. Let's get a place together."

Remaining true to the culture of the early 1970s and desperate to escape the crowded house, it sounded like a perfect solution. My sister and I began looking in earnest while he was again away on business.

I contacted an old family friend who was a realtor. As fate would have it, she had that very day received a rental. It was an old farmhouse and barn on 45 acres just out of town. Sally and I drove the 10 minutes it took to get there and fell in love before we ever saw the inside. The realtor rented it to us with the understanding that the property was for sale. No doubt someday a developer would buy it, but for now it was ours. By the time Charles returned, we had created a warm and cozy place for all of us. Never loquacious, he remained taciturn about his trips south but he seemed to be well compensated. He was generous with his money, giving Sally and me sufficient funds for household upkeep. Charles was enthusiastic about the farm and when he wasn't flying, he was fixing the barn or clearing brush. There was always a lot to do.

One day Charles decided it was time to get a horse. He'd found one and wanted to check her out. I dropped what I was doing, nearly beating him to the truck.

She was a pretty bay mare, well-mannered and gaited. There was a little Welsh pony in the pasture with her.

"For the boy," Charles said, referring to my son.

The residents at the farm increased by two.

I felt that I was floating on a cloud. It had been years since I'd had my horse and I'd missed him terribly. This was too good to be true. My son and I spent many long hours in the field and woods around the farm that fall, riding and racing.

The farmhouse had one room we called the fireplace room. It was clearly part of an expansion of the original little farm house. It was cozy and inviting, and soon became a meeting place for what I referred to as Charles's groupies. I watched from a distance, fascinated at how people were drawn to him. He seemed to have an aura about him. The talk around the fire was always philosophical. I ate it up as much as his groupies, but it seemed to always fall short. I decided he was a master of illusion, able to avoid answering direct questions while keeping people coming back for more. He never charged for these gatherings, which seemed to naturally occur each Sunday evening. He did charge for occasional hypnotherapy counseling. He had a small metaphysical library which I devoured. But whenever I'd attempt to engage him in conversation about what I was reading he'd shrug. It made me wonder if he'd read any of the books himself or if they were just props.

My suspicions grew as I sat reading one day about the human aura. The author told of a celebrated guru whose aura was vibrant and huge to those who could see it from the audience. During a break, the author happened upon this guru in the men's room. He was confused when he noticed the guru's aura was small and insignificant. As he observed the guru taking the stage once more, it seemed to him that the projected adoration from the audience caused the aura to expand. The thought occurred to me that Charles's aura was perhaps not entirely his own.

I had a singular experience with auras during one of these meetings as I sat watching from the steps leading into the fireplace room. It must have been during a break because everyone was quietly visiting with one another. There were perhaps eight to ten people seated around the room. Suddenly I noticed a pinkish-glow, like someone had turned on a pink light. Then each person appeared engulfed in their own egg-shaped, rainbow-colored array of lights. I blinked, wondering what was taking place. No one else seemed to notice. I focused my attention on my friend Karen, seated directly across from me next to the fireplace. She was conversing with the man next to her. Suddenly she let out a laugh at something he had said. As she laughed, bubbles of multi-colored hues followed the laughter from her mouth. The phrase "bubbling with laughter" crossed my mind.

I was seeing everyone's aura. The colors were rich and undulating, while at the same time moving and changing rapidly. Every aura contained every color of the rainbow in constant flowing movement, much like interlacing fountains, all contained within individual egg-shapes. I wondered then how any psychic aura reader could ever say they *see* a green, or red, or blue, etc., aura around someone. Based on what I was seeing, it would not be possible to *see* only one color. These colors intermingled and changed rapidly. They were vibrant and dazzling to behold.

Then I noticed something else. As people talked, a piece of their aura reached out to the one they were speaking with. In turn, a piece of the one listening, reached out to the speaker. It resembled intercourse. Was this the origin of the term "social intercourse"? I simply could not take in all that I was seeing. As suddenly as it began, it stopped.

I sat staring at the group.

Karen noticed my stare. "Suzanne, what's wrong? You look like you've seen a ghost," she exclaimed, laughing softly.

Remembering the bubbles of her laughter I'd seen a moment before, I said, "No, no, I'm just feeling tired."

I stood up and stepped into the kitchen for a drink of water. It was not possible to share what I'd just experienced. Nor did I want to. I simply said a quick prayer of thanks. Now, without doubt, I knew what auras looked like. I would never see one again.

Maybe because of his silences, maybe because of his inability to talk to me about such things, I never shared much with Charles about my own psychic abilities or meditations. Intuitively, I understood that I was not altogether safe with Charles on a psychic and spiritual level. I considered it curious that all these people were gathered around him for spiritual teaching and yet it was the very thing he avoided with me.

Periodically, on a moonlit night Charles would spontaneously announce it was flying time and a group would head to the airport. We'd fly toward the stars, dancing from wingtip to wingtip in the moonlight. Because of my earlier plane crash, I hated flying. But it delighted whatever handful of people happened to be with us.

One woman who hung around on Sundays, Rae, began to sit and talk with me. She and her husband Jerry were friends of my folks. I found her pleasant enough. Her husband was my mom's pharmacist and had indicated a desire to meet Charles because he wanted to learn to fly and Charles was a certified flight instructor. Rae was in her last year of college. She and Jerry had found the hypnosis parties at my parents' house addictive, so when they heard about our Sunday night gatherings they joined us.

Rae was one of Charles's favorite hypnosis subjects. She favored doing past-life regressions. Once that had been demonstrated, everyone in the room wanted to sign up.

I, like everyone else, had allowed myself to be hypnotized in Charles's group settings. I found the experience annoying, like a force pushing against my will. I tried the past-life regression once or twice, but again did not feel it to be real. What I did observe, however, is how suggestion itself made me want to supply an answer, even if I was making it up and how a posthypnotic suggestion was indeed a force to be reckoned with. I was troubled to realize that suggestion only worked if a subject agreed to surrender a portion of his or her will to the hypnotist. If the subject agrees to submit that portion, he might be aware that the offered apple is, actually, an onion but is willing to accept the hypnotist's word over his own. If the subject is unwilling to offer his will, the hypnotist is unable to carry out the suggestion. What I found so disturbing and repugnant was that a person would naively relinquish his free will, his most precious gift. Touted often as entertaining and silly, I viewed this violation of will as seductive and dangerous.

One afternoon I confronted Charles about the process of hypnosis. I wanted a greater understanding of the psychic and energetic exchange that took place between practitioner and subject. He became defensive and stonewalled me. He implied that I would never be a good student and that's why he wouldn't teach me.

I continued meditating. I had no more dialogues with my inner voice, but felt the comfort of its presence during my meditations. I also had the peace of the beautiful farm, my horseback rides in the quiet woods, my zany sister who really could not care less about metaphysical chitchat, and my beautiful son, who was becoming very active in school. All of these things I held onto. They kept me grounded.

Charles was gone on one of his flying trips when the phone rang early one morning. It was he.

"I need your help," he said. "You've got to wire me some money."

"What... what for? Where are you?" was my sleepy reply.

"I'm in jail. It's a long story. Don't worry, they've got me covered. I'll fill you in when I get home."

And so, my farm haven began to fall apart. He flew home on a commercial aircraft. I picked him up at the airport.

"Where's the plane?" was my question.

"It's been confiscated. But look, don't worry. I'll get it back," was his confident reply. He continued, "Remember when we first met I told you I worked for the FBI sometimes? Well, it's a new branch of that called the DEA. The past several months I've been planted in a......" I didn't hear the rest. My world was spinning. It was all a bad dream.

This is not really happening, I thought. But indeed it was.

When we got back to the farm, my dad and sister were waiting.

As Charles's story unfolded, I heard only pieces of it, my head still reeling. "Under the radar... Mexico...dry lakebed."

According to him, the DEA had to make the bust look real so as not to blow his cover. His plane would be returned soon. They'd use him again. He assured us he'd been through this many times with the Bureau, that none of us was in danger, and that we lived far from where it all took place.

Somehow life resumed, but not without a cloud or shadow lurking over us. Every so often Charles would be visited by men, sometimes one, sometimes two. They'd talk, cloistered in his office, for a while and then leave without a word. He described the visitors as his Bureau contacts.

Soon after his grounding, he began writing a book. He said his many students needed a handbook. He would shut himself away in his office, typing. No one was permitted entry.

On one of those days when Charles was writing, I heard a knock at the front door. I recognized the caller as one of the DEA agents who'd come to visit him. I invited him in. As I turned to let Charles know of his guest, the man stopped me.

"Actually I'd really like to speak with you if you don't mind," he said.

"Me? What for?"

"We need him to cooperate with us. He made some bad choices. He's going to do some time for them, ma'am," was his stoic reply.

He expressed his hope that I could urge Charles to cooperate. If not, he had grand jury subpoenas for my entire family. Trembling, I sat down. My sister entered the room, curious to know who our visitor was.

The agent filled in the missing information from Charles's prior account. It was true that Charles had been "walking the tightrope" for the DEA, working as a civilian operative undercover with an agent and entering the employ of drug runners. Lured by the money offered by the drug runners, Charles had flown the last mission unauthorized by the DEA, for his own profit. He was busted. The betrayal was incomprehensible to me. How could I have gotten myself and my family in such a mess?

At the completion of the agent's explanation, the typing ceased and the door to Charles's office opened. His face dropped as he saw the three of us sitting there. The game was over.

He fully cooperated with the agents and flew out of our lives to serve his time. He contacted us a few times asking us to please store his things with Rae and Jerry. There were several groupies who refused to believe the truth about him. They continued to support him and believe he had been set up by a bust gone badly. He'd done a pretty good sales job. Several had asked for copies of his book, which he had completed. As I was packing up his office I found the copies. I also found the book he'd plagiarized, almost word for word.

I am embarrassed to admit that I had fallen prey to one final con job from Charles. On the insistence of his attorney that a married man would be viewed more credibly in his pre-sentencing hearing, I, incredibly, consented.

I am a slow learner.

A significant downfall of being psychic is that I *see* and believe in the potential in a person, ignoring their actions in the present…and their rap sheets.

After Charles left, my sister decided it was time for her to go as well. She needed to become an adult and have a real job. To that end, she moved to downtown Portland with her friend Dave who owned a business setting up sound systems for concerts and events. Sally would work for him.

I stood alone on my beloved farm, my eyes sweeping the lengthening grasses. The horses were gone. I could not afford to keep them and had given them away, rending my heart. The barn was ramshackle again without Charles's care. My German shepherd whimpered his sympathy.

Nine

I was floating over Mt. Shasta. Suddenly, I became aware of another presence floating next to me. I'd had many floating dreams throughout the years but had never encountered any other presence. Usually I was merely an observer. I spoke to this presence, asking who it was and why it was in my dream. He opened a large telephone-type book, pointing at a certain page and underlining a name. The book was full of nothing but names. As I watched, he underlined the name "Bob Finnell" then closed the book. He said he was there to show me some things. With that we turned and were hovering over a small village which I assumed to be Shasta City.

He said, "Watch this."

Suddenly it was like looking through a telescope. I could see people walking along the streets and moving in and out of shops. As I watched he said, "Now watch this." As he spoke, everyone below froze. Turning to me he said, "I want you to tell me their next actions."

"The dog will frighten the child in the red dress and she will bolt into the street," I responded.

He started the scene moving again and we watched as the events unfolded as I had seen that they would. The rest of the dream was just that, a series of stops and starts with my making predictions.

The exercise was entertaining, but as I awoke, what astounded my consciousness was that I had actually *met* someone in spirit. Making a note of his name, I shrugged it off as perhaps a spiritual guide. God knows I needed one after all I'd been through.

Even before Charles and Sally moved out, I had maintained my house-cleaning business to supplement the household income. Now as I was the sole support for the farm, funds were slim. My mom, ever helpful, suggested that I sign up for welfare. My thought was, how humiliating, and yet, I had heard of some good training programs available through that system. I made my appointment and steered my old truck down to the welfare offices. As I sat filling out all the required forms, dirty-faced children ran between the chairs, and women who seemed to know each other sat on the outside steps smoking cigarettes, talking and laughing. I felt unreal. I didn't recognize myself anymore. I didn't recognize my life. I was a stranger watching this unreal fiction play out in front of me. Eventually my name was called by a short, round woman about my age. She was holding my file. I recognized her by her long, stringy, oily brown hair. "Gwen?" I said. She looked up at me with a triumphant smile, recognition dawning on her face.

After an awkward moment she asked me to follow her into her office. Taking a seat at the desk, she motioned for me to sit.

Not looking up from the papers she was reading she said, "What are you doing here? As smart as you were, I thought you'd be married to a doctor or an attorney by now."

Gwen and I had been in grade school together. She remembered me as a rally girl and athletic star. I remembered her oily hair and dirty fingernails and clothes. What a strange junction. I don't recall ever seeing her after grade school. Maybe she'd moved. I didn't care. I didn't ask.

After a quiet moment or two in which she seemed to be assessing me, her gaze shifted to my eyes and she spoke.

"I'm afraid we won't be able to help you much. Based on your weekly income, your assets and the fact that you have only one school-age dependent...." Her words trailed off.

Great. I sat there suffering unbearable humiliation in front of an old classmate and for what? My assets? The clothes I owned and a broke down pickup truck. I could feel tears beginning to well up in my eyes.

Slowly and precisely I spoke again, "But what about job training? I understand...."

She cut me off curtly. "You don't get it do you? You don't qualify. I can authorize some food stamps but that's it," she said, closing my file dismissively. From somewhere deep inside me an unfamiliar boldness spoke up.

Very quietly I said, "I'd like to speak to your supervisor."

"What?" she responded incredulously. I repeated myself somewhat louder this time. Pushing herself away from her desk, she stopped and smiled.

"Fine. I'll refer you on to our training program, but don't expect much." Pulling out a pen and paper she scribbled a name and phone number. We both stood now.

Handing me the slip of paper she smiled condescendingly and said, "Good luck. Nice seeing you again."

Paper in hand, I walked away. I must have been holding my breath the entire time I was in there because as soon as I was behind the wheel of my beat-up truck, I let out a loud scream. I sat there, hands on the wheel, head down, tears streaming. "I will never go through that again," I vowed. I tucked the referral slip into my wallet.

Later that evening, as my son and I finished dinner, the phone rang. It was my sister wanting to know how my interview had gone. Hearing the details, she uttered a loud sympathetic groan. Then, changing the subject she asked if we were going to be home. She and a friend were at Mom and Dad's and her friend wanted to meet me. She said she'd told him all about me and that she thought I'd like him because we were into the "same stuff." Assuming she meant metaphysical stuff, I laughed and told them to come on up.

Soon, I heard the dog barking his greeting at my dad's car and moments later the front door opened. In walked Dad, Sally and a geeky-looking guy. He reminded me of a college professor. Certainly not the kind of guy my sister hung around. He was clean-shaven, short haired and be-spectacled. Oh, this ought to be interesting, I thought.

"Suzy, meet Peter. He's Dave's partner in the sound business." Sally's glib introduction was said as she breezed past me into the kitchen. "What's for dinner?" came her muffled voice as she rummaged through the refrigerator.

"Among other things, I'm Dave's partner, among other things. Nice to meet you." He held out his hand. I motioned for him to have a seat at the table. We were joined around the table with Dad and Sally quizzing me about my day. Peter watched my disheartened account of the events at the welfare office.

"Sounds like you've been through a lot. Maybe we should leave so you can get some rest," Peter remarked kindly.

I declined and assured them that I was glad for the

company.

"If you would allow me, maybe I could help," said Peter taking my hand to guide me to a clear area near the fireplace. "I'll show you a re-energizing movement." His arms traced patterns in the air with a slow, fluid motion. "It's called Tai Chi. Here, follow my moves."

For the next 15 minutes or so I did just that and began to feel rested.

"Wow. Where did you learn that?" I asked. He just smiled.

Over the course of the evening I learned that he lived in San Francisco and ran a recording studio there. The Bee Gees were among his clients. As he named off several other groups, my blank stare and sister's laughter made him stop.

"Have I said something funny?"

Sally shook her head, still laughing. "Save it," she said. "She doesn't have a clue what you're talking about."

It was true. My life had been such a mess for so long, damage control was all I knew. Frivolities such as popular culture never occurred to me.

"Sorry," I shrugged, "but she's right."

He grinned. A beautiful grin I thought.

"That's okay," he said. "It's refreshing to meet someone like you." When it was time for them to leave, my sister hugged me, promising to call soon. Dad's hug carried the same message. Surprisingly, Peter hugged me also, telling me that it had been a pleasure.

Yeah, right, I thought. The Eagles. Lynyrd Skynyrd. Who are they? I shook my head as I closed the door behind them. I'd been so busy taking care of everyone the last few years. Who had time for such trivia?

I thought of Peter several times over the next few days. Sally said he'd be back in town in a week or so and that he thought I was nice. Peter and I hadn't talked much metaphysics that night. He'd mentioned he belonged to the Arica group in San Francisco, whatever that was, and had studied some of Gurdjieff, whom I had at least heard about. He also said he knew some researchers at the Stanford Research Institute and had participated in some of its studies. After what I'd just been through with a so-called teacher who'd made many such claims, I was cautious. Despite myself, however, I liked him.

As the days passed following my welfare fiasco, my fear escalated. How was I going to support myself and my son? I cried myself to sleep many nights. I didn't know how to handle a job interview or apply for work. Besides, at 28 years old, I had no work experience. How did my life get so hopeless?

I had thought a few times about the slip of paper with the phone number Gwen had given me, and her cryptic words, "But don't expect much." Well, it was time for me to find out how much not to expect. I opened my wallet to reveal the pink memo slip. I held the phone for what seemed like hours trying to think of what to say. Finally, I just dialed. A pleasant woman answered, identifying herself as Maria, and asking how she might help. I stammered a bit until she interrupted and said she'd like to meet with me. She also said she'd come to my house for the interview. I was taken aback by her cheery and optimistic attitude after what I'd experienced with Gwen. We made a date for the following week.

In the meantime, Peter had called. He was back in town. Would I like to go out with him over the weekend?

What a surprise. Since my son was going with his dad, I jumped at the chance of something to do, something to look forward to.

"Sure," I said, "what did you have in mind?" He had an event to set up at the Euphoria (a hippie club), but we wouldn't want to stay there, he said. Since he didn't have his own transportation, he asked if I could pick him up at the club and we could go somewhere else. I hung up, elated. I phoned my sister and told her.

"Really? Peter?" she said. "You? Wow. What a surprise."

"Yeah, I know. Should be interesting," I said happily.

I was at the Euphoria at our agreed upon time. Once past the bouncers, I scanned the noisy crowd for Peter before realizing that he was probably in the sound room. Suddenly I felt a hand on my shoulder. "Let's get out of here."

Once outside, in the quiet of the night we stopped. He turned to me, his big smile saying it all. "You look great. It's so good to see you. I've done nothing but think of you since we met." He spoke softly, seductively stroking my cheek with his hand. His words and voice took my breath away. Over dinner, I was enthralled by Peter's easy charm. He spoke at length about his metaphysical and other interests. I was more than a little impressed. And smitten.

After dinner we went dancing. He spoke passionately about the high profile musical groups that he worked with. After a wonderful evening, it was time to go. As we climbed in my old pickup, he leaned over and kissed me.

"I'd like to go home with you," he whispered. I nodded.

Peter stayed at the farm the entire week. I chauffeured him to town in the morning and picked him up in the afternoon. Toward the end of his stay he mentioned moving to Portland as his business continued to increase in Oregon.

One evening, we sat together before the fire as he played the recorder that he always carried in his briefcase. (It's a recorder not a flute, he'd corrected me.) I cautiously asked him if he felt we'd been together before. I'd just finished a book about soul mates and I was intrigued with the idea of reincarnation. Laying his recorder down, he pulled out pen and paper.

"Well, let's look at a few things," he said, acknowledging the possibility. He asked me my full given name, birth date and place of birth, and scribed numerical notations as I spoke. Then he wrote *Peter DeBlanc. November 17, 1944.*

"No way!" I exclaimed. "That's my first husband's birthday."

He started, then paused. Looking beyond me into the fire, he seemed pensive for a moment, after which he hesitantly turned his efforts back to his numbers. Fantastical charts appeared on the page, engaging and intriguing me. Finally pushing it all aside, he announced that he would have to finish it later. He was unusually quiet the rest of the evening. I felt baited and stymied.

Thus began again the metaphysical seduction to which I had proven to be so vulnerable.

The next afternoon as we drove home together, Peter suggested we stop at the grocery store and dine in that night. I pulled into a small shopping mall that had a food store.

As we walked through the mall, Peter abruptly stopped in front of a piano and organ shop. A salesman was plunking away at "In the Mood."

"Mind if I try?" he asked the salesman. For the next 20 minutes he played everything from Bach to Dylan. Enchantment filled the mall, causing a crowd to gather. The salesman puffed out his chest as if he'd arranged the concert. Peter finished, breaking the spell, and applause erupted. The salesman approached with his hand extended.

"Bob Rogers. Nice to meet you. That was some playing. Who *are* you?" he asked, as if expecting that Peter must be famous.

"Oh, I just enjoy playing," Peter said casually as he took my arm, steering me toward the grocery store.

"Well, come play anytime," Bob Rogers called as we walked away.

Later that evening, beside the warmth of the fire, I turned to Peter and asked the same question. "So who *are* you, Peter DeBlanc?" He was quiet for a long time, as if pondering his answer.

The silence created an aura of drama.

"I'm going to tell you a story. It's something I don't share with everyone." For the next hour he revealed intimate details of his childhood, his dreams and his experiences. The story ended with what I assumed was his last girlfriend, as he went into great detail about the two of them. She was a singer and they'd enjoyed a lot of drugs and booze together. After too much of that lifestyle, they'd checked themselves into a hospital to dry out. Soon after, she returned to Texas to be with family and he returned home, but not before asking her to marry him. Although they lived in different towns, they maintained their relationship through letter writing. But something changed after he had proposed. She started writing about wanting a house with a white picket fence and all the trimmings. He realized he could never share that dream with her, so he broke off their engagement. He felt badly about that, but couldn't live a dishonest life. The last time he'd seen her, a few years back, he'd gone backstage after one of her concerts. She was wasted, and he told her if she didn't change her lifestyle she'd be dead soon. She died shortly after. He paused for an emotional breath. "Her name was Janis Joplin."

I was speechless. Even I knew who Janis Joplin was.

He went on to imply that she was the link that had gotten him into the music business. He named the musicians he knew. "Sometimes we'd hang out with Bobby Zimmerman and his girlfriend."

"Who?" I asked.

"Bob Dylan," he said casually. He continued, "Through the years Janis's biographers have tried to purchase her letters from me. I'll never let them go. *Never*. I would never betray her like that."

I must confess I didn't entirely believe his story. I am not sure, though, that I cared if it was fact or fiction. It certainly made him more interesting.

One morning after driving Peter into Portland, I returned home to find a car in my driveway. Damn, I'd forgotten my appointment with Maria, the welfare program counselor. I jumped out to greet her, pulling my German shepherd away from her car. I apologized profusely. She just grinned and gathered up her briefcase.

As we sat down, I realized I liked this woman. She was well dressed and cheerful. She seemed so positive. Without knowing why, I began to feel hopeful. Finally, we took a break from the long questionnaire she had brought. As I prepared tea, she stood and stretched. She scanned my bookshelves.

"Oh, I see you like all the same books my brother reads," she exclaimed. "I'll have to introduce you two."

Oh great, I thought, just what I need, another introduction. I smiled, not taking the bait. We finished our interview and Maria promised to get back to me the following week. I was certain she would.

As she left she repeated enthusiastically, "I'm going to tell my brother about you." I just smiled and waved.

Closing the door, I thought of Peter. He had continued to talk about living in Portland, once saying, "When I move up here we've got to get a piano." On his last visit, he'd bought my son a recorder and promised to teach him to play.

Over the next couple of months, Peter visited several times. He'd always stay about 10 days. When he wasn't there he'd usually telephone daily. Strangely, he'd never given me his phone number and, naively, I had never asked. We'd become a couple.

Of one other thing I'd become certain: he was psychic. One morning I had a dream.

Peter had come and sat on the edge of my bed. We were talking. He was telling me something of great importance. I could feel him there. When he touched my arm, I felt it. As the dream was ending he said, "Remember these words…fly like an eagle…." They were words from a song by the Steve Miller Band.

As I lay in bed thinking of this dream, the phone rang.

"So what did you think of my visit?" Peter asked.

Startled, I sat up. "What visit?"

"Oh, come on. Don't tell me you didn't talk to me as I sat on the bed next to you. What did I ask you to remember?" he quizzed.

My silence said it all.

"Well?" he prodded.

"You said….you said remember these words."

"Uh huh. And what were they?" he pushed.

"Fly," I said.

"Fly...like an eagle," he finished.

Silence again on my end.

Finally I asked, "How did you do that?"

"It was nothing," he boasted. He changed the subject, refusing to speak of it again.

How bizarre, I thought. I had just left a man who claimed to be a teacher and had the groupies to prove it, but whose best efforts were only hypnotic parlor games; now I was with a man who claimed nothing, was obviously psychic, but refused to talk about it.

Peter's next visit would be his last.

"Am I dropping you off in town?" I asked after picking him up at the airport.

"Uh, no," he responded. "Let's just go to your place."

I looked at him. He always went to see Dave first to talk about the jobs they'd work on while he was in town.

"Dave and I haven't been communicating very well," he said, turning to look out the window.

The next day Peter stayed home all day. At one point he asked me to drive him to a small nearby town to speak to a man who owned a music store there.

"It's for sale," he told me. "Just looking."

Now I knew something was definitely up. Finally Peter told me he and Dave disagreed about how to run their business. I had the feeling finances were involved. I also began feeling a rock in my stomach. We sat across from each other. He held both of my hands, silently gazing into my eyes. When he spoke again, he told me he didn't know what the future held. Peter said that Dave and he were to meet the next day. The outcome didn't seem positive. A sense of panic engulfed me.

"Does this mean what I think it does?"

He nodded yes. He wouldn't be coming to Portland as often, if at all.

"We can work it out," I said desperately. "You can still move up here."

"No," he said still gazing into my eyes. "All of my work is in San Francisco." Tears filled his eyes. "It feels like I'll never see you again."

"But Peter, why? We can work this out. I'll come down there, you can come…."

He stopped me, shaking his head.

"You can't come to San Francisco. I…I live with a woman." He spoke quietly, his eyes cast down to the floor.

"You what!" I shouted in disbelief. Once again, in less than three months, the bottom fell out of my world. I sat back horrified, speechless.

"It's not what you think," he protested. "We just live together, but we live separately. It's her house. She has her living space. I have mine."

"But you're a couple?" I whispered.

"Well, some people think so, but not really, no," he

said evasively.

"So that's why you never gave me your phone number?"

He nodded.

"What's her name?" I had to know; it was like picking a scab.

"Her name is Mary." He spoke now with a firmness I'd not heard before. "I'm not willing to discuss any more about her."

"Does she know about us?" I pressed.

He rose and stepped away in an attempt to end this discussion. "I believe she suspects," he admitted. "Look, I don't like this anymore than you. I hate it, in fact. But there's nothing I can do about it. At least not right now. Do you want me to leave? I can go get a room. But I can tell you with all my heart, I don't want this, what we have, to be over."

As he spoke tears again welled up in his eyes. My heart was breaking. I couldn't let him go.

"No, stay. Please stay."

For the next three days we attempted to function as normally as possible. He and Dave indeed, parted ways. I didn't ask the details, knowing Sally would fill me in later.

Then the day came. Peter had booked a late flight so we could maximize every moment. I came to comprehend the meaning that day that "parting is such sweet sorrow." We laughed and cried.

At one point, he held me at arms' length, hands around my waist. Tilting his head slightly as if looking beyond me, he exclaimed, "You have another child coming."

"No way," I said. I diligently took birth control pills.

He said it again, adding that he could not be the father. "I can't be a father to another child."

"You have a child?" I asked, surprised. I'd certainly learned a lot about this man on this visit. He confirmed that he had a daughter, about nine years old, near my son's age. He told me her name and admitted he was a failure as a parent, which caused him a lot of pain. He said he could not go through it again.

"It doesn't matter if you use a dozen different types of protection," he said, "this child will come."

I let it drop then, and reasoned later that he'd told me that to comfort himself about going away. Then with many tears and promises, he was gone.

I continued to hear from Peter. He phoned every day for a while. We made plans to meet in L.A. but they fell through.

Ten

Shortly after Peter left, I received a call from Maria persuading me to join her and her brother for lunch. "Good then, I'll pick you up tomorrow."

I hung up. Maria was so happy, so up, so chirpy. As glum as I felt, I didn't know how I'd get through a lunch with her.

The next day, she filled me in about her brother. He was a math teacher at Portland Community College's Sylvania campus, where we'd be meeting him for lunch. He was knowledgeable, she said, about psychic things, so she was confident we'd have lots to talk about. As she parked the car I began to feel a bit intimidated. I'd never been on a college campus before. Pushing past us were scores of energetic, laughing students, bright futures shining ahead of them. I felt awkward and out of place.

As we walked across the campus and into the commons building, I hoped lunch would be brief. I was out of my comfort zone.

"Oh, there he is!" Maria exclaimed, waving to a man who stood up from his table to greet us. He smiled, extending his hand to me as we approached. He was shorter than I, "like a leprechaun" he would later say about himself. He shared Maria's smile and twinkling eyes, and as I would discover, her cheery optimism.

"Suzanne, meet my brother, Bob Finnell."

Bob Finnell.

My heart began beating wildly. Since my dream, the name Bob Finnell had haunted me.

I shook hands with the man who'd been with me over Mt. Shasta! I was tongue-tied. Fortunately, the two of them were not. They had some catching up to do. Maria took the seat beside me; Bob sat down across from us. As they chatted, I suddenly realized Bob had asked me a question.

"Excuse me?" I said.

"Would you like some coffee?" I nodded and he hastened to the counter.

Maria looked concerned. "Are you okay? You look pale."

I assured her that I was fine, just a bit overwhelmed. Thinking I was referring to the two of them talking so much, Maria began to apologize.

"No, no. It's – it's something else."

I pulled myself together and the rest of the lunch was pleasant. As we finished up, Mr. Finnell asked about my psychic abilities and studies. He suggested we meet again.

As he and I exchanged phone numbers, he announced, "I think we may have some work to do together."

If you only knew, I thought. Something told me to keep the Shasta dream to myself, for now.

A week later, Mr. Finnell telephoned, inviting me to lunch. We met at a café across from the school.

He thanked me for meeting him off-campus. "There are too many ears…most of my colleagues know nothing of my involvement in psychic studies," he said.

I understood well the need for safety. This would be the beginning of a lifelong friendship.

After I briefed Finnell about my life to date, he asked

about the hypnotist I'd lived with. He spoke at length about hypnosis and the psychic and etheric forces involved, using big words and phrases I didn't understand.

This dynamic became the nature of our meetings. I would ask questions or make small talk, he would respond with amazing knowledge of what he referred to as the "supersensible world," and I wouldn't understand. Frequently, I'd drive away from our lunches without a clue about what we'd discussed, but something kept me coming back for more.

Finnell began giving me Rudolf Steiner books. He insisted that I read *Knowledge of Higher Worlds and Its Attainment*, a book that was of particular importance to him. Trusting his guidance, I tackled it. At first I couldn't understand a word of it. I complained that after a sentence or two, I would fall asleep. He would only smile and say, "Keep reading. You don't need to understand it. You won't get it. It will get you." He was right, and for the next several years I would devour Steiner's work.

Finnell kept our meetings professional. Although he was curious about my personal life, he would usually just shake his head and chuckle as I told him about it, and then continue on with some talk of early Atlantis or Buddha on Mars!

Then one day he made a proposition. He wanted to conduct a telepathy study. Would I be interested in working with him? I eagerly consented, and in the following weeks, he formed the basis and set up for the study.

JOURNAL ENTRY

Date: March 1977

TELEPATHY EXPERIMENT

Objective: To see if images can be transmitted psychically between two people in different locations.

Materials and Methods: The subject and I convened weekly on Sunday evening to establish a categorical baseline and compare observations from the previous week's experiment. During the Sunday meetings we decided the category to be focused on and we assigned a sender and a receiver. The role of sender and receiver was alternated each week. Anything was fair game in the categories of food, color, song, book title, and object.

Tuesday, 3:00

Sender: Bob	Receiver: Suzanne
Image: Pink rose	Image: Pink tulip

Summary: Initially, we would be fairly accurate with color and less so with the exact nature of the flower. Reception improved with time. After the third week, we noticed that more than a simple image began to be transmitted and received. Observations about feelings, environment and ambient experiences began to come through. If the sender was feeling particularly harried one day, the receiver felt the anxiety. Clarity was enhanced by music. If either participant was humming at the time that he was sending, the music seemed to carry the images more easily and provide a very accurate reception. It seemed to ride on the "waves" of the music. Often the specific song left an impression as well. Visual observation of the transmitted object (looking at a rose) also delivered clearer reception.

Suzanne missed a 3:00 p.m. appointment and
transmitted at 7:00 p.m. instead; Bob, who
did not know of the schedule change, was able
to receive the image in the form that it was
sent. The necessity for a dedicated time became
irrelevant; the Intention and category were
sufficient to achieve communication.

At one of the Sunday sessions, Suzanne's
nine-year-old son asked to participate. It
was decided that he was to send an animal on
Thursday. Suzanne received the image of a brown
bear; Bob received the image of a bear in the
snow. Suzanne's disappointed son told them that
he had been thinking about a dinosaur. When
Suzanne asked her son where he was sitting when
he sent the message, he answered that he sat
on his bed and took her to show exactly where
he sat. They both discovered that from the
place where he had been seated when he sent the
dinosaur, his line of sight was focused directly
on a poster of a polar bear in a snow-covered
wood.

This experiment extended over a year and became the
basis for our weekly get-togethers. We began meeting at
the farm on Sunday afternoons or whenever Bob could
get away. Although Bob was married, he never revealed
much about his personal life. Our relationship was definitely student and mentor. Aside from my father, it was
also the first safe relationship I'd had with a man.

A few months into our study, during one of Bob's
weekly visits, I decided it was time to confess about my
angel dialogues and the journals I had kept years before.

I hesitantly detailed to Bob how my meditations had
evolved from quiet, reflective time to conversations with
an inner voice that would respond to my questions. I also

recounted to him the *fire* that only I could see, which had sparked my decision to meditate. His eyes widened and a smile crossed his face.

I could see a plan forming under the calculating demeanor of the professor. He found a pause while cleaning his immaculate glasses as he carefully formulated his next request.

"How would you like to try another experiment? I wonder what would happen if, instead of pen and paper, someone were to sit with you as you meditate and ask the question for you? I'd be honored to sit with you and be the one to ask the question."

Reason was overcome by terror. I was back to the days of my youth, suddenly hearing again my mother's demands not to take home the prizes…and later, the damning words shouted by an ex-husband who'd read my private dialogues. I couldn't bear another humiliation, especially from an esteemed college math teacher.

But Bob was kind. He had earned my trust. And as I pondered what he asked, a voice said, "Just do it."

"Yes, I would like that," I agreed. The following Sunday we began.

Our experiments took us to unknown realms. Seated in the corner of the plush sofa in my living room and embraced by a quilted blanket beside the crackling fire, I would quiet my mind. Bob would occupy a chair about three feet away. A candle between us added its flame to the glow and provided a point of focus for us both. I would settle my breath and eventually began to tremble. My shivering was Bob's cue to ask if I was ready. Just above a whisper, I breathed out a single word, "Yes."

He would pose a question and I would listen. The answers might be phrased as a concise affirmative or negative or extend for several minutes. I would speak the response I *heard,* so Bob and I started to call these sessions "speakings." I had become a foreign interpreter after all.

In the midst of these experiments, Maria had found a work-study program for me that was to begin in the fall.

Eleven

"Hey, I got something I want to show you. Meet me at Billy Bang's later," my sister said excitedly over the phone.

I hadn't had the heart to venture out much since Peter left. And staying home with Rudolf Steiner was not exactly a party. As I walked through the mall that led to Billy Bang's, I rounded a corner and stopped cold, arrested by a pair of portraits in the window of a portrait studio. Next to a very large semblance of Walter Cronkite, with his genial smile, was a nearly floor-to-ceiling image of a beautiful woman. Dressed in black, her long, blond hair cascading over her shoulders, she was breathtaking. Her gaze was ethereal and she mesmerized me. I knew her. Although we'd never met, I knew her.

My sister's voice snapped me back to the present. "There you are. What the hell are you doing?" she asked, following my gaze. Noticing the portrait that held me spellbound, she tugged on my arm, "Mmmmmm, pretty girl. Come on. We got the last seats in the house. I don't want to lose them."

What could be so important, I wondered, following her into the bar, that she would come looking for me. As we sat down Sally placed a letter addressed to her on the table.

"So, what do you hear from Peter?" Sally asked.

"Not much," I shrugged. "What's up?"

As we drank the wine that she had ordered, she opened the envelope and handed me the letter. Reading the words that were clearly meant for her eyes only, I shook my head. "What's this? Who is this?" I asked, "Why am I reading it?"

"Read the last line," she said. I did. Whoever it was would be in Portland soon, arriving on Flight 704, and he wanted Sally to pick him up. I laid the letter down and looked up at her.

"Well?" I demanded.

Lifting her glass of Chardonnay, she stammered an explanation. For the last month she'd been writing to a man, Rick, who'd befriended Charles in jail. By the sound of the letter the relationship was fairly advanced.

She had already responded to the letter and told Rick she would pick him up. However, she had no car. "So," she wheedled, "you won't mind taking me to get him?"

"To get him?" I echoed.

"Yes, just back to my place. He's going to stay with me for a while."

I gulped my wine. "Are you out of your mind?" I hissed. "He's been in jail."

Sally lowered her eyes. When she raised them, they were wet with the hint of tears. She described how his romantic letters had revealed his true heart. And she dismissed his crimes: he was an artist, owner of a gallery in Red Lodge, Montana, he had told her. His crime was forgery. She assumed he'd forged a Van Gogh or something. She didn't care.

"It's not like he's a murderer or something," Sally argued as I put my head in my hands. I looked up at her. She seemed so happy. How could I say no?

On the day of Rick's arrival, we waited at the airport gate, our eyes following every single guy who exited the plane, since we had no idea what he looked like. Finally, a tall linebacker sort of guy, carrying a duffle bag, stepped toward us.

"Sally?" he spoke tentatively.

"Rick?" She responded. He gave her a warm hug.

"Uh, you must be Sally's sister," he said stretching out his hand with a dimpled smile. His blue eyes shone with kindness. He had a mane of curly blond hair cut short. I suggested we move on to the luggage claim.

Chuckling, he proclaimed as he lifted his bag, "This is it. You're looking at my luggage claim. Let's find the bar instead. I need a Scotch." Sally and I exchanged a quick glance.

"Sure, why not," she said as he put his arm around her waist. Looking back over her shoulder she mouthed, "Come on!"

We found a table by a window overlooking the tarmac. When the waitress appeared for our order. Rick told her what he wanted, reached in his wallet, tossed a $50 bill on the table, and excused himself to visit the men's room. .

As he walked off, Sally let out an "Argh!"

I knew where this was going. I'd been watching her body language.

"He can't come home with me! He's so not my type. He's so...so..."

"Straight?" I finished her sentence for her.

"Yeah, straight," she nodded. "If I let him in the house, my roommate will shit! He looks like a narc. What am I going to do?"

"What do you mean 'What am I going to do?'" I asked,

gathering up my purse. "We're getting out of here."

She grabbed my arm. "No, sit down. We can't just leave. We can't just dump him here. Let's at least go to Mom and Dad's for a while. That should be okay," she reasoned.

I looked up as Rick returned to the table. He had a great smile.

On the drive to Mom and Dad's, Rick did most of the talking. His crime, he said, was not even a crime in most states, but it was in California. Apparently he liked to copy things. He was eager to return to his gallery in Montana, but just had to stop in Portland to meet the lady he'd been writing to. Sally rolled her eyes. When we pulled up in front of Mom and Dad's, Mom opened the door and yelled a greeting. The house was full of friends.

"We thought we should give you an Oregon welcome," was Mom's greeting to this man she'd never met.

Rick was introduced to all and greeted warmly. Somewhere along the way he acquired a glass of wine. Oddly enough, he fit right in. I watched him mingle.

"Well, he's in," I lamented to Sally. She was not happy.

As the afternoon went on, Sally finally stood up and said, "I've got to talk to him. I've got to tell him." Setting her glass down, she headed to the group of men gathered together listening to Rick tell football stories. My son, too, was all ears. Sally interrupted and asked Rick if she might speak to him alone. They went back to the den and closed the door.

Mom wandered over to me. "What's going on?"

"He's not her type. She's got to ditch him," I said apathetically. As much as I loved my dear sister, she was more like my child than my sibling. I'd come to her rescue so many times through the years. We couldn't have been more different. Her lack of responsibility was equal to my need to take care of her. It was a vicious cycle.

"What? He's so nice. So friendly," Mom insisted. "What's the matter with her?" She huffed off to the other guests. After an hour Sally and Rick emerged from the den. Rick went to refill his wine glass. Sally sat next to me on the sofa. Mother materialized next to us.

"Sooooo, did you tell him?" I asked.

She said he took it well. But he didn't know what to do in Portland the next few days or where he'd stay. She stopped, looking down at her hands now and fussing with her rings.

"Uh, I mentioned he might be able to stay with you at the farm. You've got plenty of room," she said quietly.

"That's a great idea!" Mom blurted. "We can't just kick him out."

I shook my head. "You're kidding. Right? Both of you?" How was this suddenly my problem?

"That settles it then," Mom said. Drink in hand, she walked away.

Sally, too, stood now. 'It'll be okay," she said. "He's a nice guy, and it's only a few days. Thanks. I owe you big time." Her smile returned as she left me to refill her wine glass.

I sat stunned, laughter and chatter encasing me in a lonely shell. Numbness grew. I was surrounded by laughing, joyful people and I could not be more disconnected from them. My mother and sister had converged to remove, in one instant, the tenuous grasp that I then had over my life. I had done nothing to deny them, to resist their idea of placing a strange man in my house, in my life, with my son. It was as if a great wind had blown in and I was just a leaf floating on it. I was defeated.

An unfamiliar voice roused me. Rick was thanking me for agreeing to let him stay at the farm for a few days.

"Yeah, sure. Whatever," I muttered.

Rae and Jerry came to sit with me. "It's great you're going to let Rick stay. We've been talking to him and he seems like an okay guy," Rae said. "Funny too. And boy can he drink," she continued, lifting her glass to no one in particular.

My glum look must have given me away.

Jerry patted my leg. "Now don't look so concerned. We're going to keep a close eye on him," he chuckled re-assuringly.

"Yeah," I shrugged.

On the way home my son and Rick talked about sports. Rick promised to play catch with him in the morn-ing. I was tired, really tired. After getting my son to bed, I placed a pillow and blankets on the sofa in the fireplace room for Rick. He'd lit a small fire. As I turned to go he said, "Hey, thanks again. I promise to stay out from un-derfoot. You have no idea how great it's gonna be sleep-ing by this fire tonight. Thanks." I waved him off. Walk-ing down the hall to my room, I missed Peter. It had been days since his last phone call.

The next morning I woke to the smell of bacon, coffee and pancakes. Startled, I jumped up just as my son burst through the door.

"Mom, get up. We have a surprise for you." Slipping on my robe I followed him to the kitchen. Rick handed me a cup of coffee and pulled back a chair for me at the table.

Someone had set the table. I glanced at my son. He was smiling.

"I hope it's okay. We took the truck and went to the store," Rick said apologetically. "Man. You had nothing in this house to eat. But we fixed that, didn't we?" he said to my son, as he ruffled his hair. My son opened the refrigerator.

"Look, Mom--food!" he exclaimed. On food stamps, my cupboard often resembled Old Mother Hubbard's. The vision of all that food reignited my shame.

The front door opened and in walked my dad. "Just checking up on you all," he said, smiling. I smiled back, wondering what was happening to my life.

My son, father, sister and mother had decided Rick should stay. Who was I to have a vote? Rick stayed.

From the first day, he began the arduous tasks of cleaning up around the house, making repairs, painting walls and mowing the lawn. One day he appeared with an enormous brown parcel under his arm. He opened it to reveal canvases, paintbrushes, oils and acrylics and promptly began to create a beautiful landscape. He soon became the local source of entertainment as neighbors and friends appeared each day to observe this linebacker of a man cradling a paintbrush; landscapes and seascapes emerging from the canvas. His artwork began generating income. Before long, my garage looked like a framing shop.

Everyone who dropped in was enamored, charmed by Rick's teddy bear mannerisms. He was never at a loss for stories of his adventurous life and never at a loss for an audience.

He enjoyed his Scotch, wine and beer. Since I seemed to be taking my cues these days from the people around me, it never occurred to me that his drinking could be a problem. More than one person commented on how good Rick was for my son. I began to ignore my feeling of discomfort with him.

Rick remarked that everyone could see we were destined to be a couple, everyone, that is, except me. I felt swept along by this force that had joined my life. The people surrounding me were captured by Rick's charisma; since each one seemed drawn to him, they gave no credence to my hesitations or feelings. Rick was my savior, in their opinion, rescuing me from poor past choices and a life of economic bleakness. The pressure was palpable.

Bob Finnell and I continued our weekly sessions in the midst of all of this. He had met Rick and found him talented and fascinating. Bob would frequently sit and watch Rick paint. Sometimes they would discuss the angelic realm's influence on art, but mostly it was guy stuff. Rick had worked in computers at one time, so he and Bob frequently spoke about math and science. Rick never intruded on the time Bob and I spent together. He had only a mild interest in what we were doing or discussing. I was grateful Rick did not harbor the same hatred for all things psychic, as had so many others, because those sessions with Bob felt like the only normal part of my life.

Twelve

One rare afternoon when it was just Rick and I, he stood up from his canvas and stretched. "Come on," he said. "We need to go to the bank."

"What for?" I asked.

Reaching in his back pocket, Rick pulled out a long white envelope. "It's a check for $20,000. I sold my share in the gallery in Montana. I need to bank it. I thought we'd just put it in your account so you can pay bills and we can start going to some art shows. I need to buy supplies."

"$20,000?" I exclaimed, stunned.

After a moment's consideration he suggested, "On second thought, why don't you just give me a deposit slip. I'll run to town while you get cleaned up and changed, so I can take you to dinner."

After the back door closed, I flew down the hall, excited. Maybe this was going to work out. Maybe there was hope for my life after all. I began humming as I searched my closet for something to wear. Suddenly I stopped, overwhelmed. Tears stung my eyes. I hadn't hummed or sang for such a long time. Maybe, just maybe, things would be okay. I allowed a sliver of joy into my soul.

The art shows began. It was summer and we'd pack up Rick's canvases and travel to mall shows around town and further away. It was fun for a while. I became an accomplished salesman. And the extra money in the bank account took the pressure off.

Then, one day we came home from a weeklong show out of town when my dad called. "I need to talk to you, alone, and soon," he said urgently.

When I arrived at my parents' house, they were sitting at the kitchen table looking grim. Dad stood to greet me.

"What's going on up at the farm?" he said.

"What do you mean?"

"Well, I was up there feeding your dog, and some man from an art supply store showed up. He was looking for you. He said you owed him money for a bad check." Dad's voice shook.

"What? That's not possible," I said, completely confused.

"So I went to talk to George at the bank. He confided that you were seriously overdrawn. They've sent you numerous notices, but you ignored them so they closed your account."

This couldn't be true. I shook my head.

"No, there has to be some mistake," I insisted. I told them how Rick had put his $20,000 check for selling his gallery in my account.

Dad cleared his throat. "There is no gallery in Montana."

After leaving the bank, Dad had made some phone calls checking up on some of Rick's claims. "There is no Red Lodge Gallery." He'd called the Red Lodge Chamber of Commerce. They'd never heard of Rick.

I shook my head. "But I've received nothing from the bank. No notices or phone calls...." Then I stopped, remembering. Rick had been checking the mail every day. He had also been grabbing the phone when it rang. "Oh no," was all I could utter.

Mom was crying now. "We're so worried for you," she said reaching over to touch my arm. I just stared at her.

"How much...?" I wondered, trying to remember the checks I'd written. The scene in front of me began to blur. Dad was attempting to reassure me now. I could hear him saying we could work it out with the bank somehow.

"I'm going home with you. We need to find out what's going on," he declared. He got in his car to follow me home.

Driving back to the farm, I said a prayer to spirit. "Please help me if you can," I whispered. I turned on the radio. Paul McCartney was singing, "Let it be...." A message from spirit perhaps. Or just a coincidence. Either way I felt comforted.

As I got out of my truck, Dad pulled up beside me. Rick was in the garage, unpacking from the art show. He walked over to greet us. I looked around for my son.

Rick answered my look. "He's in watching TV." I was relieved. I didn't want him part of what was about to happen.

Dad initiated. He recounted to Rick what he'd told me, ending with, "We need to know the truth. We all care about you. Just tell us what's going on."

Rick looked at us in disbelief. "Well, the bank's made a mistake," he said. "It wasn't a check I deposited but a bank draft. Sometimes it takes longer for those monies to be released. It has to be some kind of mistake." He paused. "I'll go in tomorrow and clear it all up," he said with such certainty that Dad appeared satisfied.

As the two continued talking, I went in the house. I felt nauseous and wanted to lie down. It was Sunday and Bob Finnell would be over soon. I was desperate for our sessions now. They brought sanity and sanctuary. Unfortunately, the rules of the dialogues were clear about daily life. Cosmic truths were available, but, when asked about help for specifics of day-to-day living, the response was disappointingly consistent: "You must trust you are being guided, guided at a very high level."

Great consolation. How do I pay my bills? More than once, I'd felt abandoned. I was lost in a world where everyone else seemed to know how to live; I hadn't made that prebirth meeting that explained how to live and thrive. Life had become terrifying. If it were not for Bob's and my spirit sessions and the still, small voice inside that reassured me that God loved me, I would not have survived.

As the week went by and no more bank notices arrived, I began to believe Rick had taken care of it. He assured me repeatedly that it was a misunderstanding and the bank would clear it all up. I continued to believe him; at that point, I really needed to. I had no way of paying those checks and bank charges. I'd also been sick. Summer flu had been going around.

One morning toward the end of the week, I was home alone. The dog's barking alerted me to a visitor. Opening the front door, I was surprised to see George, the branch manager of the bank walking up the path. He'd been a casual friend of my dad's for years.

"George. What a surprise! What are you doing here?" I greeted him.

"May I come in?" he asked curtly.

"Of course," I said. "Can I get you some coffee?"

"No." He wasn't smiling. "I've known your family for years," he began, "and that's why this is so upsetting to me." As he spoke he opened his briefcase and laid out copies of all the checks I'd written, all the checks that had been returned with NSF — "not sufficient funds" stamped on them.

"What's going on here?" he demanded. "You could be in very big trouble."

"But I thought Rick came in to the bank and cleared it all up," I stammered.

"Who?" he asked.

I told George what Rick had told me about bank drafts and the amount he'd deposited into my account.

Shaking his head, George spread out my bank statements on the kitchen table. "There have been no deposits in your account for weeks," he said grimly.

I stared at the statements.

"Look," he said, "here's what you need to do. And you need to do it soon. This is serious. You need to personally contact all these businesses and make arrangements to pay them back. I'll vouch for you at the bank. I'll waive some of our bank charges, but, Suzanne, you will have to make good on the rest." He was stern but helpful.

Somewhat relieved, I promised George that I would follow through immediately. As I walked him to his car, he turned and looked at me.

"I might be out of line," he said, "but lose the guy."

Nodding, I thanked him again. At least now I knew what I had to do.

I left the bank statements and checks lying on the table after George left. When Rick returned he saw them and asked, "What's this?"

I explained. He assured me we would cover all the checks. I told him that from now on it wouldn't be "we," it would be I who would handle the finances. It was my name and well-being on the line. He continued to assure me it was all a big mistake. I just wanted him to leave, but I also needed him to clean up this mess he'd made of my life. He begged me to trust him.

Later that afternoon Rae and Jerry came up to the farm. They had purchased one of Rick's paintings and had come to collect it. Part of the payment was a bottle of Scotch. Rick opened it and began drinking. Within a few hours he was drunk. Then he seemed to snap. He became loud and angry. He said we were all ignorant and didn't know whom we were messing with. As Rae attempted to reason with him, he grew more agitated. Finally, throwing his glass against the wall, he grabbed my car keys and stormed out. Jerry tried to stop him, but Rick shoved him off. I watched this taking place as if it were a horror movie. The sound of truck tires on the gravel driveway brought me back. I looked at Rae. "He can't drive in that condition. It's my truck!" I shouted, trying to shake off the hysteria creeping in on me. I was weeping, and my stomach was heaving. I headed to the bathroom, feeling like I was about to vomit.

Rae followed. "Are you okay?" she asked. "You haven't been drinking. Why are you sick?"

I told her I'd been sick all week.

"We need to get you to the doctor," she said firmly. "You look horrible."

Protesting weakly, I let Rae take my arm. She grabbed my purse on the way out and escorted me to her car. Several hours and tests later, the results were clear. I was pregnant.

Rick was gone for three days. In many ways I was relieved and hoped I'd never hear from him again. After the initial shock I'd come to accept that I could deal with the pregnancy. All of it. By myself. This child had been foreseen. I thought of Peter's words many times. Despite my precautions, this child had been conceived. It was meant to be. Knowing this brought me comfort and even a peculiar sense of stability. This child had been predicted. My life must somehow then be on track.

On day four, when Rick sheepishly entered the kitchen, I informed him I was pregnant. He became emotional and begged me to let him stay. I really just wanted him to go. My life had been nothing but chaos since he'd arrived and I knew I could never pay off the debts I owed because of him. He swore off drinking, promised to get a real job and said we could get married, which was the last thing I wanted. I hung my head, ever the victim, and feebly agreed that if he drank again it would be over. If he was arrested, it would be over. I would absolutely not stand by him in either of those conditions.

A few days later he phoned my friend Pat who owned a trucking company. Pat had earlier offered him a job. Rick was hired and began driving a truck locally. Soon we were able to pay off all the mess. He threw out the booze. It would be several years before he drank again.

By the fifth month, I was blossoming and enjoying my pregnancy. I also seemed to be getting more psychic. Despite disheartenment from the critics in my life, I had immersed myself in the world of metaphysics without a clear purpose or direction, desperate to know myself. But under Bob Finnell's tutelage, my psychic journey found a coherent direction. He coached me to evolve my spiritual side, leaving the psychic part of my nature to its own unfolding, a natural side-effect of spiritual growth. A new understanding of life was beginning to dawn in me; a clearer, more practical awareness. Thanks to my relationship with Bob Finnell, who remained unwavering in his support, I was sensing an authenticity, vague though it was, in my being.

It was during this time I had amazing out-of-body experiences and visions. *One morning as I cleaned the kitchen after breakfast, I saw a curly-haired, blond girl, about two years old, run past the kitchen table and down the hall.* I knew it was my unborn child. Even when the doctor kept predicting a boy, I'd shake my head and confidently say, "Sorry, doctor, it's a girl." I had seen her.

Rick and I managed to have a relationship of sorts. Sober, he was a great guy. My son adored him, and once through our crisis, my parents even accepted him back. He continued to paint but there were no more art shows. Life was marginal. I lived in fear that he would drink again. I remained vigilant.

I still thought of Peter often. One day while visiting with my sister his name came up. She'd taken a call from him for Dave. She seemed hesitant.

"What?" I pushed.

"I don't want to stir things up," she said, "after all that you and Rick have been through."

"Well, what?" I demanded. "You can't not tell me now."

She relented. "He asked about you. He said he'd phoned several times but each time some guy answered and said you'd moved. The last time he got upset with Peter and told him to never call that number again. When Peter tried a few weeks later the number had been disconnected." She stopped and looked at me.

"I see," was all I could say. We both knew the story. Rick had been intercepting my calls during the check-writing fiasco.

"Sorry," she said, taking my hand. "Well, I filled him in and told him you were pregnant. He didn't seem surprised."

I told her about his prediction.

She smirked. "Sounds like Peter."

I started to give her a message for him, and then stopped. It didn't matter now. Futility was my constant companion. My life had again taken a new form and shape. Literally! I took small comfort in knowing that he had sought me out and wanted to talk to me again.

Much later in my life, I learned the rest of the story about Peter. Leafing through a *People* magazine, a name caught my eye. I turned back the few pages to it. Janis Joplin's love letters were to be auctioned. Fifty-seven love letters between her and fiancé Peter DeBlanc were being sold by Peter's ex-wife. Twenty-two years earlier, Peter had insisted that he'd never sell Janis's letters to her biographers. I was stunned. He'd told me the truth.

I thought of attempting to contact Peter. We had, after all, never really said goodbye. I remembered he was from Philadelphia. I spoke with a relative there who graciously brought me up to date. Peter was living in St. Thomas, where he'd been for the last 20 years. He was married and had his own business. Mine was not the first phone call they'd had about him since the article came out. I hung up with his phone number and email address in hand. I never called.

Peter died in 2002.

Thirteen

My relationship with Sally had been tense during the check-writing episode. She'd been angry at Rick and felt responsible for introducing him to the family. She was among those who'd encouraged the relationship initially, for my son's sake. Now she just barely tolerated Rick. She appeared to be excited about the baby, but I sensed an unspoken hesitancy in her.

During my pregnancy, Sally and I had not been able to spend much time together. She had worked in retail or waitressing, but had decided to go for a job that might become more of a career and had gotten a secretarial job at Jantzen, the swimwear manufacturer. Bored after several months of that, she decided to apply for a higher paying, more challenging position as the assistant to one of the company's vice presidents. As she told me about the position, she said she didn't feel qualified or hopeful, but ended with a glib "but I'm cute!"

Sally was trying to get straight, in her own way. She dressed in more stylish and sophisticated clothing, got herself a new "grownup" hairstyle and started wearing makeup.

I encouraged her attempts to clean up, but Sally struggled. Through the years, she had used a variety of drugs, and she also enjoyed her alcohol. She confided that she felt she was just pretending at work, like she was trying to be something she was not, trying to fit in, to be a "good girl." It was only on the weekends that she felt she could be herself. She was a hippie, a flower child, pressured by friends who were artists and entertainers to not abandon the lifestyle. She began feeling alienated by them as she attempted to be what she thought was "normal."

Oh, how well I understood.

One evening in mid-October she called me, sobbing. She had gotten the position as executive secretary to the vice president a few weeks earlier. Now, she realized, she was in over her head.

"I don't know how to take a letter. I don't know short-hand, or how to use a Dictaphone," she moaned.

By Christmas I'd become very concerned about Sally. She lacked her usual sparkle, rarely smiling or joking. When I'd inquire about her friends, she'd just shrug. An old musician friend, Will, had moved in with her and her roommate Dave. His arrival seemed to only slightly re-juvenate her. Her slight frame became emaciated. She missed a lot of work because of stomach pains yet refused to see a doctor. My concern escalated.

I wanted to help, but she had shut down and become unreachable. Overwhelmed in my own daily struggle, I quit trying.

In late January I awoke to an early morning phone call.

"Suzy, we're at the hospital with Sally." Mom sounded anxious.

"What? What's wrong?" I asked, a feeling of dread coming over me.

"We don't know. Will phoned a few hours ago; he couldn't wake her. He heard her alarm go off and when she didn't turn it off, he went in to check. She wouldn't wake up. Dad and I got there just as the ambulance arrived. Don't worry. She's awake now, but they're going to keep her a few days."

By now I was up and getting hastily dressed. "I'll be right there," I said.

"No!" Mom cut me off harshly.

"What do you mean, 'No'? I'm her sister. She needs me!"

"Stay home. Take care of yourself. They won't let anyone see her right now," Mom said firmly.

I replaced the receiver, tears falling freely. "What have you done, Sally? What have you done?"

Sally remained in the hospital for two weeks. Mom said she'd had a nervous breakdown. But actually she'd swallowed a bottle of Coricidin, and washed it down with furniture stripper. Her stomach had been pumped. For the duration of her hospital stay, she had seen only Mom, which was surprising and upsetting, considering the volatile history between them. I suspect it was Mom who requested "no visitors."

The hospital would not release Sally unless she had a therapist to work with her. Mom and Rae conspired to have her released to Rae's care since she was a certified geriatric counselor. I was troubled by this decision. Rae worked at a senior center, for God's sake. My sister needed real help.

Eventually, Sally was released and went to stay with Mom and Dad. We were given orders to never speak to her about the incident, as it might cause a relapse. She could go nowhere without Mom or Dad and was never to be left alone. I was never allowed to be with her privately.

During my visits, she would sit and stare, offering only minimal responses. I missed her laughter.

One time when I was visiting, Mom was talking on the phone with a neighbor about a young man a few blocks down who'd killed himself. Sally had gone to high school with him and knew him vaguely.

After Mom hung up she turned to us and said, "Can you imagine? He gassed himself in his parents' garage. What kind of person kills himself? And the poor parents….. What a mean thing to do. He must have been a real sick…." Her tactless tirade continued.

Sally, who was sitting by the window, just pulled the curtain back and looked down the street toward the young man's house. I wanted to get her away from my mom. Maybe she'd snap out of it then. But Mom had a tether on her. "Doctor's orders," she said.

When I left that day I hugged Sally and whispered, "If you need me, call, please." A blank stare lacking any recognition was her only response. Mom demanded to know what we were whispering about.

I asked Rae what she was doing to help Sally. She laughed and said, "Oh, I take her a bottle of wine. We sit and talk. Don't worry. She's okay."

I wondered if the whole world had gone crazy.

In the meantime, Rick was working hard and we were getting along. My birthday at the end of March was quiet. Mom and Sally came to visit briefly. Sally gave me an enameled teapot. She and I had a history of always trying to outdo each other at birthdays and Christmas with unique, unusual gifts that only we would like or understand. The teapot was a huge statement. It was void of thought or feeling, a passionless gift from a passionless soul.

I was so scared for her. For the first time in our lives, she was unreachable.

When they left I cried. "Where has Sally gone?"

My due date, April 12, came and went. Two weeks later, my doctor spoke his concern. By his estimate the baby weighed nearly nine pounds. We began to talk about my having a C-section, finally scheduling the surgery for Tuesday, May 2.

The last time I saw my sister was Friday evening, April 28, 1978. I had stopped by my mom and dad's on my way to a UFO lecture close to their house. Sally declined my offer to go with me; the Portland Trailblazers were in the playoffs and she wanted to watch the game. She was looking good that night, with a little of the old sparkle in her eyes. As I walked down the stairs to the front door, she reached through the stair railing and touched my hand. She smiled and told me to have fun. I'll remember that touch forever.

Sunday morning, April 30, I awoke to sharp contractions. Without even calling the doctor, Rick said, "We're getting you to the hospital now." As pre-arranged, we dropped my son off to stay with my friends Del and Ted. By noon I was being prepped for my C-section.

The nurse monitoring the baby's heartbeat kept saying, "It's a boy." I'd shake my head. At about 2:30 p.m., my doctor showed up. As I was wheeled to surgery Rick held my hand.

At the door he kissed my forehead and said, "See you soon. I'll go call your folks now."

I woke from the anesthetic to find a nurse pressing

on my stomach. She smiled when she saw my eyes open. "It's a girl," she said, but I passed out from the pain. I floated in and out of sleep the rest of the day and night. I barely recall Rick coming into my room holding a baby, all smiles.

The next morning I was awakened by a fuss of nurses changing my bed, taking vitals, doing what nurses do. I wanted my baby. Where was she? One of the nurses placed her hand on my arm.

"Be patient," she said. "We're getting you ready. She's beautiful. We've all had fun with her while you've been resting."

I wondered aloud why I'd been asleep so long, why she wasn't with me, why I'd had no visitors. The nurses exchanged glances.

Then the door opened and in walked Rick holding a pink bundle. He laid her down in the crook of my arm.

"This is my baby?" I said in wonder. "Are you sure? She's so…so beautiful!" I exclaimed.

"She looks just like the Gerber baby food baby," said the attending nurse. We've all commented on what a beauty she is!" She straightened my covers. The other nurses had quietly left.

After a few sweet moments with my baby daughter, Rick cleared his throat. I looked up. "Where is everyone?" I asked. He seemed pensive. "I thought Mom and Dad would be here first thing."

"Uh, Suzy, there's something I've got to tell you…." His voice trailed off as he looked at the nurse. As if on cue, she came forward, reaching for the baby.

"Here, let me take her while you two have a talk," she said.

"No," I responded. "She's okay here."

Rick touched my arm, "Let her go with the nurse for now." Something in his voice alarmed me.

"What's wrong?" I exclaimed. "Is there something wrong with her?" Panic filled my throat.

"No—the baby's perfect," Rick said reassuringly. "It's…it's your sister," he continued quietly. "She's dead. She shot herself."

It was a typical spring day. Large puffy white clouds floated on a crystal blue sky in the windows behind Rick. Someone had sent a bouquet of daffodils and hyacinths. The fragrance of the hyacinths seemed to merge with his words. His face was in so much pain. "Sally's dead," he said again.

"No," I said quietly, shaking my head. "No," I repeated, as tears of disbelief filled my eyes. I grabbed his arm. "This is not funny. Don't keep saying that," I ordered him. He held my hand as he pulled up a chair. The message had made him weak.

"She's gone. She put a gun to her head. I'm so sorry." Tears filled his eyes. From somewhere deep inside I heard a shriek. Someone, a woman, was screaming and screaming and screaming. As the screams became sobs a nurse entered with a syringe. I felt a sting somewhere in my body. Then I slept again.

A few hours later I woke up. I was lying on my back looking up at the ceiling. Something was different. I was in the hospital but couldn't recall why. Something in me was broken, shattered forever. Slowly I looked around. More flowers had been delivered. I tried to sit up, but the pain in my stomach stopped me. That's right. I'd had a baby. I started to smile at the thought of her, but the broken part interfered. Oh my God. Sally.

Clutching the blanket as if it were a lifeline, I turned my head into my pillow as hot tears returned.

My nurse came in, full of warmth and kindness. "We are all so sorry for your loss," she said as she poured fresh water in my glass and sat a fresh box of tissues nearby. "Do you want another sedative?" she asked.

I shook my head.

"You have visitors. Would you like to freshen up a bit? I'll help you if you'd like." Her voice sounded far away, distant.

Humbly, I nodded. I was moved by her kindness and began to cry again. As she fussed with me she talked, "None of us can possibly imagine what you must be going through. Birth and death all in one day...." She was musing as if to herself. She shook her head. "It's too much," she said looking me straight in the eyes. Tears welled up in her own eyes. "But I know this for sure. You have been blessed with a beautiful baby girl who needs her mommy. As soon as you are ready, I would love to bring her to you," she said taking the hair brush from my hand, I nodded.

"Thank you," I whispered.

My first visitor was Bob Finnell. As he approached my bedside, flowers in hand, he shook his head. "My God," he said, "what a strange turn of events." The sentiment brought tears to my eyes.

"You have a beautiful baby girl," he said. "No doubt she had an angelic escort this day." I nodded. Life was spirit to this man, and as he'd reminded me so often, it had a perfection.

But it was too soon to talk about that. He stayed only

briefly. Shortly after he left, my parents came. They were grief-torn. Dad had collapsed while looking at his new granddaughter at the nursery window. It was too much for any of us to hold, this joy and this grief. As evening approached I asked for no more visitors. I wanted to hold my daughter. Rick had brought my son up and he wanted to hold her too.

As I held her in my arms, she opened her eyes and looked at me. She was so clean, so pure, and so full of joy. I knew then it was my promise to her to keep her life full of love and joy. I did not want this day casting its long shadow on her life.

Over the next few days, details of Sally's death came creeping in. After Rick saw me to surgery he'd called my folks, but there was no answer. Then, after the baby had been bathed, weighed and swaddled tight, he'd left to phone them again. It was about 4:30 p.m. Still no answer. About 5:30 p.m., he tried my folks again and Mom answered. She was hysterical. She kept repeating, "It's Sally. Something's wrong. She's dead. She's been shot!"

A neighbor took the phone from Mom and confirmed her words. Rick left for my folks' house immediately but not before telling the doctor and nursing staff what had happened. That's when it was decided to keep me sedated.

Apparently, Sally had planned her suicide for a while. On Friday she'd received a call from a friend, Carl, who wanted to visit on Sunday. She told him no because she'd made plans with Mom and Dad. She told Mom and Dad she couldn't go with them on their planned outing because she'd made plans with Carl. They were glad she'd agreed to see Carl; they thought it would do her good.

So she'd cleared Sunday up to be alone. This was clearly something well thought out. When I last saw her, Friday evening, a bit of sparkle had come back in her eyes. In a strange way she had taken her life back.

The coroner placed the time of death between 3:00 and 5:00 p.m. Sunday. I have a feeling it was closer to 5:00. That's when Mom and Dad returned. Her bedroom window overlooked the driveway. I think she waited until they returned to pull the trigger. Dad found her sitting on the edge of her bed facing that window, slumped over on the pillow. He thought she'd passed out, so he straightened her legs upon the bed and lifted her head to the pillow. When he drew his hands back he saw the blood. And the gun. His gun, kept hidden away in the attic. My poor father. He'd yelled for Mom to bring a cold cloth. Now he was yelling for her to call the police. A neighbor phoned just as she was reaching to call the police. He came over immediately. When Rick called from the hospital, they had just found her.

It was not possible for me to attend her funeral. At the time of her service, we requested the hospital chaplain to pray with us that we might share in some form of ceremony and prayer. My son was given the choice to attend her funeral or stay with us. He chose to join us. So did Bob Finnell. Later that day, and for several days after, friends and relatives called. It was good to reconnect with them.

The most significant visitor was my cousin Bess, my mother's cousin. As she bid me farewell, she leaned over close to my ear and whispered, "When you are feeling up to it, we need to talk, really talk."

With this parade of visitors, reports about the funeral trickled in and it helped me to hear everyone's picture of it. James, our family friend from long ago, reemerged to sing, "I Can See Clearly Now." Poetry had been read, including some of Sally's. She was a good writer.

I also heard some reports about an after funeral party at my folks' house. Mom's festive party attitude (she must've been drunk) stunned a few people, while Dad sat alone weeping. Two of mom's cousins from Illinois were especially put off by her behavior. It didn't surprise me. That was Mom. They felt bad for my dad who was so obviously in grief. Mom kept telling him to quit crying. Several of the visiting relatives looked to me for answers. I didn't have any. I could only shrug and remind them Sally had done a lot of drugs. She was trying to turn her life around, but it seemed the more she tried the less she felt like she fit.

Maybe my 10-year-old son said it best. When I asked him how he felt about losing Aunt Sally he'd shrugged and said, "She must have been sick. Only sick people kill themselves." That seemed like a whole lot of understanding for one so young.

I was in the hospital that whole week. It would be 20 years before I could visit my sister's grave.

Somehow life went on. It always does. It surprised me, though, that people could go on working and laughing, that news kept being made, that songs kept being sung on the radio. Didn't they know my sister had died? More than once something happened that prompted me to rush to the phone to call Sally and tell her. Then I'd freeze as I dialed her number. What was I thinking? She's gone.

My little girl was always the picture of joy. She made me smile. She warmed my heart. She knew nothing of this tragedy and I was determined to keep it that way. She was the dawn who lit up all our lives. All except Mom. Those first few months she refused to even hold her. Dad would coddle the gurgling baby before offering her to Mom to hold. Mom would sit looking defiant with both arms folded across her chest. "I'll hold her when I'm ready," she maintained.

I began to feel protective of her when my folks were around. I remember visiting Mom and Dad when she was about 10 months old and beginning to walk, holding onto furniture. Mom had a coffee table with crystal coasters and a crystal ashtray on it. As she toddled around the coffee table she reached for the coasters.

My mom pointed her finger at her and said "No!" My beautiful, wonderful little girl pointed her finger right back at mom and said a jumble of something unintelligible. I laughed at her mumblings and defiance.

Mom just glared at her and said, "I'll break that spirit. There's not a child yet I've not been able to break."

Horrified, I stood, gathering my baby up. "Not this one you won't," I said snatching up my purse and car keys.

As I left, I walked past a large vase of yellow roses Mom had brought home from the florist, where she worked part-time. Each yellow bud had been tied snug with nearly invisible string.

"What's this?" I asked, "Why are these buds all tied up?"

"So they won't bloom."

It was time to get away. Far away.

Fourteen

Why didn't I fit in my family? ...in my life? Was I so different?

I sought understanding and remembered Bess's tantalizing whispered invitation to talk. Perhaps it was time to call.

Bess was a few years older than my mother, but a personality of easy acceptance and compassion had aged her little.

Bess seated herself sedately in my living room and wasted no time. "I have heard that you are special, psychic. Is this true?"

Taken aback, I replied with a simple yes.

"I assume that you have never been told of your maternal ancestry?"

Excited by the implications, I confirmed her assumption.

She began, "Let me tell you about your Great-Grandma Jones."

For the next several hours her stories provided me with missing pieces of my heritage. Great-Grandma Jones was a beautiful girl, born Addie Ford. Like most young women of her time, Addie was married in her teens and began bearing children immediately. Shortly after her daughter's birth, her husband had Addie committed to a mental hospital for reasons that remain a mystery. In those days it was not an uncommon occurrence as a means of getting a divorce. Ultimately her parents rescued her and brought her home. Soon she was courted by James Jones and re-married. Great-Grandpa Jones was a mild-mannered man who lived in the woods. By trade he was a timber cruiser which meant he would find and mark trees to be felled. He and Great-Grandma lived in a horse-drawn wagon in the woods until their third child was born. She bore him eight daughters, for a total of nine altogether includ-ing Great-Grandma's first. Like me, Great-Grandma felt at home with horses and trained all of Great-Grandpa's work teams.

Great-Grandma had other talents and these are the ones that intrigued me. She was a midwife with an in-tuitive nature that served her well in her profession. Bess remembered staying with Grandma Jones as a child and waking up in the morning as Grandma was returning home, medicine bag in hand. She'd awakened in the night *knowing* it was time for so and so's delivery.

Often, Grandma would set extra dinner plates for the guests she knew would arrive, despite the lack of tele-phones and proximity to any neighbor. Bess fondly re-membered that when she was really, really good, Grand-ma would take her to the attic and let her look into her special chest full of all kinds of wonders; but off-limits unless Grandma was with you. What was most memo-rable about Grandma Jones, however, was her smell. She smelled of the earth because under her apron she wore a medicine belt; in its many pouches were roots and herbs used in her midwifery work.

At the conclusion of her tale, Bess leaned into me and with a reassuring touch softly spoke, "You are not alone. It is who you naturally are and who others before you have been."

I needed to know more. What could I find out about my paternal side? I was committed to uncovering details about the Murphys and contacted Grandma Murphy soon after Bess left.

My meeting with Grandma Murphy held stark contrasts and startling similarities with the visit I had with Bess.

After the usual pleasantries and many offerings of tea, Grandma Murphy wandered to the topic she had been nervously avoiding. "Your cousin tells me you're a psychic fortune teller," she said, turning to look at me in the eyes.

Thanks cousin, I thought. These were relatives who, in their born-again zeal, were praying for my heathen soul. My face burned hot as the old guilt and shame grabbed at my throat. I took a steadying breath.

"Grandma, I'm not a fortune teller. That's not what I do. I...." I began to explain but she reached across the table and touched my hand.

"It's okay," she smiled. Then after a moment she went on. "I've never told anyone this story, because it's so odd," she confessed. I waited.

"Your grandfather, my husband, used to talk about his Grandmother Murphy doing strange things. They lived in Tennessee, you know," she said as if that should imply something. I nodded.

"He said she would do 'this thing' where she would put an iron on the stove. It was one of those black cast-iron

irons women used to heat on the stove to press clothes."
Again I nodded, not daring to interrupt. She looked at me
now as if deciding whether she should go on. I smiled
calmly to reassure her, all the while trembling on the
inside, knowing this was a secret I needed to hear. Grandma cleared her throat, sitting up straighter now.

"Well, apparently then she would lie down on the floor
and at the right moment signal her husband who would
take the iron from the stove and place it on her stomach.
She would then fall into a sort of trance. The iron never
burned her stomach or clothes," she stated, resting back
into her chair.

I couldn't believe it. My great-great grandmother was
a trance medium. My mind raced. What else could she tell
me? What else did she know? Not wanting to sound too
excited I nodded as if it all made perfect sense. A hot iron!
That's a new one, I thought.

Instead I questioned, "Do you know what else she
would say or do? Did people come to her for information?"

Grandma shook her head. "Nope, that's all I know.
But your grandfather swore it was true."

Fifteen

After Christmas 1978, my little family moved from my beloved farm. The farm was in such disrepair and Rick no longer had the time or desire to keep up with it. A friend had a lovely rental home she offered us. It was in a nice neighborhood in the inner city. Located on Alameda Ridge, we were three blocks from the home of Portland's mayor. Alameda Grade School was a picture right out of Beverly Hills, as was the house she offered. We couldn't say no. What a contrast it was moving from the country to the city.

Then one day shortly after our move, Rick came home from work bent over and carrying a bottle of painkillers. He'd lifted a huge tire with a buddy, loading it onto a truck, and the buddy lost his grip. Rick had been seriously injured. After a series of doctor and hospital visits, it became clear he would not be driving professionally or lifting again. This was a huge blow for a man who'd prided himself on his physical prowess. So he converted the downstairs of our new residence into an art studio and began painting again. I became concerned that he would start drinking as the two pastimes were intimately connected for him. Thankfully, he didn't.

Finnell and I had resumed our Sunday evening "speaking sessions." Because of my increasing confidence, I would occasionally invite friends to join us. It was much as I'd imagined Edgar Cayce's sessions to be when he would enter a sleeplike state and *see*, offering intuitive insight.

On one evening, things took an unusual turn. Bob was posing questions or concerns and I sat ready, my task to hear the responses and recount them.

With a group of six tonight we had taken up our usual location beside the hearth.

Bob phrased his first question. "Can you offer information regarding a past life of anyone among us seated here tonight?"

Normally, my responses were that of the detached reporter. This night was different. I began itching and scratching, clearly experiencing discomfort. Bob inquired to the cause of my discomfort. Apparently, I stopped squirming and seemed surprised by his voice.

"What?" I called out looking around, disoriented, "Is someone there?"

Bob continued with intrigued trepidation, "Where are you?"

"I'm in the cellar where they've tossed me," was my irritated response, "and I hate these wool robes," I added, resuming my itching.

"But who are you?" he pushed.

As though I were explaining patiently to a small child, I described at great length that I was in a convent in the Pyrenees Mountains of Spain. I had been placed there at a young age because I knew things and could see things. The priest of my childhood village had become enraged with my *seeing* and had sent me off to this convent for my own protection. I hated it, but had also come to accept my place there. Occasionally, though, I was disciplined because I was caught conducting one-sided conversations during prayer.

Bob pursued by asking who it was I would converse with at those times.

She (I) replied with a question, "Is it you? Are you the angels I talk to? If you are, I just got tossed down here again." She continued with an indignant shrug, complaining about the dampness and stench of her accommodations. And the rats. She hated the rats.

Uncomfortable at this unexpected development and worried for my safety, Bob thanked her for listening and asked that Sue might return.

I blinked my eyes and asked for a glass of water.

Unnerved by the tension and stunned glances I demanded, "What's going on?"

Finnell had regained his composure and with unhidden glee, recounted for me what had just occurred. He hypothesized that the question must have triggered an automatic regression for me personally. The aspect that proved most intriguing to Bob was how time and space seemed to collapse and realities intersected.

What if our voices were the voices that she had been hearing? Voices from the future...multi-dimensional realities...all fascinating, but also exhausting and I was tired.

Later that night I dreamed about snow covered mountains.

Sixteen

My daughter's first birthday was a grand affair. She took her first toddling steps and shook her mane of golden curls. She already resembled the flaxen-haired angel that matched my earlier vision of her.

Since my sister's death, Mom viewed every holiday or celebration as an occasion to leave daisies on Sally's grave. It was a touching gesture and one I wished I was capable of. I knew that a visit to the cemetery would swallow me in grief. I just couldn't go. Working in a floral shop, Mom would prepare a bouquet to be left at Sally's grave, and would bring the remaining daisies to the gathering, reminding those in attendance of our loss. Normally, it was fine. On this particular day, on the anniversary of my mingled grief and joy, however, it was not fine. Sure enough, though, she arrived at the birthday party, flowers in hand, and announced they were from my sister's grave bouquet. The room full of people exchanged awkward glances. I snatched them away and jammed them into a vase on the front porch.

"Not here, not today."

She went into a snit and sat in the corner for the rest of the party. Dad, always apologizing for her, said quietly, "I told her not to bring those in." How could a man so kind and gentle stay with a woman so mean and hateful?

Russ remained oblivious of the altercation. I glanced at my brother, down on the floor playing with the birthday girl. My brother, the gentle giant.

Later that evening, after everyone had left and the children were in bed, Rick and I sat by the fire talking.

"This isn't working," I said to him. "I think we need to move further away."

He nodded agreement. He had decided to avail himself of the state workers' compensation program that would assist him in returning to employment. No longer able to do heavy physical labor, he intended to pitch to them the idea of helping him establish his own art gallery. "They might just go for it."

We had heard about a town in the North Cascades of Washington which boasted art galleries and tourist festivals. We settled on the little town of Leavenworth, Washington, enamored of its beauty and possibility.

With vigor, Rick researched his idea thoroughly. He created spreadsheets for costs for two years, and lists of suppliers and vendors; he'd even found a building for lease on the main street. His presentation was flawless. It looked like an attorney's brief. The state could find no argument and they agreed to his proposal and secured the business lease.

The only remaining task was to find a home in that quiet mountain village. The week between Christmas and New Years we ventured up to Leavenworth again. We trudged from rental to rental in snow that advanced halfway up our chests. We finally decided on a newly built home that was to remain for sale. That was fine, it was clean. We moved two weeks later in a snowstorm. The exhilaration of a new life in this wintry town straight out of a Dickens novel was tainted only when we had to share the news with Dad. It was January 1980.

For the next two years life in the mountains seemed to heal me. With few distractions, I could now be a fulltime mom to my two wonderful children. My son, in the sixth grade, seemed to flourish. The children in that small village ran free. Everyone knew everyone else and looked out for each other's kids. He hiked, had a trail bike, swam in the rivers, hunted with friends' families, camped and skied. It was awesome. I enrolled our nearly two-year-old daughter in the local preschool. We met new friends. Ironically, those who became our best friends were a retired L.A. police officer and his wife.

Bob Finnell would venture up our way every few months and spend a three day weekend. He always arrived laden with heavy volumes of Rudolf Steiner's work. I read them all. Looking back, it was like being given a two-year study period. In a way, it was like a seminary. God lived in this splendid land. The aurora borealis reflected over the unbroken white expanse, the seasons in hyperbole, the abundant wildlife--these powerful forces of nature converged to heal my soul. I told no one in this new community about my psychic interests. I enjoyed the restfulness of the environment, the quietness of snow falling.

The gallery did well, carrying itself after the first year. It was, however, Rick's domain. I respected that to a point, the point being, of course, his way with a checkbook (which had never again been a problem) and alcohol. He seemed to hold court there. Artists would stop in and talk for hours. He was always on display in the gallery window, painting at his easel.

One fall day in 1981 marked the demise of our idyllic life and a return to chaos. Our friends Rae and Jerry came to visit. Rae was a woman ahead of her time. In Portland, she'd been successful remodeling old homes in the inner city and turning a nice profit before it had been the fashionable thing to do. Now she had her designing eye on our little village. She wanted to purchase an old hotel, gut it and start over. She had an investor in Portland who liked her work and told her to go for it. The hotel was on the main street, two blocks up from the gallery. A month after negotiations with the hotel owner, she moved a crew in from Portland and the demolition began. Rick was drawn to the project. His interest in the gallery waned. He hired a woman to work for him so he would be available to help Rae. Jerry never did move up. Eventually Rae promised Rick gallery space in the new hotel. She put him on the payroll. He returned home after 10:00 p.m. every night. Our lives would never be the same.

One night a few months after Rae had moved up, I had a dream.

Rae was driving a hot new sports car along the winding canyon road that follows the river into our town. She was speeding. As she rounded a curve, her car lost control. The car was spinning, then...

Later that day I recounted the dream to Rae.

She laughed, saying, "That will be the day. Me driving a sports car! Someone my size doesn't fit into a sports car."

"Well, just be aware on these mountain roads. You drive too fast anyway. Maybe it's just a warning," I said.

On occasion, I would stop in at the hotel to check its progress. Work began November 1981 with plans to open later in the spring of 1982. By late January it was beginning to take shape. The gallery, on the other hand, was dwindling. Rick kept assuring me it would be fine once he got it moved into its new location. But that old anxiety, which I'd not felt for a few years, was creeping back in. Something was slipping away.

The grand opening of the hotel was in April 1982. It was a sight to behold and the talk of the town. Rae had accomplished what she'd set out to do and now had to decide about the business of running it. She decided to stay on and do that herself. She asked Rick to be her assistant. He was there all the time. One evening in late May, he didn't come home. By 1:00 a.m., I'd become very concerned. Finally, about 2:00 a.m. he came in. I was still up reading. As he walked through the door, he looked at me and walked past me to the kitchen. I could tell he'd been drinking. I said nothing as he reentered the living room. He accused me of accusing him of drinking. I said nothing. I was scared.

Then he put his face inches from mine and snarled, "You think you know everything, but you know nothing. You and your stupid angels and your goddamn books." He grabbed the one I'd been reading from my hand and launched it across the room. He was too big and too drunk to reason with. I said nothing, but sat very, very still.

"You think you're so smug, you bitch," he raged; he drew back his fist and let fire. I ducked and his fist collided with the back of the chair. My heart was pounding out of my chest. Tears filled my eyes. I knew with certainty not to move. In this state anything could incite him.

"I'm taking my daughter and leaving," he stormed. Panic seized my heart. How could I stop this man? My head snapped around when I heard my son's bedroom door open. His fearful eyes peered through a small gap. I shook my head barely perceivably and motioned him back. Then I took the only action that remained to me, I quietly said a prayer, "Dear God please distract this man for a moment."

Miraculously, seconds later Rick stepped into the bathroom and slammed the door. My son came out. I ran for the phone. Trembling I called Mike, the retired cop. He could reach us sooner than the county police. "Mike, it's me. Rick's drunk. Get here quick. He wants to take my daughter. Someone's going to die here tonight – hurry!"

He was at least 10 minutes away. I turned to my 13-year-old son.

"He mustn't see you," I hastily whispered, fearing Rick might take a punch at him. "When Mike gets here, take your sister out your bedroom window, get in his car and lock the door. Do not let Rick see you," I repeated, shoving him back into his room and barely controlling my trembling voice.

"But Mom," my son pleaded.

"It will all be okay. Just do this. Do what I told you." He nodded and softly shut his bedroom door. I heard the toilet flush and scrambled back to the big chair.

Rick sauntered back in the living room arrogantly brushing past me. He returned from the bedroom, suitcase in hand.

"What...what are you doing?" I spoke for the first time.

"What am I doing? You stupid bitch. You're pathetic. Look at yourself sitting there with tears in your eyes," he hissed at me, grabbing a handful of my hair and pulling my head back.

Once again putting his face inches from mine he sneered, "I told you what I'm doing. I'm taking my daughter and getting the hell out of here."

With that he let go of my hair pushing me back into

the chair. He went to our daughter's bedroom, opened the door and woke her.

"Mike, hurry, for God's sake, hurry," I prayed.

A few moments later my daughter stepped into the living room, long nightgown touching the floor, blankie in hand.

"Mommy, where are we going?" She asked, rubbing her sleepy eyes.

Rick followed, suitcase full of clothes he'd thrown together for himself and her.

"You and Daddy are going on a trip," he cooed, taking her hand now. The fear and panic rising up in me was indescribable. If he headed out the door before Mike arrived, I would need to make a scene, create a distraction. But my daughter did that for me.

"No, no, not without Mommy and Brother," she said breaking free of him and rushing to me. She sat next to me in the chair, clutching tightly to my hand. Rick had her little coat in his hand. He sat the suitcase down and kneeled in front of her to help her with her coat.

"They can't come with us," he explained gently.

A moment later the front door swung open and Mike stepped in. I've never been so glad to see anyone in my life. Rick was a big man, but Mike was bigger. He loomed in the doorway, an angel from heaven. Rick, alarmed, bolted to his feet squaring off with Mike. As if on cue, my son's bedroom door opened.

I whispered to my daughter, "Go with your brother now!" Her eyes lit up at this and she ran to him. I heard the bedroom door close behind her.

"Thank you, God," I said.

Rick had seen none of this taking place behind his back. Mike was asking him what the problem was as he reached in his pocket for his cigarettes.

Rick, seeing his reach, said, "Don't go for a gun, man. I'll ice you."

Mike, cool as ever, held up his pack of Marlboros and shrugged. He looked at me and motioned with his eyes for me to get out. As he engaged Rick in conversation, I stepped behind them and slipped out the front door. His new Audi was parked out front and my children were safely locked inside. My son unlocked the front door as I approached. Sitting in the front seat, I noticed Mike had left a set of car keys on the floor. He'd thought of everything.

I turned to my children, "Thank God you're safe," I spoke softly. While we waited for Mike, I filled my son in on what had happened.

"What are we going to do now, Mom?" he asked. His life in this town was full. He had a girlfriend, a part time job. He was a popular athlete about to enter high school.

"I don't know," I said shaking my head. Just then Mike emerged from the house. I unlocked his door. There was no sign of Rick.

As he turned on the ignition I said, "Well….what happened?"

He smiled, a bit smugly, I thought, and said, "He went to bed."

"To BED!" I nearly screamed.

Nodding as we pulled away, he said, "Yeah that's what they usually do…if they don't go to jail."

We spent the next three days with Mike and his wife Vicki. I refused to see Rick, but Mike spoke with him several times. Sober, he had no memory of the event. Great. He could traumatize our family on a drunken whim and be granted immunity the next day simply because he couldn't remember. Mom had done this to me when I was a child. Then, I could do nothing. Now, it was unacceptable.

"He wants you to take him back. He wants you to come home," Mike reported after his visits with Rick. I shook my head. I felt trapped. I couldn't stay and I couldn't leave. I had no way to support myself and my children. I didn't know what to do.

"He swears he'll never drink again," Mike added. "He says he'll do anything you want."

On the third day we returned to our little house at the edge of the mountains. Rick was apologetic and humble. As I sat listening to him go on about his promises and how it would all be different now, I knew I could not stay. I would never again trust him and I refused to live with the quiet terror of always wondering. He had come too close to damaging all of us beyond repair. I had to get out while there remained a window of hope. But how? Something he was saying brought my attention back.

"We'll go to the beach for a week. Maybe your friends at Cannon Beach will let us use their cabin," he said.

"Okay," I nodded.

It would give us time away. It would buy me time to think. I needed a plan. As much as I loved this little town, I knew the children and I could not remain here. Overnight it had changed. The dream had shattered.

I sensed a now too familiar physical force that pushed me away, unyielding, when spirit made it clear that I must move on. Thankfully, I was powerless to resist this force.

I looked out my kitchen window across the river and the mountains beyond. How often I'd stood there watching the snow fall as it quietly soothed my soul. I would never again see the full moon rising over the mountains, its first light glowing on the snow like some mystical god. How could I live without this place, this sanctuary? I cried. Rick put his arms around me in comfort.

"We'll be okay, you'll see," he said. But his touch made me freeze.

No, I thought, we'll never be okay again.

We stayed at the beach for a week. Bob Finnell joined us for a day or two. While Rick was down at the ocean with our daughter, I explained to Bob what had happened. I could see his sadness and sympathy. I told him I had to move back and would need to find work. He suggested it was time for me to start doing readings. I shook my head.

"I need a real job. I've got to take care of my kids. Tell Maria I could sure use that help now."

"Yes, yes, I will. Sue, I'm sorry this has happened, but I must admit it will be good to have you back," Bob said encouragingly. It was the ray of hope I needed. I smiled.

On the drive back to Leavenworth I told Rick I could no longer live there. "When do you want to move?" he asked with resignation.

"Now. The moment we get back to the house," I emphasized.

He nodded. "I can move you and the kids, but I'll have to return. I'm committed to Rae for a couple of months yet," he spoke quietly.

I knew they had yet to get the new gallery location up and running. It would take a while to close out the old location and get commissions paid to artists. I was grateful he'd not be moving with us.

Later that night as we packed and loaded the U-Haul, a sheriff's car pulled up front. A deputy, Jake Brewster, knocked at our open door.

"Wow, looks like somebody's moving," he said, letting himself in.

"Hello," I said as I walked past him, arms loaded. "Rick's in the kitchen." I motioned with my head.

Soon, indistinguishable, quiet voices came from that direction and a few minutes later he walked back past me.

"Goodbye Sue, and good luck," he said sincerely as he put his hat back on. I flashed him a quick smile as he walked away. I had always liked Brewster. He'd often come in and sit at the gallery on his breaks, visiting with the rest of the locals, before Rae had moved to town and it all changed. It didn't occur to me to ask Rick what he'd wanted. We were busy packing. Later Rick told me Jake had delivered an eviction notice. It was indisputably time to move.

The children and I left the next day after a tearful goodbye to friends. I cried all the way to Oregon. It was decided we'd stay with my parents and to put everything in storage.

It was my hope to find work. The last thing I wanted was to be stuck at my parents' house. On the second night, there was a knock at the door. Two Oregon police officers were looking for Rick. He went to the door and slipped outside to speak with them. He returned inside escorted by both officers.

"They have a warrant for my arrest. Forgery," he stated dispassionately. He had written a few bad checks over the last few months. Washington state wanted him back. As the police handcuffed him, I grabbed his arm, angry tears in my eyes.

"You've broken both of our agreements. You drank and now you're going to jail. Don't come back. I will *not* live this way!" I shouted after him as they led him off. "Stay away from us!" I continued to scream at the closing door. I collapsed on the floor, heaving with sobs.

"I'm so tired," I said to my dad as he helped me to the sofa. I was grateful my children had not witnessed this event. My daughter was next door, playing, and my son was at the video arcade. I sat shaking my head and trembling. What was I going to do? Dad assured me we'd be fine with them for however long we needed to be there.

Seventeen

For the next couple of months I laid low. I saw a few friends and, of course, Bob Finnell. He began referring me for readings. Someone would have me over to his or her house where several others had also signed up for readings, a "reading party," so to speak. These were psychometry readings. I would hold a personal object belonging to the one being read; images and impressions would begin to form in my mind. I charged $20 for a one hour session. The readings were enjoyable for me, but I didn't take it seriously. It was play. I needed a "real" job.

During this time several paranormal events occurred. One afternoon, I was alone in the house. I'd been reading *The Road Less Traveled* and wanted a place to stretch out. The bed my daughter and I shared was a hide-a-bed and tucked away every morning. So I went in to my parents' bedroom, stretching out on their bed.

After a few minutes of settling in with a comfy afghan, a movement at the foot of the bed caught my eye. Looking up from my book, I saw a woman standing in the doorway of their room. She was clothed all in white, and a veil covered her head, falling around her shoulders and down to her feet. But she had no feet. She just floated in the doorway. Her face was clear. Her lips displayed a comforting smile, her arms tenderly outstretched. She resembled a hologram. I'd just seen "Star Wars" and was reminded of the hologram of Princess Leia.

I sat up and looked over my shoulder to discover the source of the projection, needlessly, as I was up on the second floor, so it would have to have been a hovercraft! Furthermore, the blinds were closed tightly to keep the glare of the sun off the book I was reading. I warily turned back and she was still there. I spoke a greeting, but she did not acknowledge me. She remained unanimated. Moved to action, I cautiously rose to approach her, but when I was within three feet from her, she dissolved in glittery lights. I fell back on the bed, mystified. What had just occurred? What could it mean? There had been no overt message, but I did feel comforted and reassured. I told no one.

A few mornings later, I awoke about 3:00 a.m. As I lay listening to my sweet daughter's rhythmic, peaceful breathing something caught my eye. Turning, I saw two light orbs hovering in the doorway. The door was closed and I searched for the light source. The drapes were closed securely. I watched the lights bouncing slowly, about four to five feet off the floor. One was slightly larger than the other, but both were similar in size to large beach balls with undefined, hazy edges. While I was mesmerized by the orbs, I heard my dad get up in his room across the hall. He went to the bathroom. He flushed the toilet, then walked down the hall towards the kitchen. As he did, the orbs disappeared. A few moments later I heard him return to his bedroom. He must've needed a glass of water, I thought as I drifted back to sleep.

The next morning as we sat around the breakfast table, I asked about his wandering in the night, and asked if he'd had a headache. He glanced at me and then at my mom who was at the kitchen sink. I knew that look. It meant *Mom won't approve of this conversation.* He spoke anyway.

Shaking his head, Dad said, "It was the darndest thing. The bathroom door was open and as I washed my hands, I glanced in the mirror. I couldn't believe my eyes, but I saw two figures standing in the door of your bedroom. A woman and young girl, both dressed in white, both with long hair. It looked like the woman was brushing the young girl's hair. When they saw me watching, they turned and walked down the hall past the bathroom door. I thought it must be you two going to the kitchen, so I followed to see if you were okay. When I got to the kitchen it was dark. No one was there! Then I realized it wasn't you. It didn't even look like you. I guess I was trying to make sense of it," he ended glancing again at Mom who was drying her hands and walking toward us now.

"What are you two talking about over here?" she demanded. Ignoring her, I told dad what I had seen on my side of the door at the same time of his apparitions.

My God, I wondered, all the years I'd seen the orbs, could it be I was just experiencing the back side of something else?

"You two are making me nervous with this talk. Stop it now." Mom's command broke my reverie.

A few weeks later in August 1982, I woke abruptly one morning just before sunrise. There was a cloud, a mist, at the foot of my bed. It was short and round and made me think of Rae. She was short and round. I lay there thinking of her and dozed back to sleep. A couple of hours later the phone woke me. It was 9:00 a.m. I heard Mom answer.

"Sue, it's for you."

I slipped on my robe and took the phone. It was Denny, the accountant from the hotel in Leavenworth.

Great, I thought, now what has Rick done?

Denny's voice was shaking.

"Are you sitting down?" he said.

"Denny, what's wrong? Just say it," I said impatiently.

"There's been a horrible accident," he said. "Rae's dead."

I staggered and sat down. "What? What did you just say?"

"Rae's dead. She died in Tumwater Canyon about 2:00 a.m. this morning. Her new Porsche hit a boulder. She never hit the brakes. They found her in…in pieces. I'm so sorry. I know you and your family were close to her."

I was speechless. I handed the phone to Mom who had heard my end of the conversation. She was as stunned as I at the news. She thanked Denny and hung up.

"He said he'd let us know about the funeral," she spoke, wiping tears away. I sat, quiet tears falling down my face, staring at the floor. People were either leaving or dying. A few minutes later the phone rang again. It was Rick with the news. He said he'd be down for the funeral.

I didn't ask about his charges. I didn't care. Something in me was going numb.

Later that week I collapsed at Rae's funeral. Her investment partner caught me before I fell. He and Rick helped me to my parents' car. I motioned them both away. I just wanted to be alone. That evening I told my parents I needed help. I wanted to find a therapist. My life was swallowing me.

My first therapist was Jim. He was nice enough, but after our few first visits I felt an awkwardness around him. Therapy is awkward enough without feeling it from your therapist! Then I understood: I'm nearly six feet tall and he stood around 5'4". He would not stand up when I was standing.

I wanted a woman therapist anyway and began working with Margaret. I liked Margaret, but she cried a lot. She said my life was painfully sad and she cried for me. I shrugged it off. It was just the way my life was; nevertheless I considered it sweet of her to cry for me; odd perhaps, but sweet. We worked well together for a few months. She encouraged me to speak more directly to my mother. She also encouraged my job search efforts and allowed me to call her whenever I felt out of control. She usually made sense, or would at least cry for me! I never told her about my psychic life. Then she moved to St. Louis, and I didn't have the heart to try another therapist. Besides, I was feeling better. I'd been dating an attorney friend, who was also going through a divorce, and I had an upcoming interview for a job. Ultimately, the job came through. The attorney didn't.

It was now February 1983 and my divorce from Rick was nearly final. It had been arduous and time-consuming to locate him. After Rae died, the hotel fell apart and had been repossessed. Rick had already closed the gallery. I'd heard he'd gone to Canada and pulled some sort of art scam up there. He was wanted by the Royal Canadian Mounted Police; I knew because they'd called me looking for him. Rick had posted a letter to Bob Finnell bearing a postmark from Anchorage, Alaska. I called information to gather a list of the most upmarket hotels in the area. Looking at the list, I intuitively knew which to call and phoned the hotel asking for him by name. The kindly woman there advised me that he would return later that day and she would happily give him a message. I declined and hurriedly phoned my divorce attorney who immediately began the process to serve him the papers there before he fled again.

Meanwhile, I was working at Safeway checking groceries, and although it didn't pay enough for me to move out on my own yet, I enjoyed it. It was busy and that's what I needed. Busy.

By September 1983, I'd become well established in my work routine, I'd received my first raise, I had health benefits and I felt a certain pride in my paycheck. I was becoming responsible for myself. At this rate, however, it would be another year before I could think of getting my own place.

Eighteen

Finnell and I continued to meet a few times a month. Nothing of this "unnatural" nature, as my mom called it, was permitted in her domain. Some friends, Liz and Jack, offered their home for our Sunday night meetings. One such evening when the wind was extraordinarily fierce, we gathered in the comfort of their living room. Terminating our speaking session in the usual manner, Bob handed me a grounding glass of water, but, uncharacteristically, he looked distraught. Questioning him as to the content of the night's speaking, I learned that it was to be our final session. No explanation was provided, just that it was time for the meetings to end. We were saddened, knowing we would no longer have access to this source. It had been six years.

I have my own opinion as to the reason behind the cessation: a true teacher provides only enough direction for the student to stumble to find her own path toward the truths of her own life, and then removes himself discreetly from the student's journey. I believe that spirit sought to maintain my purity and innocence. Times had changed and the New Age was upon us.

It was a few years later when the first channelers appeared on the New Age scene. In the 1980s, metaphysical bookstores began opening, and with them came a new level of social acceptance for the psychic. Suddenly, everyone was a gifted psychic or healer or teacher. At first I was delighted with this new public awareness. Maybe I could now feel safer in the world. Then I realized it was Pandora's box. They'd all been let out!

Through all my metaphysical wanderings I had been blessed with a protective force guiding me away from influences that were not true or genuine for me. It enabled me to *see* the psychic fakes. I also began noticing a difference between the natural psychic--someone born with the ability, and the unnatural psychic--someone who just took a lot of classes. Generally, those born with it didn't want to talk about it. I understood that valid reluctance. The self-made psychics seemed boastful and pushy, requiring psychic props like crystals, candles, beads, sage, prayers-of-protection (From what!? I always wondered, the bogeyman?).

After my initial gratitude for the metaphysical bookstores and the presence of increasing numbers of "my people," I realized I needed to distance myself. These weren't "my people" after all. They were scary, dangerous, misleading and cloaked in the promise of love, oneness and unconditional acceptance. It's all very seductive. Beware the gossamer veil of self-enchantment!

The naturalness of my gift could be threatened by fears, rules and conventions foisted by so-called "masters" promoting the "correct" way to do things. I learned that my ability functioned by instinct.

I saw an illustration of this natural instinct at a barn where riding instruction was offered. A young girl entered the barn; she easily approached and mounted a large mare. The two raced across the pasture, seemingly as one.

Later, I saw the girl taking lessons to make her a better rider. "Hold your hands lower, change the angle of your head...."droned the instructor. The girl seemed awkward now, as if it was her first time atop a horse. Her natural instincts were removed, to be replaced by showmanship.

The more I learned of these different modern practitioners, the more grateful I was for the grounding influence of Bob Finnell and the teachings of Rudolf Steiner.

At one tearful, pained moment, I had asked Bob if I could *see* so much more than everyone else, why was I so easily duped by people. Logic would dictate that a path that could be *seen* should be easier to navigate. I could accurately guide others on their path with the night vision of a jungle cat; however, on my own path I was "as blind as a bat."

Bob's patient explanation turned to reincarnation. He quoted Steiner's teachings that describe the natural psychic as a child in the reincarnation cycle. The natural born psychic is less evolved than others; since he exists in an earlier state with fewer incarnations, he lacks the accompanying experiences and learning. These "children" should be nurtured and guided.

In ancient times and in pre-industrial societies, children displaying signs of a psychic gift were taken away from their homes and raised in a cloistered environment where they were taught the significance of their gift and were protected. In modern times, we value independence. Those born with psychic ability are left to make their own way, even though they are markedly ill-equipped to do so. Being born a natural psychic in today's world, I was required to work harder to compensate for the current belief structure.

I felt cheated.

Nineteen

Around mid-September my friend Karen called. She was in town. I had tickets to *Godspell* at the community college that weekend so we agreed she'd pick me up Friday evening, have dinner and see the play. As we were driving to dinner, Karen announced that she would rather go dancing than see a play. Karen had just wrapped a film in Tulsa with Francis Ford Coppola, working as a go-fer, and was still on what I called a Hollywood-high. She wanted to dance. I knew of a nearby cowboy bar, but winced at the thought of cowboy dancing, only because I didn't know how. She laughed.

"Dance is dance. You'll have fun!" she said as she signaled her turn into the club parking lot.

"But I'm not dressed cowboy," I protested.

"Don't worry," she replied. "You still look like Lindsay Wagner." I groaned. With my hair down to my waist and my size 10 pants tucked into knee-high boots, I had been mistaken for the bionic woman more than once. She had, after all, gone to school in my part of town and still owned property on Mt. Hood.

Giving Karen a playful fist to the shoulder, I opened the door and got out. "Lead on," I said as she opened the club door. Stepping in behind her, I couldn't believe my eyes. All those cowboy hats moving around the dance floor in one singular motion; it was a cowgirl's dream!

"Are they all real cowboys?"

Laughing, she said, "Haven't you seen *Urban Cowboy*?"

I shook my head. Taking my hand, she led me to a table. "Girl, you got to get out more often," she said, shaking her head.

We no sooner had ordered our drinks when a tall, lanky "cowboy" stepped over and took my hand.

Tilting his hat, he said, "Let's dance." As he led me into the sea of cowboy hats, I looked over my shoulder at Karen. She was laughing.

Needless to say, I had two left feet.

"Haven't danced much," he said, more to himself than to me.

"Not like this," I answered. He was very good and I caught on fast. As the music ended, I started to walk off the dance floor.

"Not so fast," the cowboy said holding my hand. Rosanne Cash singing about "the seven-year ache" brought the dance floor alive again. The following song, "Swingin'," however, made all the hats form a line. I shook my head no, so the cowboy followed me back to my table and sat down.

"My name's T.J.," he said.

"T.J., that's it?" I responded incredulously.

"Yes, ma'am, just T.J.," he nodded.

"What do they call you for short?" I asked with a laugh. Lifting his head, he looked me straight in the eye.

"I can see we're going to get along just fine." And so it was I met my next husband.

I know, I know. I am a REALLY slow learner.

T.J. was not a cowboy. I was briefly disappointed. He was, however, the most normal man I'd been with. In other words, he matched the middle class checklist of society's standards. He had the same job for 10 years. He had a mortgage, a car, truck and boat, and his ample suburban home had a view and a swimming pool. He'd been married once with no children.

On our second date, I told him about my special interests and involvement in the paranormal. I was taking a chance, but he just shrugged, asked a few questions and changed the subject. He also asked me out again.

A few months later, my children and I moved in with him. He was kind to them and funny. They liked funny. I was content to live together. He was not. We married shortly after. That first year we seemed to play a lot. There were always groups of people over in the summer around the pool. It seemed all too good to be true.

Finally, my life was normal.

After we'd been together a few months, I began to notice a habit of T.J.'s. He would frequently begin drinking on Thursday evenings and have me call in sick for him Monday mornings. I'd never been a drinker, but my wine consumption had gone up since we'd been together. It seemed normal. Everyone else around us was drinking. It was the social evening and weekend thing to do. But it made me sick. Although I never addressed it, I just quit drinking whatever was poured for me, consuming only a few sips all evening. That's when I saw how drunk he would get.

When I asked T.J. if he thought he had a problem with alcohol, he laughed and pointed out how well he could control it. After all, he didn't drink *all* the time. He could quit whenever he wanted. He just didn't want to. That seemed reasonable compared to what I'd been through with Rick. T.J. was a mild drinker by those standards. I let it go. We were happy and life was good for the most part.

Then, in late spring of 1984, a strange event took place at work. I had been at Safeway over a year. When you work in a place like that you become aware of people and their shopping habits. I noticed familiar faces and knew many customers on a first name basis and what they usually purchased. As a rule, I noticed when people did their large weekly shopping. It was the same people week after week. They were loyal customers. That's why this was so odd.

One afternoon a man came through my check stand with two carts loaded with food. I'd never seen him before. I made the usual small talk, but he wasn't friendly. He was wearing a baseball hat pulled down over his eyes so I didn't see his face entirely. He was alone. As he handed me the money, he looked straight into my eyes and said, "What are you doing checking groceries? You're supposed to be doing readings."

With that he took his carts and walked away. I was speechless. I had never seen him before and I never saw him again.

Later, I recounted this incident to Bob Finnell. He was intrigued, both by the encounter and the concept.

"Well, with you, nothing would surprise me. Maybe it was your angel."

I remembered then one of my favorite Bible passages from the Old Testament about not closing your door to a stranger for you never know when it might be 'an angel unaware.'

"Hmmm," I said, "an 'angel unaware,'" more to myself than to Bob, who smiled and nodded.

I quit my job at Safeway.

And so began my part-time business. By word-of-mouth referral, I was soon seeing three or four people a week and began feeling more comfortable with my decision.

Somewhere along the way, my name and phone number were sent to a man, Arthur Myers, in Boston who was writing a book about haunted houses. He called to see if I had any stories to contribute. Having things go bump in the night from my childhood days, I had always eagerly gone to explore other people's haunted house stories. I developed a few theories on the topic. I came to realize that what I thought had been a haunting of our house when I was a young teen, was in fact me, poltergeisting. The excess energy of adolescence doesn't sleep. In its restlessness, it knocks and raps and bumps and walks. There is no ghost involved. It is a normal teenage phenomenon. In the developing psychic, however, this energy can run rampant. And that, indeed, was what my family experienced in the home of my teenage years. Today when I receive a call about a haunted house, the first question I ask is "How many teenagers live in the home?"

So when Arthur requested tales of hauntings, I sent him a few of my favorite stories. They were later published in his books, *The Ghostly Register* and *The Ghostly Gazetteer*.

Twenty

By the end of 1985 we were looking at a move. The state needed our property to expand a freeway and offered true market value. We decided to try country life, since my daughter had become a horse lover and was taking hunter-jumper lessons. We found a beautiful place on five acres just outside of town. It was lovely.

The house sat on a small hill overlooking a trout pond. A natural stream flowed through the back pasture and fed the pond after a series of small waterfalls. In the back were also a small well-kept barn and several fruit trees. The front pasture was ample and well fenced. Soon a little gray half-Arab, half-Welsh mare completed the picture. I was in heaven!

A few months after moving in, I was rummaging through memorabilia I'd kept since high school. As I lifted a stack of old report cards and photos, a postcard fell out. Turning it over, I caught my breath. It was the postcard I'd carried from house to house as a child, a photo of the house on the hill overlooking a pool and pasture with horses! I sat down as tears formed. Closing my eyes, I held the postcard to my heart.

"Thank you God," I whispered.

Over the next five years life just kept getting better. My work/hobby of readings moved along quietly. I was quiet about it because my mother still asked me not to tell any of her friends and T.J. had picked up the same attitude. I continued to be an embarrassment to the people who loved me. In spite of that, I persevered. T.J.'s work became more lucrative, but the more money he made, the more he seemed to drink. I still cringe when I hear someone dropping ice cubes into a glass, because that's the first thing he'd do when he got home.

A chilly distance grew between us. I could no longer talk to him when he drank. We would go for days without speaking. Ironically, the better we looked on the outside, the more pain I experienced on the inside.

I began sleeping a lot. When I wasn't working or involved with my children's activities, I was sleeping. It was the only way I could cope with the emotional pain.

T.J. refused to quit drinking. "It's not my problem," he said. "It's yours. Get over it and quit trying to control me."

When I threw booze out, he bought more. I threatened to leave and he smirked, sweeping his hand across the room, knowing I wouldn't leave all that we had. And he was right. I felt captive to the lifestyle we'd created. So I slept more.

On my annual physical, I mentioned to my doctor how much I'd been sleeping. She did a series of tests to rule out any physical problem, then sat me down and said, "Have you thought of changing your lifestyle?"

My lifestyle was fine, I protested; it was great actually, and so what was she suggesting? She did not pursue it further. This was before the days when doctors began handing out antidepressants as if they were Skittles. I am grateful for that because it left me to deal with my problem. It forced me deeper into myself, and each time

I got there my doctor's words were waiting: "Have you thought about changing your lifestyle?"

How could I change anything? So much depended on my staying the same. I'd mentally list everything I and my children would lose. It wouldn't be fair to anyone. I would have to stay.

Soon, however, resentment began creeping in. I became quietly angry at T.J. If he would just quit drinking, I could be happy and enjoy life again. I became mean with my words towards him. I lost all respect for him. He was the problem. I hated what I was becoming and it was all his fault. I prayed harder.

Ironically, as my personal life was taking a nose dive, my reputation as a psychic was growing. My personal problems did not seem to disturb my abilities to do readings. T.J. and I could be having a heated fight minutes before a client arrived, and when the doorbell rang, I could shift into reading mode and feel wonderful. It amazed me but also saddened me. I wanted that feeling all of the time. How could I be so split? It was as if I had two selves at war with each other, which of course, I did. It had been set up a long time before.

A few friends had gone to different psychic healers and encouraged me to try some of their esoteric techniques. I was desperate, and willing to try anything--aura-cleaning, soul-retrieval, karmic readings, Kundalini healing, Reiki treatments. All well-intended, but nothing substantial.

That's not entirely true. In these techniques, I did learn new ways of justifying the situation I was in and blaming myself. It was my fault that I had allowed those "thoughts" which turned my aura muddy brown; if I could only hold loving thoughts and project a golden light around him; if only I had repented in that previous incarnation when I was burned at the stake; had I not betrayed T.J. in a previous life, I would not be bound to him in this one. I learned new reasons to find fault with myself while gaining no new ways to remedy the situation. All that, and how to form a perfect downward dog pose.

About this time I met Ann, who would have a huge impact on my life. She was a manicurist; we met at a beach retreat for women at which we'd been hired to work. I'd spent the weekend doing 15 minute mini-readings. Ann had done manicures.

As the weekend came to a close Ann said, "Well, do I get a reading?" I was tired but agreed. I'd watched her all weekend and was drawn to the way she talked.

After her mini-reading, I said, "So tell me how you learned to talk the way you do." She smiled and suggested we get together sometime. A few weeks later I called. We met for lunch and soon realized we had much in common. We'd even gone to the same high school, many years apart. I asked her again about her confident use of language.

"It's my recovery," she said simply. She handed me a card. The card read Caroline Derrickson – Addiction Therapist. I looked at Ann, puzzled.

"Why would I need an addiction therapist?" I asked, adding quickly, "I'm not addicted to anything."

"Yeah, I know," she said with a soft chuckle.

Twenty-one

"It's not normal."

Those words resonated in my head. Those words defined my life.

It was 1989 and I had been on a high from my validation with the Lee Iseli case. I had been proud.

I had spent years being "normal" with T.J., being a perfect suburban wife. Well, except for my dirty little secret. Why did normal feel so abnormal for me and why did the abnormal feel so right?

T.J.'s inability to accept the accuracy of my visions in the Lee Iseli case widened the chasm that divided us.

A few days before Christmas 1989 my mom's sister, Juanita, died. Aunt Juanita was an alcoholic. We had been close when I was young, and she'd been quietly supportive of my paranormal interest. I loved her, but was so saddened by her alcoholic lifestyle I couldn't be around her as an adult.

One evening the phone rang. T.J. was in our bedroom napping. I answered and heard Mom's tearful voice say, "Suzanne, your Aunt Juanita just died." Addiction had claimed her. She was 54 years old. I was saddened, but not too surprised. Hanging up, I went to sit by the lights of the Christmas tree and pray for my aunt. I was interrupted by T.J. He looked like he'd seen a ghost. He had, as a matter of fact. A woman standing at the foot of our bed had awakened him. As he described her, he added, "And she had red hair."

I started to laugh but stopped. I knew he was scared. I told him about Aunt Juanita's passing and that she had red hair. This really shook him. When he could finally master his voice, he muttered, "Who are you people?" and stomped out of the room. We never spoke of this again.

By spring 1990 I was certain the marriage was over. I was desperate to save it. When T.J. and I married seven years earlier I vowed I would never again leave. I'd done that too many times. I would make this one work. It was also clear I could not stop T.J.'s drinking.

Then one afternoon, as I watched a talk show, a miracle occurred. A woman was talking about living with an alcoholic. She mentioned "codependency" and attending Alcoholics Anonymous meetings. This woman on this afternoon talk show had been watching my marriage. She described it perfectly.

After the show ended I rummaged through my books until I found one I had but hadn't yet read, *Codependent No More*. I sat down and began reading. It read like a textbook on T.J. Some passages described him perfectly. I was onto something and determined to know more.

We had seen marriage counselors through the years, off and on. Not one had ever suggested alcohol could be the problem. The last counselor had even suggested that T.J. was allergic to alcohol.

I decided to attend Al-Anon meetings. There, I heard people recount how they live with their alcoholic spouses. After my third or fourth meeting I quit attending. I didn't want to know how to live with his drinking; I wanted to know how to stop him from drinking. Finally, in midsummer I hit a wall. I'd been sleeping on the sofa for weeks, we rarely spoke and none of it seemed to bother him. He continued his lifestyle as if nothing was wrong, while my soul carried an incapacitating pain. I'd heard that Kaiser Permanente had an outpatient intervention clinic. I made the call. When the information packet arrived, I set it on the table in front of T.J. and stated resolutely that either we do it or I was leaving.

He shrugged and said, "Fine." So, for weeks that summer we went to evening appointments with Kaiser. We were separated in groups, the alcoholics from their spouses. It was a fascinating educational process about the disease of alcoholism. But when our group counselor talked about the disease of codependency, she lost me. How could that be a disease, for God's sake? It's life. I just wanted T.J. to get fixed so our marriage could work. I was getting pissed and more depressed. He wasn't getting it.

Then in August another miracle occurred. It was a balmy evening. The air was full of the smell of fresh mowed hay and overripe fruit. The sky was clear and the moon barely new. T.J. had phoned hours earlier saying he'd be 30 minutes late. It was nearly midnight. I stepped outside to enjoy the evening. Our pony whinnied from the gate. I walked over and stroked her, taking in her wonderful smell. As I spoke to her, I burst into tears. I knew my life was dangling by a thread. I knew I was about to lose it all. I walked back to the house and sat down on the picnic table. I lay back to look at the stars. I wanted to die.

"Dear God," I prayed, "please give me a sign, some kind of hope to keep me going. I am so painfully unhappy. My heart is breaking." I had no sooner spoken when a brilliant display of shooting stars lit the sky above me.

"Oh my God," I whispered, "You are so beautiful." I sat up weeping, and as I wept I saw a business card in my mind: Caroline Derrickson, Addiction Therapist. I'd forgotten about Ann's advice. It was time to make the call.

Twenty-two

My re-birthday was August 21, 1990.

Caroline's office was in an old renovated house, blocks from Portland's Providence Hospital, where my sister had been taken years ago. Walking up those steps that day was terrifying. Although I'd seen many counselors through the years, something about this put butterflies in my stomach. After passing through the rose garden out front, I opened the door. A bell tinkled, a small set of chimes at the top of the door alerting the house that I had arrived. To the right was a set of stairs. To the left was an archway leading to what was once a living room. It was now a waiting room. A small handwritten sign on the mantel told me to please wait, my therapist would be right with me. Taking a seat in an overstuffed armchair, I smelled pipe tobacco. Beyond the softly playing classical music I could hear the murmur of a man's voice coming from what I assumed was the kitchen. In a small frame on a side table were words crafted with calligraphy: *"Easy Does It,"* next to a vase of lovely, fresh roses from the small rose garden out front, I surmised. There were a few magazines, mostly about health and wellness, and a newspaper. What struck me about this moment was how un-cliniclike this waiting room felt. I took a deep breath and sat back, allowing myself to settle into the familiar classical piece now playing.

A few moments later my reverie was broken by a door opening and voices coming from upstairs, fol-

lowed by footsteps. A woman came down the stairs. My
heart began to race. Our eyes met for a moment before
she looked away. At the bottom of the stairs she moved
hastily to the front door. The bell chimed her departure.
I shrugged and leaned back once more. Within minutes
footsteps, brisk and purposeful, descended the stairs, followed by a cheerful voice.

"Hello, Suzanne. I'm Caroline," she spoke as she
crossed into the waiting room, hand extended. I stood up.
She had a willowy, thin frame, auburn hair cut in an attractive chin-length style and a sincere smile. When her
eyes met mine, it felt like I'd been run down by a bulldoz-
er! My palms began to sweat. I could feel my feet becoming cement.

Turning, she said, "Let's go upstairs to my office." I
glanced once more at the front door. I could still bolt, I
thought. But just as quickly, I admonished myself to not
be foolish. After all, I'd been with therapists before.

At the top of the stairs, she turned left and went into
the only open door. Several other rooms lined the hall, all
with closed doors. Caroline took a seat in an old silver-
blue, wingback chair. There was another chair and a loveseat I could choose from. I sat on the loveseat and wondered if which seat I chose signified anything to Caroline.
She smiled. I smiled.

"So, tell me about yourself," she said. "What brings
you here today?" I told her I wasn't sure why I would
need an addiction therapist but described T.J.'s drinking problem and how it was killing me and how I wished
he would change. She asked if I'd been married before. I
dropped my eyes and nodded, reporting this was my fifth
marriage. She asked about my childhood, my siblings and

my education. She asked about my career. I told her I was a homemaker. I was not ready to tell her about being psychic.

The extraordinary part of this initial meeting was how Caroline named everything. Terms like "emotional incest," "rageaholic," "emotional abuse" and "narcissism" were used to define events and conditions I was describing. I was intrigued. "This stuff has a name?" She nodded. "But who or what gives you permission to name it all? None of my other counselors have ever done that."

She shrugged. "It is what it is," she said firmly.

"I'd like to come back next week," I said, noticing as our time drew to a close that she had not reached for her appointment book. Her arms were folded across her chest. As I spoke she held up one hand.

Shaking her head she said, "Well, I don't know if I want to work with you. You have a lot of problems."

What kind of therapist was this, telling me I had a lot of problems!

"To begin with, you have a relationship addiction...."

"I have a what?!"

She looked at me, lifting one eyebrow. "Well, Suzy, nobody gets married five times," she said with a note of incredulity in her voice.

"That's an addiction?" I asked, truly astonished by this news. She nodded.

We sat quietly, my mind reeling. I knew that I needed what this woman had but I could feel the opportunity slipping away. I had come to her because of T.J.'s drinking and she had turned the tables on me. She was stating that I had an addiction. Why hadn't anyone told me this before? Who was this audacious woman anyway and how can relationships be an addiction? My eyes darted around the room looking for her license or diploma. Maybe she wasn't really qualified for this kind of work.

After several extremely uncomfortable moments, Caroline leaned forward and spoke again. "Here's the deal. If we are to work together, I need a few things from you. First off, are you willing to admit you are 50 percent of the problem in this marriage?"

Did she not hear anything I'd told her about T.J.? Did she not understand how much pain I was in because of his behavior? And now she wanted me to admit to something I absolutely did not believe was true! I could feel my face burning and tears emerging. Don't cry. Don't cry...I told myself. Intuitively I knew the correct answer at this moment was yes. Quietly I nodded.

"I'm sorry," she asserted. "I didn't hear you."

I forced my gaze to meet her eyes. "Yes," I said directly at her, forcing sweetness.

She smiled. She wasn't done yet. "Good. Now there are a few more things. For the next two years you won't drink, you won't date, and you will attend a weekly 12-step meeting."

"But I don't have a drinking problem," I protested.

"Good, then that won't be a problem for you. You need to be available for your feelings while we work together. Alcohol, even a glass of wine occasionally, will numb your feelings. So, no alcohol."

I agreed, grudgingly.

"But dating?" I asked, reminding her I was still married.

She shrugged. "You never know what the next two years might bring."

I was less receptive to attending the12-step meetings. I didn't have a drug or alcohol problem. I'd already tried Al-Anon. The thought of attending these meetings scared me. She smiled as she reached for her appointment book.

"Addiction is addiction," she said. "You might try ACOA for now. So, when would you like to come back?"

We scheduled for the following Tuesday.

Later that evening I phoned Ann and told her about my meeting with Caroline. I told her how surprised I was at her directness.

"Yeah, that's Caroline," Ann agreed. "She's the best. She knows what she's talking about." She invited me to go with her on Saturday night to her "home group" ACOA meeting. Hanging up, I felt some relief. At least I wouldn't be going alone.

My next appointment with the Kaiser counselor was the next day. She had a shiny office with a functional desk, behind which she remained for the entire hour. She was young and well-schooled, judging from all the books on her shelves and the certificates on her walls. She was perky and positive. She asked if I'd been reading the books she'd suggested. I nodded. She asked if I'd begun to identify my feelings. I nodded.

"You know you need to work hard at this," she lectured from her perch behind her desk. I looked at her and realized I was experiencing a feeling. A feeling called shame. She was somehow shaming me, and I was an awkward little girl in her sage presence. On the walk back to my car, I mulled over the glaring difference between my experience with her and my experience with Caroline. Caroline had given me something, although I couldn't quite yet be sure of what, but it felt strangely like hope. This woman, a highly qualified addiction therapist employed by this very large hospital had reinforced my inadequacy. I cried all the way home.

On Saturday, I met Ann in the parking lot of the church where the meeting was held, nervous and scared. She reassured me, saying that I didn't have to talk if I didn't want to. The room was filling up with people. Someone went to get more chairs, which were placed in a circle. People were visiting quietly. A few sat alone. Promptly at 8:00 p.m., a woman stood and welcomed everyone. Then she said something that would have a powerful effect on my recovery.

"I especially want to welcome newcomers tonight, and I want you to know that if you can come to at least 10 meetings, you may not 'get' the program, but the program *will* get you." Then she added, "I want you to look around at all the faces here and know that you may not like us all, but you will come to love us."

In that moment I only wondered what the hell I was doing there. I didn't belong. I was "special." As the evening went on and people spoke about their feelings, and told the stories of what had happened to them, I wondered why they didn't just get over it like I'd done. The past is past. Let it go for God's sake! Quit whining. Move forward.

As I sat there, I realized I was having trouble taking a full breath. The room was closing in on me. I was grateful when they took a break. I made for the door and fresh air. Ann followed me outside.

Smiling, she said, "This is probably one of the most powerful groups in town. People get a lot of work done here."

I looked at her, not really understanding what she'd just said. Work? It sure sounded like whining to me. After the break, we went back in. The group was a little smaller now. As people took turns speaking, others cried from time to time. It made me uncomfortable. What a bunch of softies, I thought. No wonder they're messed up. They can't cope. When the meeting closed with the serenity prayer, I thought, Oh brother, now this, how corny!

As I uttered my goodbyes, I thanked Ann and asked if I'd see her next week. She wasn't sure, but reminded me that I knew my way there now. Great. The thought of showing up by myself was terrifying, but I'd made my promise and meant to keep it.

The following Tuesday I was eager to report to Caroline about my first meeting. She listened and smiled when I commented about all the whining. "Well, just keep going," was her only comment. We spent the rest of the hour talking about boundaries, something I'd never been taught. So when she suggested I needed to start setting boundaries with T.J., I freaked.

"That will just cause problems," I said.

She raised her eyebrow in her trademark look. "Oh?" she queried. "How so?"

"Well, he'll get pissed off," I replied shifting in my seat.

"Oh, that," she said, nodding her head knowingly. I breathed a silent sigh of relief. Thank goodness she understood.

After a few seconds of silence, I heard her say, "Sooooo?"

"What?" I said, somewhat startled.

"So *what?*"

"What do you mean 'So what?'" I said nervously.

Silence again.

"He'll get angry," I said once more.

"Yeah, well he has a right to respond however he wants. But you have a right to set boundaries and take care of yourself based on his actions."

"I do?" I said with surprise. "Really?" This was new to me.

"Of course you do. It sounds like you let other people's anger control you," she mused, with a slight hint of concern in her voice.

"Well, yeah. Doesn't everyone?"

She shook her head. Fear and confusion surfaced. Did this woman not care if I got into trouble?

After a pregnant silence, Caroline cleared her throat. "Suzy, which one of your parents had a rage problem?" she asked.

I broke and began to cry, quietly at first and then with sobs arising from deep inside.

"Suzy, I want to offer you something to think about. Understanding this characterization is critical to your recovery although it is difficult to define. Codependency is a learned survival behavior when we are exposed to a dysfunctional or abusive environment. It is a state of hyper vigilance to our surroundings in which we maintain an unshakable belief that we are the reason for all the ills of the world. Phrases such as "If I was good, dad wouldn't drink; if my room was cleaner, my mom wouldn't hit me" are commonplace among codependents. In this hyper vigilant state we assume ownership of the moods, feelings and actions of those around us. It is the greatest lie that we

could ever believe about ourselves and which we perpet-
uate throughout all of our future relationships."

We sat in silence as I absorbed her words and pondered how it related to my life.

And so my healing began.

After a while Caroline breathed a comforting, empa-
thetic breath. Now was the time to set my first boundary.
The issue that we had chosen to tackle was the stony silence that had settled in the house over the last few days. I
had ceased trying to engage T.J. His non-response was so
hurtful. Caroline and I spent the remainder of the session
engaged in role-playing. I acted as T.J., who would come
in from work and, without speaking to me, would pick
up the mail as he walked into the TV room, closing the
doors behind him; sometimes acknowledging my presence, sometimes not.

Caroline, as me, said, "T.J., I need you to speak to me
when I say 'Hello.' It feels hurtful when you don't."

My overwhelming thought was disbelief that this
could possibly have any impact.

"Yeah, right. That's going to go over real well," I said
nervously. She assured me that it's always scary initially
to set these boundaries, but that I really needed to see it
more as self-care.

"It's time to start taking care of yourself. You can do
this." Her reassuring voice sounded so confident.

"You're sure this will work?" I asked cautiously.

She nodded. "You can do this, Suzanne. You must. It's
really your only option if you want to do this work."

And so I experienced my first act of trust. I felt like a
child again. I wanted to go where Caroline was. I wanted

to stand where she stood. It was as if she were on the other side of a wobbly bridge over a deep canyon, the safe side. And I had wolves snapping at my heels. I couldn't go back. I had to cross over. I had to trust her words to guide me.

"You can do this," she was saying again.

"Okay," I promised her. She smiled.

That night at home, I confronted T.J. with my tenuous boundaries. T.J. accused me of trying to control him.

I repeated Caroline's words to him, "It's called self-care." He stomped into the TV room and slammed the door. His actions remained unchanged. I, however, felt empowered.

I voraciously began reading everything I could about alcoholism and codependency. I continued to set boundaries. I learned about detachment. I informed my Kaiser counselor that I'd found another therapist and wouldn't be finishing the program. She was concerned that I wouldn't get my "certificate." I told her I could live without it. For the first time in my life I began to feel authentically powerful.

Twenty-three

Early October was in the air. I do so love the warm fall days and the brisk cold mornings. The morning sun shone through the leaves of the maple outside my parlor, painting the room in golden hues. The sight took my breath away. In this room I did my readings. With three floor-to-ceiling windows overlooking the pond and stream, it was as if it were part of the outdoors. I sat in the window every morning with my coffee and journals. It was such sweet reverie for my soul.

This particular morning, however, my musings were disrupted by the phone ringing in the kitchen. I thought about letting the machine answer but felt an urgency in the ringing. It was the sister of a client whom I'll call Nancy. She sounded frantic.

"Suzanne, my name's Amy. I'm Nancy Jones's sister. I understand she's been to see you a few times."

"Yes," I replied tentatively, since my readings are private and confidential.

"I am calling out of desperation. Nancy's missing. You've heard about the two hikers missing on Larch Mountain? It's Nancy and her friend Beth."

"Oh no," I replied, sinking into a nearby chair.

The plight of the missing hikers had dominated the news coverage over the last three days. They had gone hiking on a clear fall day. Then the weather changed suddenly and became a snowy whiteout. Police and search teams combed the area but the falling snow made the hikers impossible to track. No clue to their whereabouts could be found. Their locked car remained where they'd left it in the trailhead parking lot.

"Suzanne, have you worked with missing persons before?" she asked.

"Well, yes, once, but honestly I'm not sure how helpful I can be. I would be willing to try, of course, but I'm sort of new at this missing person stuff."

We arranged to meet later that day. I asked her to bring an item belonging to Nancy, a photo of both women and a map of the area.

Dropping the receiver back on its cradle, I returned to my parlor and sat looking out across the pond. I felt scared. This was huge. Offering personal guidance through private readings was one thing, but working with families and possibly the police, that was something else. The lives of two women were at stake. I felt vulnerable. Doubts invaded my mind. What if I couldn't *see*? What if I was wrong? What if I misled them? Why did I say I would help? I took a deep, calming breath.

"I can only say what I *see*," I reasoned with myself. Besides, I really want to help if I could, I thought, as I stood to get ready for my day.

Later that afternoon Amy and her mother arrived. I led them into to my reading room. They updated me; snow had covered any tracks and hopes were fading fast. The hikers were clothed in only windbreakers and their supplies would be scarce, as they had only prepared for a day hike. Holding the photos and a bracelet of Nancy's, I closed my eyes.

The picture came quickly.

"I can see them huddled together out of the snow. It looks like they're in a one room shack or lean-to... a line-shack. That's where they are: in an old line-shack!" I spoke aloud what I was *seeing*.

"Where? Can you see where?" Nancy's mother pleaded. With trembling hands she unfolded the map on the coffee table in front of me.

Looking at the map I *saw* nothing. I shook my head. "I'm sorry," I said, although the words seemed inadequate.

I began to feel uncomfortable. I could sense Amy and her mom pressing me to see more and do more. But there was nothing. I felt their disappointment. I wanted to fix them. Panic crept in. But, after working painfully through months of therapy, I had learned to set boundaries. I could not fix anyone. Strengthening my resolve, I took a breath and looked up at them.

"I'm sorry. That's all I see," I repeated. Their heart-wrenching looks of distress tested my resolve. I wanted to embrace them and somehow magically take their pain. I could only empathize. This was so hard. Psychic ability and empathy are closely wedded. I often could feel the feelings of others so acutely that it caused me physical pain.

A few hours later Amy phoned. She'd just spoken with the county sheriff in charge of the search.

"Suzanne, I told him we'd come to you. He said we'd wasted our time and money. I told him you didn't charge us and that you'd seen them in a line-shack. He reaffirmed that I'd wasted my time. I insisted he look into any line-shacks up there. He said he'd call me back later. Suzanne, what's up with his attitude? Do police not use psychics?"

I could hear the frustration in her voice. Of course, hearing all of this only brought up my doubts and shame, the old voices telling me to keep quiet, to not "bring home all the prizes." Mostly, of course, I didn't want what I *saw* to hurt anyone. She sounded hurt.

"Amy, give him time. I'm certain they're doing all they can," I reassured her. "Let me know when you hear from him again," I added.

Hanging up, I wondered why I'd ever agreed to work with them. What if I was wrong? I didn't want to give the family false hope. I can only see what I see, I reasoned with myself again. Sometimes I'm right. Sometimes I'm not. I whispered a quiet prayer for the missing women.

The evening news reported that the police had not ruled out the possibility that the women had been abducted. With no sign of them and continued snow in the forecast, their chances of being found were fading.

The next morning Amy phoned. "Suzanne, I just spoke with the sheriff. He maintained that all of the old line-shacks up there had been removed years ago. He checked with the utilities, and their maps confirmed it. There are no line-shacks." She spoke calmly, but she was crying.

My heart sank. "Oh Amy, I'm so sorry. He's sure of that?" I asked feebly, not knowing what else to say.

"Yeah," she said, disheartened. "He also said he wished people wouldn't use psychics. His exact words were, 'Let the police do their job.' It sounds like he may call off the search soon. Suzanne, do you think they could have been abducted?" I heard the desperation in her voice.

"I don't know what to think now," I admitted. "I saw them so clearly, huddled in some kind of shed or something." My mind walked back through what I'd *seen*.

It felt like I was being stonewalled. I knew what I *saw* and that I needed to trust it, but there was a person with authority telling me it wasn't possible. I felt torn. My rational mind was trying to agree with the authorities, but my intuitive mind was screaming, "They're in a line-shack!"

Amy politely thanked me for my help and asked that I call her if anything, no matter how trivial, came up.

Following the call, I reconsidered what I knew. Maybe they were abducted. Maybe what I saw was the women being held somewhere against their will. I tried to convince myself that it was plausible. As I sat with that thought, I began to picture the scenario playing out. I saw the hikers return to their car and two men asking for help to jump a dead car battery. Then I saw them grabbing the women and throwing them in the back of a van, and driving off to the east.

That's it. They were abducted!

Wait a minute, I thought. I felt like I'd made up a story. My imagination had gone into overdrive. This second "acceptable" version felt wrong and contrived, not natural like my line-shack vision.

The difference was like watching a scripted movie, versus a quick snapshot. My mind was reeling with confusion and uncertainty. A few hours later my confidence was further eroded as I answered a phone call from a county sheriff's detective. Apparently, Nancy's family had insisted he call and speak to me. He was annoyed and told me so. I repeated again what I'd seen initially.

He interrupted. "With all due respect," he said, with no respect at all in his voice, "we are clear that no line-shacks exist. We are shifting our investigation now to possible abduction. Do you see anything around that?" he queried dismissively.

I thought for a moment. His intimidating manner had me completely off-center. I had never worked with police before. I promised myself I'd never do it again.

"Well, actually, when I thought about it later, I could see two men...." I went on to give him an account of my other vision. Who knows? Maybe it was the accurate one. I was, after all, new at this psychic detective work. His enthusiasm increased as I provided the version he was seeking. I, however, experienced a sick feeling in the pit of my stomach.

I wanted to be done with all of this psychic work. Maybe it was time to go find a "real" job.

The evening news program was interrupted by a phone call from Amy. She was barely understandable through her hysterical sobs.

"They've called off the search. The sheriff instructed all the searchers to go home, including the helicopter from the air base. HE CALLED OFF THE SEARCH!" she shouted in disbelief.

As we spoke, the sheriff appeared on the news.

"Amy, he's on the news now. Let me call you right back," I said. Before I could call Amy back, however, my phone rang again. It was my friend Debbi who worked with search and rescue.

"I heard the family had contacted a psychic. Was it you?" she asked.

"Yeah, but I guess I wasn't real helpful," I answered.

"Tell me what you saw," she said.

I told her about seeing the women huddled in a shed or shack.

"Are they still alive?"

"Yes," I responded without thought. "But the sheriff insists that there are no shacks up there. I believe that it's an old line-shack. I can see utility poles," I added.

"Listen," Debbi said firmly, "after our experience with the Iseli case, I trust what you see. Our group is going back up there at dawn. This is their fourth night in the cold. They don't have much longer," she added grimly.

"But what about the sheriff's orders?"

"Screw the sheriff," Debbi said. "We're working for the family now. I'll talk to you soon."

Hanging up, I could feel my heart racing. Holy cow! What have I gotten myself into, shaking my head at my friend's audacity. I'd been raised to respect authority. This was bringing up so much for me.

The ringing phone startled me. I jumped. Man, this is getting to me, I thought. It was Amy. I'd forgotten to call her back. She had just spoken to search and rescue, who had assured her that they were going back up in the morning.

"Suzanne, they're going back up because they trust what you saw," she said.

"I know," I answered quietly.

"Thank you," she said gratefully.

The following day, my noontime program was interrupted by breaking news. The two women hikers had been found. Details were sketchy, but they were both alive! My legs crumbled. On my knees, in front of the TV, I wept.

Before the excited reporter finished his interviews, a call came in from Debbi. Based on what I'd *seen*, the search and rescue team followed an old utility road and were within a half mile of the rescue site when they heard a chopper overhead. The 304th Air Force helicopter rescue team had also gone back to search at daybreak, acting on a hunch, a gut feeling. Around noon, the helicopter crew had spotted H-E-L-P spelled out in the snow. Putting down, they saw a woman waving her arms near what appeared to be an old line-shack. Search and rescue converged on the site minutes after the helicopter team had put down.

"The shack was there, Suzanne, just like you said," Debbi excitedly yelled into the receiver. "How do you do that?" she added, not waiting for an answer.

Both women were alive but suffering from hypothermia. They would not have made it through another night.

A few weeks after Nancy and Beth had been rescued from Larch Mountain, Nancy called to invite me to a "welcome home" party. As I pulled up in front of her house, I wondered if she'd be comfortable talking about the ordeal. A young man answered the door and escorted me into the dining room. Nancy sat, laughing with friends around the table. When she saw me, she stood and rushed over.

Crushing me with a big hug, she whispered, "I have something to tell you. Let's talk." I followed her to a quiet place in a corner of the living room. She smiled. "I want to thank you for working with my family during this ordeal. You'll never know how comforting it was to have someone willing to talk to them. Apparently the police don't really talk much about what they're doing."

We both agreed on that point.

"Suzanne," she continued, lowering her voice, "the strangest thing happened to us. I really need your take on it. After we found the hut we soon realized it would keep us out of the snow, but not out of the cold. That first night we huddled together to stay warm. Amy said you saw us huddled together in a shack. Well, we were. We did calisthenics to stay warm the next day. We were crestfallen when the sun came up and it was still snowing. Later that morning we heard the search helicopters but never saw them. We decided to take our chances spelling out HELP in the snow. We dug out the letters then filled them in with tree branches." She smiled wryly, "I guess it worked."

I shared her smile. "Thank God," I said, reaching over to touch her hand.

"Well," she went on, "digging in the snow got our clothing wet. We were freezing. As we huddled in the corner I knew we might not make it through the night. I was really concerned for Beth. She seemed to be having a more difficult time with our predicament." She stopped, her voice quavering with the memory.

"Anyway, I began to feel a strange sense of peace which overtook my fear. It was almost as if a reassuring presence had joined us."

I nodded, remembering that same sense of peace I'd felt as our small plane had crashed in Reno years ago. Had it been an angel?

She went on. "Suzanne, somewhere in the night or early morning the strangest thing happened. Across from us appeared an old-fashioned potbellied stove. It was burning hot. I could distinguish the glow of red-hot coals inside it. There was, of course, no stove in the shack. I was obviously hallucinating. But I could feel slight warmth from it." Nancy paused a moment, taking a breath.

When she continued it was with a question. "Is it possible for two people to have the same hallucination?"

"What do you mean?" I asked.

"As I quietly watched the glowing stove, Beth stirred. I thought she was asleep, but then she sat up and started to stand. I asked her what she was doing and she said she was going to stand by the stove to get warm. Instinctively, I pulled her back down beside me, stunned that she could see it too. A feeling emerging from deep within me impressed upon me a knowledge that if she went to that stove she would die. The stove seemed to beckon to us with warmth and comfort. I kept chanting, "There is no stove, there is no stove." Beth finally quit struggling.

"We both must have fallen asleep because the sound of the rescue helicopter woke us. I confess I was afraid to move at first, fearful that it too, was a hallucination. When I heard the rescuers' voices, I knew we were saved." Her voice tapered off.

We both sat quietly for a moment. Clearing her throat, she added, "The doctors said we were near death. I knew that was true. Our death had taken the form of a potbellied stove calling us home."

I quietly pondered what she had shared with me. I knew that symptoms of hypothermia include a point at which the body does begin to feel false warmth and hallucinate. But I'd never heard of a shared hallucination.

Life is such a grand mystery. The more I learned about it, the less I knew. Perhaps the hallucinations of the dying are in fact the other world showing up to take them home. What if the other world does just pick up where this one leaves off? What if it does meet us right where we stand?

Twenty-four

I could no longer withhold my true nature from Caroline despite my overwhelming fear that she might be unable to accept me. The search had both drained and energized me, psychically and emotionally. As I drove to my appointment with Caroline, I contemplated how I would tell her. Would she suggest that maybe I wasn't psychic but psycho? Would she want me to try medications? I thought of Great-Grandma Jones whose first husband had put her in an institution. I thought of people through the years who'd fallen away when I'd revealed this part of myself, people who'd literally stepped back from me when I told them my career, like I had some strange disease. Would Caroline step back? God, I hope not, I thought.

I had to trust.

We sat quietly for a few minutes, Caroline across from me, smiling expectantly, waiting. I cleared my throat.

"Caroline, there's something I need to tell you about myself. Something that could risk our future work together." I paused. Taking a breath, I continued, lowering my eyes. I couldn't bear watching her reaction to my words.

"I'm psychic. I mean I am a psychic. That is what I do," I said quickly and quietly.

She waited expectantly, lifting her eyebrows in a manner that urged me to continue.

"That's all, I mean that's it." I stammered. She was still smiling.

"Well, Suzy, that's great! Tell me about it," she said, adding that she'd visited psychics a time or two herself.

"You have?"

She nodded. And so the floodgates opened. After all those years of hiding in the shadows, I stepped forth into the light that day. Caroline, being Caroline, threw me a suspicious curve.

"Suzy, when you're doing this, do you hear voices? Tell me how it works for you." Her inquiry felt leading. All my defenses flew up. I had been tricked. She had gotten me to confess and now she was going to medicate. How could I have been so stupid, so trusting?! Damn! She was good. Very good.

I sat still and silent. No one spoke.

Finally I confessed, "Yes, I do hear voices. But not like hearing someone speak. It's a different kind of hearing," I said, using my best professional voice. "It's an inner hearing."

She nodded. "Do these voices ever tell you what to do?"

Now I was getting pissed. I could feel tears and shame welling up inside. "No, Caroline, it's not like that," I defended.

"Suzy, I know it's not, but I have to ask these questions. Let me explain. In psychology, the schizophrenic is referred to as the drowning mystic. The difference between a mystic-psychic and a schizophrenic is often only that the mystic-psychic knows how to turn the faucet on and off." Her compassion was evident.

I nodded, loving that explanation.

She leaned forward in her chair, "So tell me about this missing person case."

I found a new confidante that day. She even shared some of her own psychic experiences. On the drive home, I felt embraced by the lightness of having confided in someone who accepted that part of me. God had truly sent me an angel. I felt that my heart and soul were expanding, welcoming me home.

Later that evening I shared some of my excitement with T.J. He brushed me off with a feeble "great" as he looked through the day's mail. This time his brush-off didn't devastate me. I could go on. I had Caroline. I had my meetings. I had new friends like Ann. My path was beginning to emerge as footstones in the mist before me. I was learning that I could trust the steps.

Then the day came when it was time for T.J. to leave, even though his drinking had abated as a result of the Kaiser program. The more I set boundaries with him, the less we spoke and the more assertive he became with my 13-year-old daughter. It was making me uncomfortable and she had complained he was being mean to her. She ended her complaint, saying, "I wish he'd just drink again. He was nicer when he was drinking."

Caroline and I talked about it. She explained how the addict will have arrested emotional development based on the age he was when he began using. "So if T.J. was 13 when he took his first drink, that's how old he is emotionally. He's about 13. He's in competition with your daughter. Unfortunately, he's in the body of a 42-year-old." She added, more to herself than to me, "It is truly a cunning and baffling disease."

"So what do I do?"

The room was silent. Caroline seemed to be thinking. "Well, you might try a trial separation. A lot of couples who enter recovery together have to separate for a while. It's hard enough doing this work alone, but having two people in it at the same time...." She shook her head. "It's hard."

"Oh, great," I said, "now I have to ask him to leave?"

"Well," she said, shrugging her shoulders, "it might be just as uncomfortable for him being there right now. It can't hurt to make the suggestion."

I had been noticing a sinking feeling every day when I saw T.J. driving up the driveway. It was time for some distance. To my surprise, he agreed. A few hours later, I watched as he drove away. Sadly, it felt more like I was watching a child leave home. It was October 1990.

For the next few months I immersed myself in my recovery work. My times with Caroline continued to support and reveal me. My daughter and I both began to experience some peace and serenity at home. It felt good not having someone else to bump into, either physically or emotionally. For the first time in my life I was experiencing life in my own space. I loved it. I was taking care of myself. It was the little things like paying the bills, taking out the garbage or hiring a repairman that felt so good. It was those same little things that made me more aware of my codependent behaviors and my unrealistic expectations of others. I began to see and experience the 50 percent of the marriage that was my fault and how covert and manipulative I'd been in all of my relationships, born out of the lie that other people's feelings and well-being were not only my fault, but my responsibility.

With Caroline's help, I was learning to become honest with myself in every situation. She was giving me self-care tools. I felt like a child again but sad for all the years that now seemed wasted. She reassured me they were not wasted, that timing is everything. I had not been ready until now. I had not had the tools until now.

We talked about the spiritual and metaphysical studies I'd done through the years. I laughed when she suggested I was spiritually top-heavy! I knew how to live in my spirit; I just didn't know how to live in my body. She refused to talk about dreams or other out-of-body experiences. More than once as I began to recount a dream or some other mystical event, she'd wave it off and tell me she didn't want to hear about it.

"Stay in your body," she would say.

I had friends who were telling me of their healing experiences with soul retrievals, shamanic journeys, or aura cleansing. When I shared these ideas with Caroline, she said, "Do you like being hypnotized?" (ouch!) "STAY in your body!"

I should have known better, also, when the same friends asked me what I was doing to make such positive changes in my life and I handed them Caroline's card. Several said, "Oh, I don't need THAT." The few who did go see her fled after their first session.

When I asked her about that, she smiled and said, "Well, Suzy, it's not for everyone." Then she added, seeing my puzzled look, "Not everyone can do this work. It's very hard."

"Yeah, tell me about it," I agreed, rolling my eyes. And so I continued, head down, shoulder to the task. I lost some friends along the way. It made me sad, but I also understood. One of the things that began to stand out for me was how my friends didn't seem to like or understand the idea of boundaries.

I heard a lot of empathizing with T.J. Things like "Oh, poor man, he must be having a hard time. You know, you two might have karma to fulfill. Maybe you're being too hard on him." These words spoken purportedly out of love and concern scared the hell out of me. They brought up feelings of guilt and responsibility.

Sitting with Caroline one afternoon I mentioned this to her, adding that perhaps I had been too hard and maybe I should be taking care of T.J., since, after all, he was my husband. I'll never forget what happened next. After a few moments of silence, I began to squirm. Something didn't feel right. In fact, something felt very wrong.

Then Caroline spoke. Brow furrowed, eyes intense, she looked at me and said, "Well, after all, he is your responsibility. You know he can't take care of himself. What is he going to do?"

Had she lost her mind? What had she been telling me all these weeks? I broke. Sobbing, I struggled for breath. I felt defeated.

"C-C-Caroline, what are you doing, why are you saying this?" I whimpered between sobs. My mind was reeling with confusion. I continued sobbing for what seemed like hours, then a quiet came over me. Slowly I got my breath back. Looking up at her, she was still there, arms folded, brow furrowed, like some judging parent.

I said very slowly, almost in a whisper, "I can't take care of him."

"What?" she asked. "Did you say something?"

Sitting up straight now I repeated myself, louder this

time. "Caroline, I can't take care of him. He's not my responsibility. You know that. What's wrong with you?
I thought you were teaching me how I'm not responsible...."

Her smile cut me off. Shaking her head, she said, "There
you are! For a while there I thought we'd lost you."

Oh, the relief I felt. She had only been doing her job,
showing me to me.

As for my psychic peers, I realized most were using
empathy to tune-in. They could not afford to have boundaries. That style of tuning-in began to feel "icky" to me
and inappropriate. I became grateful that my training had
been through psychometry, the ability to touch or hold a
thing and see pictures. True, I had indeed experienced empathy. It's, in fact, almost intoxicating for die-hard codependents to feel the feelings of others. But now it felt more
like a fix, a junkie's fix. So, along with the obvious benefits of boundary setting, the psychic benefits were a plus.
I no longer felt I had to *feel* for others. I only had to *see*. I
also became aware of how empathy turns around and becomes projection. I began to understand that I could still
have compassion without taking on the feelings of others.
I felt empowered and liberated.

Twenty-five

Bob and I met a few days later at the Horse Brass Pub, a few blocks from Caroline's office. I was eager to see him and bring him up to date. This was the first time I'd seen Bob since starting my work with Caroline. As I filled him in, I realized I was using language unfamiliar to people not in recovery. In the past, my discussions with Bob about spirit had always seemed to make my messy life more palatable. Today, however, the spirit talk seemed irrelevant, so I cut my briefing short.

"Tell me about the hallucination you mentioned earlier among the women on Larch Mountain," Bob said.

I filled him in and we went on to discuss supersensible worlds and multi-dimensional realities. Normally, I would have been totally engaged in this conversation. Today I found my mind drifting.

This feeling of disconnect to my mentor was disturbing. I seemed to have traveled such a distance in just a few short weeks.

Sitting with Caroline the following week I mentioned this disturbing distance I'd begun noticing with friends. "For one thing, my not drinking seems to bother a few of them. I wasn't aware until I stopped drinking how much of my social life involved getting together over a bottle of wine. It makes no difference to me, but I've noticed plenty of my friends reacting to it." I paused, thinking of a party I'd been to over the weekend. I was the only nondrinker.

After a few minutes of silence, she said, "Well, Suzy, you're growing and changing. No doubt that means some of your friendships are bound to change, especially the ones that were based on caretaking or neediness."

"But what about my friendship with my spiritual mentor?" I asked, my voice trembling. I had shared with Caroline a little bit about my friendship with Finnell and how important and life-saving it had been through the years. I told her I'd felt distanced from him when we had met last week.

Caroline frowned. "I wonder...," she said, pausing a moment. Looking at me as she shifted slightly, then continued, "I wonder if it's possible that part of you has been hiding in your spiritual studies. That it's been such a place of refuge for all these years that now you're experiencing a sort of awakening in your body. Perhaps you no longer need a hiding place."

She went on cautiously now. "Suzy, you are experiencing an awesome awakening that has everything to do with staying in your body and being present for yourself. The work we've been doing together is creating safety for you. Maybe for the first time in your life you are safe, here in this room and at your meetings, to be who you are. There's no mystery involved in that. There's nothing to figure out. No hidden meanings, nothing to make sense of. It's you discovering you. You're learning self-care, learning to meet your own needs. And while it is, no doubt, the most awesome journey you'll ever take, make no mistake, it is hard work, very hard. And you are doing a great job. You're getting it faster than anyone I've ever met...."

She smiled now and the warmth and sincerity in that smile moved me to my soul.

"Really?" I asked quietly. "I'm really getting it?"

She nodded and with a chuckle said, "Oh yeah."

"But it feels like I'm losing...something. My spiritual life is everything to me." My voice was trembling.

She grinned. "Don't worry, it's not going anywhere. It's part of who you are and it's yours to keep. It will always be there for you. It may have to step aside a bit, however, to make room for the rest of you. What you are losing is an old way of life, full of behaviors and habits that no longer work for you. It takes great courage, and from this moment on, a boldness and commitment to yourself like none you have ever known."

I sat back, letting her words cover me like a favorite, familiar comforter. "That sounds ominous," I said.

She smiled.

"Caroline, I have to trust you. I believe you. You're like my lifeline right now. And that feels terrifying."

"But you can do this, Suzy," she said. "You are doing it. And you're doing great."

I thought about this for a minute. "If I'm doing so great, why is everyone around me so upset about it? My family actually mocks my therapy and meetings." I swallowed hard around the lump in my throat. "I've quit mentioning my therapy or referring to it around them."

"Remember John Bradshaw's example of the family system being similar to a mobile?" Caroline asked, referring to his book *The Family*. I nodded.

"When the mobile is hanging peacefully from the ceiling, each piece stays in place. Even when a breeze comes along, all the pieces hold their position in relationship to each other. It is the same in a family system: each player knows his or her place. The whole is dependent on each one keeping their place." She held up her hands as if dangling the mobile in front of me.

"So when someone enters recovery, they begin to make different choices and set boundaries." She smiled, poking the imaginary mobile with her finger.

"It bounces around and gets messy," I replied.

She sat back and grinned. "Exactly. You're making things messy in your family system. You're not keeping your place. Your family needs you to be who they need you to be…to keep it the same."

"But I can't go back to the way I was. I am forever changed even if I quit all of this right now," I said. The magnitude of my work with Caroline was beginning to dawn on me. "And it's making everyone so unhappy. How can I do this to my family?" I began to cry, quietly at first and then deep soulful sobs.

After a while Caroline spoke again. "This is very, very hard work. Right now you're going to have to trust. Suzy, because you are doing this work, you are breaking a cycle of behavior and addiction that has been passed on for generations. Because of your efforts and commitment to yourself, you clear a path for your children and their children to do it differently. The buck stops here. Right here."

Wiping my eyes I looked up at her.

"You're sure?" I asked softly.

Caroline nodded her head.

Our hour was up and as I stood to leave, Caroline stood and followed me to the door. Impulsively, I turned and gave her a hug, something I'd never felt had been appropriate before.

"Thank you," I said. She opened the door and we stepped out into the hall.

"Next week when you arrive, just come on up and wait for me in here," she said, motioning to the room next door.

"Oh?" I said. "We're changing rooms?"

"I think it's time," she said, smiling slyly.

The holidays were approaching and I could feel the tension growing. T.J. had hoped to move back in by Thanksgiving, but I was not ready. For the first time in my life I had personal space, and emotional and psychic breathing room. It felt so good. The thought of his moving back made me sick. Everyone around us was pressuring me to let him back.

"After all it's the holidays, poor man."

I could feel the emotional noose tightening. How could I do this to him? Bowing to the pressure, I reluctantly agreed to meet with T.J. Maybe things had changed. We met at a coffee shop and as soon as I sat down, he began issuing ultimatums. I could smell alcohol and asked if he was still attending meetings and going to therapy. He looked as if I'd just thrown cold water on him.

"Not that it's any of your business, but yes I am," he responded curtly. After a few minutes of uncomfortable silence, he leaned across the table and said, "I'm moving home next week. It's my home too and this has gone on long enough." He jabbed his finger on the table for emphasis. I felt bullied and scared.

"Set a boundary or leave. Take care of yourself." I could hear Caroline's voice.

"No, you're not. I'm not ready." The words came out but I could hardly believe that it was my voice issuing this audacious statement. Did I just say that?!

He looked stunned.

"I think you're still drinking," I added. We sat glaring at each other. I stood to leave. This was going nowhere.

"I should have listened to my therapist," he said derisively, standing now too.

I swung around to face him.

"He said you're not psychic, you're crazy." T.J. threw these words down like a trump card. I was speechless.

Gathering up my purse and keys, I nearly ran to my car. I didn't look back. As I drove home his words echoed in my head, undermining everything I'd worked so hard to gain these last few months. I couldn't believe a therapist would say such a thing. What if my therapist believed the same about me? What if she was part of this somehow? How could I have been so stupid to believe her? It must be a setup. By the time I got home, panic had taken over. I was trembling. I couldn't gather a full breath. Walking into the kitchen, I dumped the contents of my purse onto the counter. My vision was blurred with tears, but I knew somewhere in this mess was Caroline's home phone number which she had given me a few weeks ago.

As she handed it to me she said, "I don't like to be called at home, so only use this in an emergency." I wondered if this was enough of an emergency. I didn't care. I had to speak to her.

"Hello," she was saying. Thank God, she was home. "Hello," she said again.

"Caroline, it's Suzanne," I spoke between sobs. "I just met with T.J.," I began, but she stopped me.

"Suzy, you're not crazy," she said matter-of-factly. My God, how did she know?

"But Caroline, he said his therapist says I am. I'm scared," I said.

"It's okay to feel scared," she said. "But you're doing great. T.J.'s just a bully, and it sounds like he's still drinking. I suggest you don't talk to him for a while. Remember, boundaries are about self-care. You're not crazy," she repeated, "you're doing great."

I was quiet for a moment. Her voice was reassuring. She sounded so confident in my ability to take care of myself.

"Okay," I finally relented.

"All right then. I'll see you Tuesday," she said.

Tuesday was only two days away. I could make it until then.

Climbing the stairs to Caroline's office, I realized I'd been so eager to see her that I'd forgotten about the new room she wanted to meet in. As I passed our old meeting place I could hear voices, one of them Caroline's speaking softly. She must have needed that office for someone else, I thought. Quietly I turned the handle of the door to the new office, but halted at the threshold.

The entire room was padded. Pads on the floor. Pads on the walls! There were no chairs, only pillows. Lots of pillows of various sizes and shapes. Oh my God, I thought, she really must think I'm crazy. I stood there, frozen, wanting to flee. Just then I heard her office door open. I could hear her say "goodbye." She walked towards me.

"Hi Suzy," she said. "Go on in. I'll be right with you."

I turned to face her. I must have looked horrified.

"It's okay," she said smiling, "have a seat. I'll be right back."

Maybe it was the tone in her voice or the twinkle in her eyes, but I felt reassured. Leaving my shoes at the door, I stepped inside.

What have I gotten myself into, I wondered as I sat on a pile of pillows in the corner. Caroline came in and sat close by, stretching her legs out in front of her.

"Sounds like you had an interesting weekend," she remarked.

I nodded. "What is this room for?" I blurted out.

"Oh, this?" she responded casually with a sweeping motion of her arms. "This is where we get some real work done. Sometimes we need more room to get comfortable, relax, express our feelings." She paused.

After a few minutes of silence she continued. "Sometimes we need to express certain feelings like anger a little more physically," she stated matter-of-factly.

I folded my arms over my chest. That won't happen for me, I told myself.

"Many of us have been controlled by other people's anger all of our lives. Some of us don't know how to express our own feelings of anger, so we swallow them," she said. "Of course that then becomes depression or sadness; kind of a chronic feeling that happiness is always just out of reach."

As she spoke these last words, my eyes filled with tears.

"Yeah," she said, wiggling her toes. "So what's up with this 'you're not psychic-- you're crazy' crap?" she asked incredulously.

I looked up at her. "I was hoping you could tell me," I said, noticing my sadness. Was it this room, or had I just not noticed it before. Caroline was talking.

"What?" I asked, "I'm sorry, I was somewhere else I guess."

She grinned. "I was saying that T.J.'s therapist obviously has his own issues with psychics."

"But he's a therapist. What do you mean 'his own issues?' Aren't therapists supposed to know what's going on, sort of objectively I mean?" I asked, feeling confused.

"Well," Caroline shrugged. "Everyone's different. We're only human you know," she chuckled and shook her head.

"So you don't think I'm crazy?" I asked. "I mean you're a therapist too."

"No," she said still shaking her head. "As a matter of fact you are far from it. It's like you're leaving 'crazy' behind and entering truth. Just remember crazy people make other people crazy. You just told me last week how peaceful your life has felt since T.J. moved out." She looked at me. "Right?"

I nodded.

"Then you spend 15 minutes with him and feel crazy again." She let out an exasperated sigh. "There's a saying in AA: if you don't want to slip, stay out of slippery places. T.J. is still a slippery place for you."

I considered her words. "So when I phoned you at home you heard the 'crazies' in my voice? That's why you said what you said?"

She nodded, smiling. Silence followed as I sat, letting her words settle in.

Finally I spoke. "You're right. I hadn't felt that way in weeks. It wasn't just his words that upset me, it was how I felt sitting with him too."

"Now you're getting it," she grinned, as she reached

for her appointment book, signaling the end of our session.

Driving home I realized there was no way I could spend any time with T.J. over the holidays. I resolved to set my boundaries and just say no.

Thanksgiving came and went without incident, at least for me. But a few days later, my mother contacted T.J. and then called me to inform me that she'd invited him to her annual Christmas party. "I just thought you should know," she said. He told her he'd be there.

"Then I won't," I said slamming down the phone. A lump formed in my throat. Tears stung my eyes. I felt so betrayed. Blessedly, I was to see Caroline the next day.

I arrived early and went upstairs. The door to our room was open so I went in and sat down, grabbing a tissue box as I took my place. She came in a few minutes later, taking her usual place. We didn't speak. I looked over at her. She was sitting with her arms folded across her chest, frowning. The silence was oppressive. Finally I spoke. Quietly, meekly, I began talking about what happened.

Caroline interrupted, saying, "Suzy, I can't hear you. You sound like a little girl. Could you speak up?" She sounded irritated and was still frowning.

I cleared my throat and started over with more volume this time. I didn't get far however because as I spoke the lump formed again and the tears came. I began crying, sobbing, bent-double sobbing.

"Why are you crying?" Caroline said as if she were truly puzzled.

"I'm just so sad," I responded, blowing my nose.

"Well, it's a scam," she replied.

"A what?" I asked, feeling anxious now. What was

happening to my therapist?

"It's a scam you pull instead of feeling your anger. You bypass it and go right to sad. Your own mother inviting your estranged husband to a traditional family party should piss you off. I know I'm feeling some anger about it. You should be outraged. Your mom's behavior is outrageous," she fumed.

"It is?" I asked.

She raised her eyebrows in response.

My tears had stopped. Caroline had my full attention. "Then why do I just feel sadness? Why can't I feel outrage?"

"Because somewhere along the way you were taught to accept the unacceptable. This is unacceptable," she declared. "And in your family the unspoken rule was that your mother was the only one who could do anger or rage. Correct?"

Her words were resonating. They were like missing pieces of a puzzle I'd lost long ago coming back to where they belonged in me.

Caroline spoke again. "It's time for you to do some anger work."

The mere thought of what she was suggesting scared the hell out of me. "What about forgiveness?" I asked. "Aren't we supposed to forgive and move on?" I negotiated, desperately trying to hide the panic I was feeling. "I could do the 'right thing' and forgive. It always works for me."

"Oh really?" Caroline responded, lifting that eyebrow.

I was 10 years old again. I could hear my father's voice telling me that my mother really does love me, she just gets angry sometimes. I could feel his hand wiping the tears brought on by the ferocious words she delivered to her young children. He was saying we need to be understanding with her and forgive her. I saw and felt the setup. Caroline's words interrupted my memory-trance.

"I'm sorry, Caroline, I was remembering...." I started.

"I know," she said softly. "Forgiveness, so to speak, became a place to hide, a place to swallow your own feelings to make life more manageable. It became a survival skill, enabling you to live with the unacceptable. It disempowered you."

Her last words startled me.

"It what?" I almost shouted. "I...I thought it made me a better person." My voice trailed off. The room was silent. A siren sped by. "Everything I've studied, all of the spiritual teachings, teach forgiveness as the high road to God, the way to overcome the pain of this world. I'm confused now...."

"There is a time and a place for forgiveness," Caroline said. "Most of us are too quick to forgive, because we don't want to feel our feelings. Feelings like anger, outrage, betrayal and resentment are just too uncomfortable. We don't know what to do with them. Some of us were even taught those kinds of feelings are bad – so we must be bad if we feel them. No wonder we walk around feeling bad about ourselves. Our self-worth has been attacked by our own 'shameful feelings.'" She was shaking her head now sorrowfully. "It's self-perpetuating, self-loathing. And it stinks." Her last words were more like a punctuation mark than a statement.

I laughed, uncomfortably. Her words were hitting home.

"Suzy, we all have a right to our feelings. They're ours. They inform us about ourselves in relationship to our environment. They're like early detection devices and if we listen to and honor them, they always take care of us. When we don't, when we deny or swallow them…"

"What?" I asked.

Caroline grinned. "Well, we end up here," she said, motioning with her arm.

"Or dead," I said more to myself than to her.

After a moment or two she spoke again, with a seriousness I'd not heard before. "Make no mistake, this work takes great courage, courage most people don't have. Just look around. Addiction of one sort or another is everywhere, destroying us. It's easier to use and numb-out, than to feel and confront ourselves and our inner demons. Some people would rather die than set a boundary and say no."

I thought of my sister.

"So what do I need to do?" I asked, with a new resolve. Maybe it was her words, but I began to feel courageous. "I want to do this work. I want to take it all the way. I want to be well and whole."

As I spoke Caroline began arranging pillows in the middle of the room. "Good," she said, looking over at me. "Let's do some anger work."

Kneeling in front of the pillows, she explained again the appropriateness of anger and how, if we let it get too big, it consumes us. She gave examples of inappropriate anger, telling me it was never okay to do it at someone. She surprised me when she said cynicism, criticism and teasing were all forms of "sideways anger" and also inappropriate.

She took a breath. "I'm going to show you some anger work. This is a way of getting it up and out of you." She rolled up the sleeves of her sweater. She said it was important to first name the pillow. It could be a person or an event. Then, with hands in a fist, she told me to strike the pillow as hard as possible, shouting something with each blow.

"You must shout something, anything," she said.

I could feel panic setting in. I cowered against the wall.

"Are you ready? Now remember I'm just demonstrating. Okay?" she said.

I nodded, terrified. Taking another breath, Caroline straightened her back, drew back her fist and let go. Screaming and punching, she was transformed into a Tasmanian devil!

Abruptly, after a few minutes, she stopped, sat back on her heels, and grinned. "See, that's all there is to it." She stood, straightening herself, and resumed her spot under the window.

I was blown away. Shaking my head I said, "No way. I can't do that."

Still smiling, Caroline said, "Sure you can."

Still shaking my head, I said, "No, no I can't. It's... it's too big in me. It feels like I'll blow up the world. I... it's too big," I stammered.

"I know it feels that way. All the more reason to do it. You can do it, Suzy. I'm right here to witness you and coach."

Silence. A long silence. Then, meekly, I spoke. My voice startled me. I sounded like a child. "But what will happen to me?" I whimpered.

Caroline thought for a moment. "Have you ever watched a child get angry and throw a tantrum?"

I nodded.

"What do they do when they're done? Usually they lie down right where they're at and cry a while, maybe even fall asleep for a moment or two. And then they're fine. They're ready to talk or play again."

I found myself envying the child she was describing. We were never allowed to demonstrate anger at any age.

"Very likely that is what will happen for you," she continued, "and remember, it's safe here. I'm here and I won't let anything bad happen to you."

From deep inside I could feel a scream building. Kneeling in front of the pillows, my hands began forming fists. The scream was pushing its way up to my mouth. I drew back my arms and let my fists shoot through the pillows. The scream followed my fists, moving through the pillows and off the padded walls. It was followed by another and another. Words came out.

"No!" "Stop it!" Unrecognizable sounds, wails.

From far away I could hear Caroline's voice encouraging, applauding. "Good anger, great, you're doing great, Suzy." Her voice was like an anchor, reminding me I was safe, holding the space open for years and years of anger.

Finally my screams and shouts died away. I fell onto the mats sobbing. A profuse sweat had erupted on my chest and throat. At one point it felt like I would vomit. My sobs turned to whimpers. I closed my eyes. After a few moments I heard Caroline's voice telling me I did great. Lying on the mats, I slowly opened my eyes. The room was still there. Nothing had changed, but I felt lighter. I didn't want to move. I knew I had changed.

Finally I sat up.

"Wow!" was all I could say. "Wow! That was…powerful. I feel…lighter," I exclaimed, the wonder of it all still resonating in me, in the room, in the air I was breathing.

"Well Suzy, you've been carrying all of that around for years," Caroline said, shaking her head as she reached for her appointment book. "It took a lot of courage and you did it!"

"Thank you, Caroline," I said.

"For what?" she said, adding, "You did all the work."

Driving home that afternoon I realized that Caroline had endowed me with a powerful tool. By giving me permission to experience my anger, my voice had been released. I would never again be able to swallow my feelings. For a split second I felt guilty, like I'd betrayed my parents. I acknowledged the guilt briefly; then felt another, less familiar feeling taking precedence. It was joy – pure unattached and unadulterated joy! Joy for the sake of joy.

Twenty-six

"So exactly when is the time and place for forgiveness?" I asked Caroline on my next session, a week after my brilliant display of anger in the padded room.

I had spent the week considering the implication of being too quick to forgive and using forgiveness as a survival tool.

Caroline seemed distracted.

"Forgiveness? Oh that," she grinned. "Here's what we weren't told. It is important to separate the person from the behavior. After all, we are all human and we all make mistakes. Because of our human frailties, we all deserve forgiveness."

I listened intently, as if my life depended on it. In a way, it did.

"But Suzy, there are certain behaviors that are simply unforgivable and unacceptable. We don't have to forgive those behaviors, nor should we. We forgive the person, not the behavior, to a point. If that person perpetuates the unforgivable behavior, we must distance ourselves. We do this to take care of ourselves."

Her words made so much sense. They liberated me. Now I could forgive in a way that offered the person the grace that they deserved, but gave me the safety that I needed.

Caroline led me back to the moment by mentioning that she was thinking of forming a small women's group.

"I think a group would be good for you," she said. "You can really get a lot done in a group."

The thought of sharing my time with Caroline did not appeal to me, nor did the idea of sharing my innermost thoughts with other women.

"Hmmm," Caroline nodded. I knew that nod. It meant we would talk about this.

I went for it. "I don't like or trust other women. I've never done well in groups of women," I blurted out.

"All the more reason to do it," she finally spoke. "Good, then it's settled. We start next week. We'll meet in here." She smiled, reaching for her appointment book.

"But Caroline, I don't think I'm ready...." I protested.

"Suzy, I'll be a part of the group too, not just the facilitator. If after a few weeks you're still not comfortable you can always quit," she said.

"Okay," I grumbled.

As usual, she was right. Group was just what I needed. After a few weeks, I really looked forward to our meetings. The five of us had all come from similar backgrounds and experiences. Safety was the concern of all of us, so we agreed from the beginning there would be no crosstalk, just women listening to women. Caroline maintained the voice of facilitator if needed, but her willingness to be a participant was empowering to us all.

On April Fools' Day, T.J. called to say he wanted to come by for a visit. He wanted to talk about us and evaluate the situation. I was outside mowing when he drove up. My heart was racing. I was still hopeful we could stay together and I thought he was too. I didn't wish to lose my dream home and I didn't want to meet failure in another marriage.

As he got out of his car and approached me, however, my dream shattered. I *saw* another woman walking with him. I climbed down off the mower, removed my glove and extended my hand in greeting. He nodded, refusing my hand.

"This has gone on long enough," he blurted, moving past me toward the house. "I need to move back home." He spoke with such assertion I took a step or two back.

It was a beautiful spring day. The fruit trees were in bloom. Ducks chattered down at the pond. My beautiful dream home. I let out a deep sigh.

"T.J., who's the woman you've being seeing?" I spoke calmly and directly, surprising both of us.

"You're crazy!" he fumed. There was that word again, the one that used to undo me with shame. I straightened my back and walked toward him, removing the other glove as I walked.

"There is another woman. I can *see* her. Who is she?" I asked, exasperated now.

"Fine," he said. "Have it your way. I met her two months ago."

His words were a knife to my heart. How could I have been so naïve, so foolish to believe he was doing his work, that he wanted to save this marriage. I fought back tears, swallowing hard.

"Suzanne, I want to be with you. I want us to be together, I want to come home. But you can't seem to get yourself 'fixed.' What am I supposed to do? Wait forever?"

I had no words. I could only stare in disbelief.

He spoke again. "Well, what did you expect? I'm only human."

Turning away from him I started for the house. He grabbed my arm.

"Wait," he said. "I love you."

"No, T.J. No, you don't. All these months I thought we were working on ourselves so we could make this marriage work. At least, that's been my goal." As I spoke I looked at his hand on my arm. Slowly he released it.

"Apparently that wasn't what you had in mind," I added, continuing toward the house.

As I walked on, his next words followed me.

"You have 30 days. Thirty days to fix yourself. If you're not ready by then, I'm filing for divorce." He was shouting now.

I turned to face him once more. "You'd better file now then, because we're done."

"We're done," I repeated, collapsing on the closest kitchen chair as I entered the back door. A few minutes later I heard the sound of tires on the gravel drive. T.J. was gone.

"What am I going to do?" I moaned. "I'm losing it all, my home, my marriage. How will I take care of myself and my daughter? What about her horses?" I was sobbing. The four other women seated on the floor with me listened and understood. One was crying too.

"I can't believe this is happening. It's like a nightmare," I groaned, holding a pillow tight to my chest as I rocked back and forth.

"What am I going to do?" I looked at Caroline now, hoping for some magic answer. My pain shifted to anger. I was so pissed at T.J.

"Why can't he quit drinking," I screamed. "Why did he already replace me? I don't get it. He loves me, but I'm replaceable?! Aaaay!" I screamed again, this time punching the pillows. Finally the room fell silent.

"Caroline," I said, "what am I going to do?"

After a moment or two she spoke. "Well, Suzy, you're going to take care of yourself. And you're going to do it one day at a time. You can do this."

The support of the other women in the room was palpable.

"But I don't want to do this again. Another divorce! I tried so hard to make this marriage work. I was determined to not go through this again."

"You can do this," Caroline repeated, "and this time, because of your recovery, you'll do it differently. You'll do it without finding another man to take care of you. You'll speak to an attorney and find out about your rights, make a plan and do it your way. This time you've got us," she said, acknowledging the group. "We won't let you slip."

And so, the dissolution of my marriage and the unraveling of my life began.

Twenty-seven

After a few visits with my attorney I realized things were not as grim as my crisis-thinking would have me believe. Financially, at least, I would be okay for a while. There was no decision about whether I would keep the farm. It was, after all, my dream house. I would make it work. Then came the subject of my career. My attorney inquired about how I planned to support myself and my daughter; eventually. I told him about my readings.

"Your what?" he said, bemused.

I explained it was more of a hobby than work.

"Good," he said. Then he quickly added, "You'll need to get a job. What training do you have? What else have you done?"

My blank stare must have given it away.

"You'll need training then, maybe college. Think about what you would be interested in studying. Don't worry. You'll be fine," he grinned.

As I stood to leave, he leaned over his desk and said, "Do you do...like, palm readings or something?"

I looked at him. I saw the smirk. "No, nothing like that. Forget it."

At the door I turned and looked at him. He'd followed me and was opening the door for me, still smirking.

"Just get me my divorce, okay?" I said in an attempt to dismiss him and maintain my dignity. But inside I was quaking and seething. Was it always going to be this way?

Later that week in group I recounted this meeting.

"I may as well have told him I'm a prostitute," I groaned. "If I'd only gone to college. What's wrong with me? How did I ever get so messed up?"

After a few minutes, Caroline spoke. "Well, what would you study if you did go back to school?"

Without hesitation I answered, "Psychology!"

"Why not go ahead and look into that? After all, you can do anything you want now."

I wasn't ready to acknowledge that buried deep inside was still a secret longing for my prince to save me.

Over the next few weeks I explored the possibility of college, checking out options at several local campuses. The more I learned, the more daunting it seemed. I was looking at four to six years of school with probably a two-year internship following graduation. I would be 50 years old by the time I was ready to go to work and would probably need a walker to gather my diploma.

As I shared this information with my group, one of the women said, "Gosh, and when you do readings now you make as much per hour as most therapists charge."

"Suzy, why don't you just do readings?" Caroline urged. "Just make it your business. Have some business cards made, maybe some brochures too. You could always take night classes if you really want to go to school."

I considered the concept for a moment. Some of Portland's New Age bookstores featured readers. "No, I can't make a living that way. It just won't work." I was still so scared to reveal myself. "I need to find a real job," I added, echoing the words of my family.

One evening in late spring a friend invited me to dinner. She owned a modeling agency in Portland and had been looking for someone she could train to run the business and fill in for her.

During dinner she offered the job to me saying, "Well, I keep hearing you say you need a real job. So here's your opportunity."

I jumped at the chance. For the next four months I got up at 5:30 a.m., so I could leave the house by 7:00 a.m. and be downtown by 8:00 a.m. to open the agency. At first, it was fun and exciting. I met interesting people. After a while, however, getting up at 5:30 a.m. and getting home at 6:00 p.m. got old, especially when I'd have a 7:00 p.m. reading booked in the evening.

Reflecting on this in group one day, I said, "This is exhausting. I work long hours and make as much in a day as I make in an hour doing readings in the evening. What's wrong with this picture? Why am I working so hard?"

"Ah, now you're asking the right question," Caroline said succinctly.

In September 1991, T.J. and I had mediation. It was time to come to terms with our divorce settlement. It was ugly. The following week my attorney called to tell me the settlement had been reached and the paperwork would be drawn up soon. T.J. wanted the house, and it had become clear to me I could not manage its care. It was a full-time job. He would buy me out as part of the settlement. It wasn't a lot of money, but enough for a future down payment. Reality was hitting hard. I was being evicted from my dream.

By mid-September I left the agency. I was grateful for the experience. Following Caroline's suggestion and the urging of my group, I had business cards printed calling myself an intuitive consultant instead of a psychic. No one in my family and few of my friends supported this idea.

I heard comments like "You've got to be kidding; you can't make a living that way" or "No one makes a living being a psychic" or my favorite: "When are you going to get a real job?"

It was hard. I felt like the Titanic going down. Everyone was jumping off.

Our divorce would be final December 31, 1991. I needed a plan. T.J. would take possession of the house the following day. It felt like I was standing at the edge of my life, the edge of my known world, and being asked to jump. I had not the slightest clue what to do next. It was time to leave my dream, to face the unknowable.

Interestingly enough, the one thing that sustained me and gave me hope was my business. My business cards were being passed around and calls were coming in, slowly increasing my clientele. It felt good to feel valued. I thought of what Caroline had once said as I complained about the "compartments" of my life. For so long it felt like there were several of me: wife, mother, friend and, of course, secret psychic. She had commented about how nice it would feel to live a seamless life in which there were no roles to play, no seams to be felt.

"Just a natural flow of who you are in the world," she said, with that twinkle in her eye.

December arrived and I still had no plan. My family was scared for me. I was terrified. In group I bemoaned getting an apartment or renting a house. I had no heart for the search. I cried and screamed a lot. My friend Ann offered to rent me a room, but that didn't feel right. Thank God for those women of my group. They understood completely.

Then an old friend in Montana suggested I come to his ranch for some R and R. At this point I had nothing more to lose. I ran it past my group first. A couple of the women were upset that I might leave, but supported my choice. It felt like the right option for the time. Some distance and rest might be what I needed, and, as Caroline reminded me, "You know your way home."

On moving day, after the last item was loaded onto the truck I returned inside. Running my hands over every wall in the house, tears streaming, I bid this dream goodbye.

Twenty-eight

The first few weeks on the ranch were hard. I missed my children, especially my daughter, horribly. I realized on that distant prairie how rejected I felt. My feelings of inadequacy as a parent and as a human being were glaring. I took many long walks and morning horseback rides, sometimes sitting for hours staring across the sage and pine-covered valley, the ache inside soothed only by the quiet munching of the horse.

Before leaving Portland I had set up an answering service for my business phone line, not expecting much activity. I was pleasantly surprised, then, when after a few weeks I checked it to find a few dozen messages for reading appointments! Somewhere in the darkness of my soul I felt a spark, a stirring.

One afternoon while kayaking with my friend something powerful occurred. I had eddied out of the main stream to watch as he and his friends surfed river waves.

Sitting in that eddy I felt the spirit of the river as she rushed along. Movement was her nature as she hurried over rocks and boulders. But so was stillness, I thought, as I sat in quiet movement in the eddy pool. Quiet movement…. Of course! She's never completely still. I realized she was showing me the nature of life. Rivers converge and separate. They fork and eddy. There are rapids, waterfalls and quiet movement. The middle or center of the river has the strongest current. Step into your center. Let the flow of your life, the river that is you, the river named Suzanne, let it carry you. You'll know you're there each time you hear and honor your honest thoughts and feelings.

"They are your current," she whispered. I looked around at the life this river's flow had created on the banks, life that would not be there had she not moved through. I looked beyond at the distant mountains and knew they too had touched this river's soul, perhaps feeding her with their spring waters.

"Yes," she whispered again. "We're all in this together. We are all connected. We are one."

That evening I told my friend it was time to go home.

I left Montana with a spring snowstorm at my heels. It was March 4, 1992. I'd been at my friend's retreat eight weeks and we'd had no snow. So why this day? I asked myself as I packed my last few things into the jeep. My German shepherd, Buddy, looked up at me, tail wagging. He didn't care. He was going for a ride! The radio said the storm was coming from the east and would hit Billings in about four hours.

"Well, at least we're heading west," I said to Buddy as he jumped in the back seat. "I hope we can outrun it."

The storm was expected to drop a couple feet of snow over the state. My friend had urged me to wait a few days to let the storm pass, but my mind was made up, feeling an urgency. I had to get home. With many thanks and goodbyes, we set off.

I kept the radio on storm watch, hoping to make it to Lewiston, Idaho for the night. I'd have to push it. We reached the Lolo Pass about dinner time. I stopped for a quick bite, filled the tank, watered the dog and decided to continue. The storm was now two hours away, but the pass was clear.

"We'll be fine," I said, patting Buddy's head. Besides, we can always pull off at a motel if we need to, I thought.

The trip down the pass, however, took longer than I'd anticipated. It was windy and slow-moving trucks forced me to proceed slowly. By 9:00 p.m. I began to feel concern. The snow had started falling, and the only sign of a motel was for a resort called Three Rivers. As the miles passed, the snow fell harder. I watched for more Three Rivers signs. Around 11:00 p.m. I saw one in the swirling snow: "Three Rivers Resort, 2 Miles."

"Good, we'll stop for the night," I exhaled. Buddy whined. It was difficult to see through the falling snow, but as I came around a bend the car lights hit another sign. "Three Rivers Resort next left" it read, with a temporary sign underneath which said "Closed for the winter."

"Oh no!" I groaned. We were approaching the turn-off. Looking over to the left I saw lights on in what must be the lodge. Lacking any more appealing options, I took a chance. We crossed an icy bridge and drove into a settlement of quaint cabins, stopping in front of the largest cabin where the lights were on.

"Wish me luck," I said to Buddy. I knocked. There was a sign in the window that read "Office" and another sign above it that said "Closed for the winter." I knocked louder. I heard footsteps. The door opened and a woman in a bathrobe peeked out.

"Sorry to bother you but would it be possible...." My words got lost as she smiled and turned away, leaving the door open a crack. I peeked in, seeing glowing embers in a fire behind her. She quickly returned with a key.

"First cabin next to the bridge," she said, pointing to my right.

"Oh, thank you!" I exclaimed, beyond relief.

"No problem," she said, adding, "there's a storm coming."

The cabin was meager, but had heat, running water and a dim light bulb dangling from the beam overhead. I crawled into bed with my clothes on. Buddy jumped up next to me, something he was never allowed to do.

"It's all right tonight," I said, enjoying his warmth as I fell off to sleep.

Sunlight streaming in the window woke me the next morning. I could hear a river close by. It took a moment to remember where I was. The snowstorm! I sat up. The room was cold. I lifted the curtain back to behold the most beautiful blue sky, a backdrop for what was now a winter wonderland. The storm had left a couple feet of snow. I watched the river moving over ice-covered boulders. A blue jay darted from tree to tree, his noisy call breaking the snow-silence.

"Beautiful," I murmured. Buddy, eager to go out, was waiting by the door. He whined, spinning in circles with his you-better-let-me-out-soon-look. I opened the door and he bounded past me to play. He loved the snow. I laughed as Buddy ran ahead of me, bouncing like a deer.

"We can't play. We've got to get going," I said knocking on the office door. The lady in the bathrobe answered.

"Thank you so much," I said, handing her the key. "What do I owe you?"

She shrugged, "How about 20 bucks?" And then, "Where you headed?"

"Lewiston, then Portland. I'm going home."

"The roads should be clear. I heard the plows earlier," she responded with understanding. "My husband's already cleared our drive," she added, motioning with her eyes.

I thanked her again and turned to see Buddy eagerly waiting by the jeep. It took a few minutes to warm it up and brush the snow off, but soon we were crossing the little bridge and turning onto the highway.

In Lewiston we stopped for gas and coffee. As the car filled, I walked to the nearby phone booth and made two phone calls, the first to my friend Ann.

"Hey wake up," I said, hearing her groggy voice. I'd forgotten I was in a different time zone.

"What's up?" she asked.

I asked if the offer to rent her spare room was still good.

"Absolutely," she said without hesitation. "When are you coming? I can have the room ready by tomorrow. And Suzy, I'm so glad you're coming back."

"Yeah, me too," I said as I hung up. Then I called my folks, who were also glad for the news. I asked them not to tell my daughter. I wanted to surprise her.

The rest of the trip was long and uneventful. It felt so good crossing into Oregon and heading west on I-84 down the Columbia River Gorge. Home.

I pulled up at my folks' about 4:00 p.m. T.J.'s car was parked out front. Damn, I thought. Buddy beat me to the front porch, glad to be home too. Home, but still homeless, I thought, walking up to their front door.

Everyone but T.J. was glad to see me. He dropped my

daughter off at a nearby horse show and decided to stop in on my folks. I suspected collusion with my mother, but didn't care.

I was barraged with questions I had no answers to. I made a quick call to my son. He was glad to hear I was back but concerned about what I was going to do next.

"One day at a time," I said lightly. What else could I say? I was clueless. I gave him Ann's phone number. Hanging up, I realized how proud I was of him. At 24 he had his own apartment, a good job and a girlfriend. As a reserve police officer, he had plans to become an officer. He knew where he was going, more than I could say for myself.

That night I had a dream.

I was riding a horse. We walked along a river bank then turned up a street. It was an old street full of beautiful Victorian homes. We stopped in front of a cottage. I got off the horse and walked up to the back porch, peeking in the windows. The horse followed me.

"This is it," I announced to my horse. "It's a keeper."

Ann's place was small but comfortable. Her spare room had a twin bed. As she helped me unpack we talked about my plans. I had a friend in West Linn who'd offered her home for readings. I would begin scheduling appointments with the clients who had had left messages with my answering service.

"I just don't know if I can make a living doing readings," I said, slamming the door of the jeep.

"Are you kidding? Of course you can!" Ann's enthusiastic response caught me off-guard.

"Really?" I said cautiously.

She laughed. "Just wait. You'll see," she said confidently.

I shook my head with a skeptical sigh. "I hope you're right. I don't know what else to do."

"Can I still be in group?" I asked Caroline tentatively over the phone the next morning, not knowing if they would want me back.

"Of course you can," she said quickly. "After all, you never really left, you just took a break. So, we'll see you Tuesday?"

How many times in Montana had her words cleared a path for my return? More than once I'd recalled her cheerful words, "You know your way home."

I hung up and breathed deeply. Thank God for her and my group. And for Ann. I did have support, good support. I could do this.

March breezed along. My friend Barbara in West Linn set up appointments at her house. She and her husband were most gracious. As the weeks passed, referrals for readings trickled in and I stayed surprisingly busy.

As I shared my surprise with Ann one evening she said, "I don't know why this surprises you. You're good. You just don't see it yet, but you will."

I thought about this for a minute. "Yeah, I guess. It's just hard being out there by myself. It's not like I go to an office every day. I don't work side by side with other psychics. I have nothing to compare myself to, no instant feedback or results to stand back and look at."

"Don't worry. That will come too," Ann said. "Look at the referrals you're getting."

I smiled at her now. "Thanks for being there for me, Ann. I don't know what I'd do...," I said quietly.

We sat in silence, a peaceful CD playing in the background.

"That's what friends are for," Ann said as she stood now, stretching. "I'm going to bed. See you in the morning."

As she walked past me, I remembered when we'd met and how I was so impressed with her and the words she used. I'd wanted to learn to talk like that, and now here I was, nearly three years later, talking the talk and learning to walk the walk. Nobody told me it would be this hard.

Twenty-nine

Ann's home had been a wonderful cushion to fall on when I returned to Portland. It embraced me as I'd re-entered my life. By mid-April, however, I began to feel restless. I missed my own things. Everything I owned was locked in storage. I'd been up to visit it once and left feeling more homeless than ever.

I needed my own place. I had enough money for a down payment, but with no job or work history who would lend me the rest? Besides, even if I could get a mortgage, how would I make monthly payments? Could my work as a psychic sustain me? I knew of no full-time professional psychics in town. I had no mentors for this part of my work. And God knows I had enough people telling me that I couldn't make a living.

I really had no choice. It was time for me to move. If I kept thinking about it, needing guarantees for the future, I'd never do it. I had to jump. Besides, it wouldn't hurt to look.

Taking a deep breath, I picked up the phone. I had a client, Ginny, who was a realtor.

"Hello, this is Ginny," she answered.

"Hi, it's Suzanne," I said hesitantly.

"What's up? You ready to buy a house?" Her enthusiasm lifted my spirits.

"Yeah, how'd you know?" I quipped, laughing now.

"Well, I saw a psychic a few years ago who told me I'd be a great realtor," she said. "And guess what... I am!" she boasted, half in jest.

She'd credited that first reading of ours many times for saving her life. She'd been depressed and without direction, desperate for a word to guide her, when I said I could "see her making money off the land." And I didn't mean farming. Ginny always looked and dressed like she just stepped out of *Vogue*.

"So what are we looking for?" she asked. "A house, a condo? I can get you into a condo real easy. What part of town did you have in mind? I've got a new...."

She talked so fast I had to laugh. "Ginny, slow down. I...I just want to look. See what I can afford," I interjected. I'd forgotten, with Ginny you always had to interrupt.

"Great. Let's get you pre-qualified. When can we get together?"

We arranged to meet the next day.

Later that evening Ann and I sat recounting our days, part of our daily routine as roommates. I would miss that. I told her I'd spoken to a realtor and had an appointment the next day. She was excited for me.

After a long pause she said, "Suzanne, you can do this. You can earn a living doing your readings. Your work will take care of you. A few years from now you'll look back and wonder why on earth you were so scared."

Ann was such a cheerleader for my work. I thought back to my first reading for her. As I'd held her ring quietly, the first words out of my mouth had been "Your parents live together but they aren't married...."

Her mouth had dropped and she uttered a loud "Oh my God!" Nobody knew her folks had divorced years earlier but continued to live together. I chuckled at the memory.

"What are you laughing at?" she now asked from

across the room. She was folding the quilt she'd been snuggled under, heading for bed.

I reminded her of that first reading. We both laughed.

"You really got my attention," she said, smiling. Then she added more somberly, "Don't you get it? You're the real thing. You're good. Your work has to succeed. It's about who you are...."

"Yeah, well, it's not exactly a career represented on high school career day," I joked.

"No, but it's your work, and you'll be fine," she yawned. "Good luck tomorrow," she added, closing her bedroom door behind her.

I sat in the silence for a while. I was headed for unknown territory, uncharted waters. If only there was some kind of guarantee.

The next day I met with Ginny. She was certain that with the money I had for a down payment, there would be no problems getting pre-qualified.

Paperwork done, she said, "Let's go see some houses." She pulled up some listings in my price range. As she thumbed through them, she said, "How would you feel about West Linn?"

My raised eyebrow said it all. West Linn was out of my price range, with the highest median income and property values in the state. "You're kidding. Right?"

"No, look. This just came on the market," she said, handing me a listing sheet.

The photo of the little cottage was right out of *Cottage Living* magazine. It was cute and quaint.

"Let's go look at it," Ginny said, gathering up her purse and keys. "It's down in Willamette. You know, down by the river?" she said, opening the car door for me.

"Yeah, I know," I said, thinking of how many times I'd driven through Willamette. It was West Linn's historic district, at the convergence of the Willamette and Tualatin Rivers, a sleepy quaint neighborhood and a well-kept secret.

I felt a touch of disappointment, however, as Ginny turned her car away from the rivers and back towards the freeway. We gave each other a doubtful look as the freeway loomed closer.

"Look, there it is," Ginny said encouragingly. She slowed and stopped in front of the cutest little house. "It looks like a beach cabin, Suzanne," she said, stepping out of the car.

We stood staring for a moment. The house sat on 1.4 acres that spread right up to the freeway. Fortunately, because of the rise in the land and the shrubs and trees, you couldn't see the four lanes, but you could definitely hear them.

I looked at Ginny. "Yeah, listen, it's the ocean," I laughed.

"Come on. Let's have a look," she said, leading the way to the door.

The house was darling inside as well. Small, but I didn't need much. To my surprise it also had a small office off the kitchen with its own entry. The room at one time must have been a porch or mud room. It was perfect. Peeking in, Ginny turned to me with a grin. We were both thinking the same thing.

"Your office, Madame Melba!" she exclaimed. "All you'll need now is a neon sign of a hand in the window and some Christmas lights. You'll be set."

We laughed, thinking of Whoopi Goldberg's psychic

role in the movie *Ghost*.

"Oh yeah, that will be a big hit with the neighbors," I added.

Back at Ginny's office later that day, I told her, "Make an offer."

A few weeks later, at closing, I handed my check over to the escrow agent and my divorce attorney's words came back to me. As he handed the divorce settlement check to me he'd said, "I just want you to know, statistically, given a check this size most women like yourself are broke within four years. Take good care of this… and yourself."

I'd left his office that day thinking he was pretty damn arrogant and determined not to become one of those statistics. Sitting that day in escrow I felt proud of myself. My money was going to work for me.

I stood alone in my new kitchen. I looked around. This house looked smaller than I remembered. How would I ever get all my stuff in here? It certainly wasn't my dream house. What if something went wrong and I needed to fix it? I could feel panic and sadness coming on. I sat on the kitchen floor and began to cry. What have I done? The tears overwhelmed me and I lay down on the floor sobbing harder. As I lay there I noticed the floor was crooked… or was it the walls? I began to laugh. How perfect did I expect this old house to be anyway? I'd just paid a lot of money for a very old, crooked house! I sat up, laughter overcoming my tears and I leaned against the wall. It was imperfect and the flaws endeared it to me. It was just like me. Flawed, but needing and deserving of TLC.

"It's home and it's mine," I smiled. Within a few days it looked like I'd lived there forever.

I'd taken a week off to move and get settled, but soon my clients began arriving at my new office. Not many, maybe five or six a week but enough to give me hope. And enough to make the neighbors talk. It was something I'd been dreading, but I knew I had to let them know about my work. I certainly didn't want them to think I was dealing drugs or something! So when I saw them standing, talking in the street after one of my clients left, I took the opportunity to introduce myself.

They watched me approach. I swallowed hard.

"Hi! I'm your new neighbor," I said with my best smile and cheerful tone. They all grinned.

"Welcome," one of the men said, extending his hand.

They introduced themselves and then the one named Jim said, "We hear you're a psychic. Cool."

"Yeah, we heard you couldn't move in until the moon was just right and you'd done some kind of ceremony in the backyard," a woman named Brenda added with a nervous chuckle.

"What?! You've got to be kidding," I said, stunned at this news. "Well, I don't know where you heard that, but it's so not true," I said, regaining my composure. "You'll see I'm pretty normal."

"Cool," Jim said.

And so I met my neighbors. They are all wonderful people, and through the years have become helpful and supportive. Acceptance was never an issue.

Thirty

Shortly after my move, one of my clients came to me with an urgent request. Her teenage niece was missing. Julie, my client, was from England where most of her family still lived. Her brother's 19-year-old daughter, who lived just east of London, had gone to a nightclub and never come home. It had been three days since she had last been seen. As I sat with Julie, my eyes closed, I saw her niece's body lying on or near railroad tracks. I looked up. This was the hard part of my work.

"Julie, I could be wrong. I pray I am. I can see her body...."

I went on to describe what I was seeing. Catching her breath, but ever practical, Julie asked if it might help to have her brother send an item that belonged to his daughter for me to hold. I agreed, seeing how upset she was and wanting to help.

A few days later Julie called again. The items had arrived. She came over that evening. With the items of her niece's in hand, once again I saw her body. Then I saw a man and young woman involved. It felt like she'd left the club with them. Julie pressed for more details.

"I can only see what I see," I shrugged, adding, "but the man's face is so clear. If I could draw, I would sketch it."

The next day Julie phoned again. "They found her body...next to railroad tracks," she reported grimly. "Just like you saw. Scotland Yard is now involved. I don't think they work with psychics."

She paused.

"Would you be willing to work with a sketch artist?" she asked. "I understand there's a good one who works with Portland Police."

"Sure," I answered, without hesitation. "Let me know when and where."

The next morning Julie left me an excited message. "The sketch artist said she'd be willing to work with you. Can you meet with her this Friday? Her name is Jeanne Boylan...."

Friday was only three days away. What had I gotten myself into, I wondered. Little did I know it would be the beginning of an amazing friendship.

Friday morning I walked through the doors of the police station. At the front desk, I told the woman I had an appointment with the sketch artist. She gave me a quick glance then pointed to the elevators. "She's up in detectives. Thirteenth floor," she said, returning to her work.

My heart was pounding as I pushed the call button on the elevator. Stepping off on the thirteenth floor, I looked around. Everyone seemed busy. A few people glanced up from their desks. As I stood wondering who to ask for directions, a nice-looking man in a suit approached me. He held a stack of papers in his hand.

"Can I help you?" he asked.

"I have an appointment with Jeanne Boylan," I said, trying to sound official.

He grinned. Pointing back over his shoulder he said, "Down there, third door on the left."

I thanked him as I walked past, noticing that he followed me with his eyes until I reached her door. Looking back at him I smiled again as I knocked softly. He was still grinning.

I heard footsteps, then the door opened. I must have looked startled, because she laughed quietly.

"Hi. I'm Jeanne," she said, extending her hand.

She was knock-out gorgeous! A stunning, shapely blonde, nearly my height, she could have doubled for Kim Basinger on a Hollywood set. What in God's name was she doing at the Portland police department? I looked back at the "suit" who'd given me directions. He was still watching. She followed my glance.

"Uh, thanks Dave," she said sweetly, dismissing him. "Cops!" I heard her say under her breath. I took a seat across from her and watched as she arranged her drawing pad and pencils on the desk. Sitting back now, we looked at each other. It was a moment I'll never forget. Somehow I knew this woman. Where had I seen her before? There was something so familiar about her.

"So you're a psychic. Gosh, I've never worked with a psychic before. This will be fun," she said, her voice barely above a whisper. I wondered if she always spoke so softly. It was a breathless sort of Jackie Kennedy/Marilyn Monroe voice and as I would soon discover, her normal speaking voice. I made a mental note to listen closely and try not to say "huh?" too much. I quickly briefed her on the case and described what I'd seen that had ultimately brought us here to work together.

"Okay," she said, "let's get started."

Placing her sketchpad in her lap she explained that she was not a "pick-a-nose" artist. I laughed.

"You know the kind? 'Did his nose look like one of these, his eyes, his mouth?' That's not what we'll be doing." She cleared her throat. "Basically we're going to talk. We'll talk about you, your work, the weather…?" she asked, her voice lifting as she saw me grimace.

We laughed.

"As we talk, I'll ask things like…would you say his eyes were nearer or farther apart? But mostly we'll just be visiting."

She'd already begun sketching. She asked if his cheek bones were wide or narrow. Over the next three hours, we talked about my work, her work and our personal lives. We had a lot in common. And just as she said, from time to time she would interrupt the flow to ask about shades or textures, wideness or lengths, circles or ovals or squares. For the most part I was so engaged in our conversation I didn't notice her interjections. I also didn't notice that she'd stopped drawing.

"Well, are you ready?" she asked, slowly turning the drawing to face me.

As she did, I caught my breath. How had she done it? She had perfectly captured not only the physical appearance but the essence of the man I had seen.

I was speechless. I gasped, "How do you do that?"

Our eyes met.

"You're psychic," I stated, realization dawning.

She lowered her eyes. "Shhh. We don't use the P word around here," she whispered conspiratorially. "Besides, I'm not, not really, not like you. Honestly, anyone can be taught to do this."

"Well, I think you are," I argued.

She stood now. "This has been fun. It's been a pleasure meeting you. We should get together again," she said, handing me her business card.

I dug in my purse looking for a card. As usual, I had

none.

"Here, write your number on the back of one of mine," she said handing me another.

I wrote my number, and giving it back to her said, "Yes, we need to stay in touch. Please do call."

She escorted me to the elevator, and as the doors opened we said goodbye. The unexpected connection we had made was broken and she quickly looked away.

"Keep up the good work."

The elevator doors closed between us. My eyes stung with tears for a moment on the ride down and I felt a jab of homesickness. I had found a peer, a sister, a "true" as I referred to the authentic intuitives, the ones I'd only read about but had never yet found. I smiled as the elevator reached the lobby and the doors dinged open. I was certain we would meet again.

Over the next few months, life settled into a routine in my new home and community. Work continued to move along. Slowly, but I was at least getting some new clients. I refused to advertise. It just didn't feel right. Especially living alone, I didn't want to be that accessible.

Then one afternoon a woman came for a reading who would change that for me. Her name was Terese and she worked at a new Portland bookstore called the New Renaissance Bookshop. I had been in it a few times and liked the feel there. Although it was a New Age bookstore, it felt different than the others. It wasn't all "woo-woo." It felt well-grounded, solid and authentic. It also felt like home.

More than once, as I'd browsed the shelves I'd thought it would be a nice place to work. Terese had heard about me and wanted a reading. When we were done with the reading she said, "You're good. I'm going to tell my boss to come see you."

She left and I thought no more of it.

When I schedule appointments I get as little information as possible from the person, usually only a first name and phone number, primarily out of respect for privacy and anonymity, but also so they can't accuse me of looking them up beforehand. For me, less is more.

So a few weeks later when a woman named Margo came in, I thought nothing of it. After the session, she smiled and told me she was one of the owners of the New Renaissance Bookshop and asked if I would be interested in coming in to the store to do readings. I was honored and delighted but at the same time hesitant. I paused, then told her I'd get back to her. She agreed, adding she really hoped I'd consider it. She loved her reading.

Sitting in group later that week I shared my excitement and fears. This felt huge. I would be coming out publicly. My face and bio would be in the bookstore newsletter. The world would see and know about me! Argh. All my shame, all the years of being told to hide, all the jokes and all the mockery rushed forward.

As I talked in this wonderful, supportive group I heard my voice speak these fears and I held the momentary prickle of panic. That voice, however, was driven back by one that heralded my confidence and pride at being recognized for having a special ability. It was time. It was time to step out of the shadows and be seen and cease the self-indulgent "specialness" that hampered my success.

I called Margo the next day and told her I'd love to do readings at the bookstore.

Being part of the bookstore family has been a great comfort through the years. I was the Saturday psychic the first four years I was there and have seen the store grow and expand over the last 15 years. It went from being housed in one Victorian home to three homes in a row, all connected. I have come to appreciate the store's selectivity and discernment in a field that seems to harbor charlatans and soothsayers. New Renaissance's reputation is impeccable. Even Al Gore made a visit to its beguiling shelves as he stumped through Portland! Although I'm featured there only a couple of times a year now, I still consider myself its "in-house psychic" as I remain part of the New Renaissance family.

By summer's end I realized I rather enjoyed living by myself. The cottage was warm and cozy. It felt as if it had been built for me. Unlike my childhood homes, it was blissfully ghost and ex-husband free.

Except for the cat.

One evening I had my family over for dinner. As we sat talking around the table my son shook his leg from time to time as if shaking something off. Finally he pushed himself away from the table.

"That damn cat keeps rubbing on my legs," he said, peering under the table. He was wearing shorts so the cat's fur was especially irritating

"What cat?" I asked, surprised.

"What do you mean 'what cat'? The obnoxious one that keeps rubbing against my legs," he replied, still looking for the poor kitty.

"But son, I don't have a cat."

"You what? Then what...." He stopped, silenced by

the implication. It was pretty funny. Since then several people have felt and even seen the "cat in the kitchen."

Thirty-one

Near the end of October my daughter and I attended a horse show in Eugene. While there my friend Debbi called my cell phone. She'd just received a missing person call. An 80-year-old Alzheimer's patient was missing from her son's home in Springfield, which was just across the Willamette River from Eugene. Debbi was pleasantly surprised to find that I was so close.

"Gosh, could you take the time to go talk to them?"

I agreed.

She made the arrangements and called back with the contact information for Tom and Valerie. It was his mother who was missing. I called Tom and told him it might be after 9:00 p.m. before I could get there. He and Valerie were fine with that and eager to meet with me.

When my daughter was finished for the day I told her I had to go on a search and rescue call and she could stay with her trainer.

"Oh please Mom, let me go too," she pleaded.

I hesitated. I had always kept this part of my life separate from my children, wanting to shield them. Being psychic was not something I'd ever really demonstrated in front of them, not wanting to impose it or wish it on them. I just wanted them to have normal lives. These thoughts swirled as I looked at her pleading eyes. I consented. She was 14 after all and should be allowed to choose for herself.

"Okay, but do exactly as I tell you. No matter what happens or what you see me do, don't react. And do exactly as I tell you," I repeated emphatically. "Now, we have to find this place. Sounds like it's out in the boonies," I said, looking at my notes. And it was.

The journey to Tom and Valerie's place was like a scene in a scary movie. The wind had picked up, moving big puffy, dark clouds over the face of the October full moon. We drove out of town then turned right at the cemetery. As we drove slowly past it, watching for our turn, barren trees blew in the wind, seeming to reach out for us. We turned left on Trail's End Road, which Tom warned was rough and bumpy.

"It was a dark and stormy night," I said in my best ghoul voice.

"Mom, stop!" my daughter said. "This is creepy," she added, sounding a bit anxious. I gave her a quick appraising glance. She was still smiling.

With the jeep bouncing over every pothole I handed her my cell phone. "I don't know what I'm getting us into," I said, "but here's the phone. Keep it with you."

"We're watching for the buckboard wagon out front, second driveway up the hill," I read, trying not to sound anxious myself now. "Ah, here it is," I said, turning the jeep up a steep slope. Outside lights flared on around the house and garage, momentarily blinding us.

A man and woman stepped forward to greet us. I pulled in next to them. The man approached.

"Hi. I'm Tom. This is my wife, Valerie," he said quickly.

I shivered. The wind had a chill to it.

"Let's step inside."

As we sat around the dining room table, Tom filled

us in. His mom, Edith, lived with them. She disappeared eight days before, driving off in her old Buick while he and Valerie were at work.

"Is that hers?" I motioned toward the road. I'd seen a Buick at the bottom of the drive as we'd pulled up.

He nodded. "Yeah. They found the car three days ago but no sign of her. We hoped search and rescue would come with dogs." His voice was weary.

"Search and rescue informed me that they would come," I reassured Tom, "but they asked me to check it out until they can get here." I paused, trying to get a sense of things. "Don't tell me any more for now. I don't want preconceived notions tainting my impressions."

He looked confused.

"You don't know?" I asked.

"Know what?"

I hadn't expected this.

"Tom, I am a psychic. On occasion I am called in by search and rescue when few tangible leads exist. Is that okay?"

Tom gave Valerie a quick glance.

"Well, my wife believes in that stuff," he hesitated. "I am worried for my mother and willing to try anything." He added, "I'm sorry, no disrespect, ma'am."

Heartened, sort of, I said, "I'd like to go down to the car. Would it be possible for me to sit in it?"

"Sure," Tom responded, standing to get the keys from his pocket.

I caught my daughter's eye.

"If you don't mind we'll walk down there alone," I said, motioning her to follow me.

We walked to the car, with only the crunch of gravel breaking the silence. A dog barked in the distance. A few feet from the car we stopped. I turned and faced my daughter.

"Mom, do you know what you're doing?" she asked cautiously. I felt for her. Why did her first foray into my psychic life have to be scripted by Stephen King?

"Not a clue," I said, "but here's the deal: I want you to stay back away from the car. Under no circumstances are you to touch it or come near. Do you promise?"

She nodded, hesitantly.

Fools rush in, I thought, unlocking the car door. I flashed my daughter a smile of reassurance that I didn't really feel, and bracingly took a seat behind the wheel.

Placing my hands on the steering wheel, I said softly, "Okay Edith, tell me what you were up to."

I sat in the silence for a moment and then heard a man say, "She was looking for me." I felt a man sitting next to me in the passenger seat, and turned to see an old man clad in a plaid shirt and suspenders.

"Who are you?" I said to him.

"I'm Clyde, her husband. She was trying to find our old place up at Falls Creek. She was looking for me. She just wanted to go home," he said quietly.

"Where is she now?" I asked.

"Close to where they found the car. She got lost and just started walking."

"Is she still alive?" I continued, but he was gone.

I felt the silence tangibly. Then the car began to sway with a rocking motion side to side. I bailed out.

"Okay. That's enough," I said out loud.

"Did you see anything just then?" I asked my daughter who hadn't budged from where I'd left her. She shook her head. I shut the car door and locked it.

"What happened?" she asked. Standing in the dark, I

touched the hood of the car. As I did, a bright light flashed inside the car like someone had taken a flash picture. We both jumped back.

"What was that?" we spoke in unison.

"Uh, let's go back up to the house," I suggested unnecessarily.

Back in the dining room I told Tom and Valerie what I'd experienced.

"So did your mom know a man named Clyde?" I began. They exchanged quick glances.

"He was her husband," Tom answered, visibly shaken.

"Well, a man named Clyde told me she'd gone to find the old place at Falls Creek and got lost."

Valerie fell onto the couch.

"Yes, that's where they lived. Her car was found not far from there." Tom's voice was quaking now. "But how could you know that?"

"It's what I do," I replied, ever amazed at how the conscious intellect stumbles over the intuitive and seeks to rationalize it out.

"He also told me she would be found not far from where the car was. A mile or so was my sense of it," I paused.

"Is she…." Valerie began.

"I believe she's dead," I said quietly. "I also believe it could be a while before she's found."

"Do you think if you went up there…." Tom asked.

I shook my head. "No, I've done all I can do."

They thanked me for my time and we headed back to town.

We drove off in silence. "Wow, Mom, that was cool," my daughter said, finally. I laughed. We both agreed the flash of light was a little too mysterious.

"Probably an electrical malfunction in the car," I said, grinning, speaking in my best scientific voice. We laughed again.

Search and rescue went to look a few days later but found nothing. Soon snow covered the ground. In the spring, they searched again. Still nothing. In the fall, one year after Edith disappeared, hunters found a woman's purse and sneakers. They belonged to Edith. As far as I know, a body was never found.

From time to time people ask if this work I do scares me. It has never occurred to me to be scared of it especially when I'm "in it" so to speak. Sometimes, afterwards, I'll get an uneasy feeling, but only in hindsight. The true psychics I've known or read about say the same thing. What's to fear? No bells or whistles, no crystals or prayers of protection. That stuff sets up or invites fear in. I'm convinced our fears are born of ignorance. It's either all God or none of it is.

Thirty-two

By January 1993, life was feeling more comfortable. After my furnace broke down and my plumbing backed up, I realized I was capable of calling a repairman and dealing with whatever emergency or inconvenience might occur. I could take care of myself and it felt so good. Work was coming along slowly. I still refused to advertise. There were days, even weeks, when my phone didn't ring. Those were the days when panic could take hold, and I would have to talk myself into gratitude.

Self-employment is not for sissies. It takes an amazing act of faith to wake up each day saying "thank you" and going to bed when your books are empty saying "thank you" again. I sat in group so many times feeling pushed to the edge, and musing that I should get a real job. Whenever I thought that might be the answer, my phone would start ringing and my days would fill up.

I employed mantras like "Life is abundant," "I allow prosperity," "My work is good and so am I," and always "Thank you."

I believed what Jungian psychologist Joseph Campbell said that when you follow your bliss, "doors will open where you wouldn't have thought there was going to be a door...and where there wouldn't have been a door for anyone else."

It had worked so far, ever since I'd begun my recovery. But I had to listen to myself and stay grounded in what I knew to be true for me. I began to refer to self-employment as co-creating with God, living daily on the edges of myself in the unknown and having to trust my higher power. This was not about willing something to happen. This was about extending myself into the world and trusting the outcome of that extending. It was hard, mostly because the world says we must be proactive and do such things as get an agent or advertise. I knew I had to listen and trust my own natural flow.

Our teachers surely do come in mysterious ways and forms.

Often when I'd become discouraged, I'd call for Buddy and we'd walk to the river. It was a 10 minute walk from the house. I found the flow and movement of the river was comforting and cathartic. Sometimes it was as still as a mirror, perfectly reflecting the sky and shoreline. Other times it moved rapidly, big waves churning and stirring up from its depths. Occasionally a light mist hung low, skimming the river's face like a silken scarf. Its moods suited me during those times.

Frequently, on our way home from the river, I'd stop at a small coffee shop. The owners, Evan and Marcia, were friendly and chatty. Often I'd sit at one of the two tables they'd squeezed into their small space and read the paper. A few other folks would stop in and we'd sit and chat. It felt good. I was getting to know my community.

One spring morning as I stepped inside their open door, a man was sitting at the table in the corner. He was very attractive in a Sam Elliott sort of way. I smiled and he nodded pleasantly, returning my smile. But something else was going on inside of me as I ordered my latte. I felt disarmed, like I'd been caught off-guard by this man's presence. As I fed Buddy his coffee shop doggie treat, the man left, stepping around us on the sidewalk. I glanced up at him, smiling again as he passed. He didn't seem to notice.

Stepping back inside for my drink, I said to Marcia, "Hmmm. New face in town?"

Evan glanced up from cleaning an espresso machine to see who I was talking about. "Who, what?" he said, like he'd just awakened from a dream.

Marcia and I both laughed at his clueless look. "She's referring to Ira," she explained. She looked back at me, smiling. "Nice looking man, huh?"

"Yeah, I guess. Who is he?" I tried to sound casual. I was way too curious, and she knew it.

"He lives down by the river. I don't know much else. He's only been in a few times. Always alone," she said, raising an eyebrow and smiling suggestively as she handed me my drink.

Over the next few weeks I hoped to see Ira again at the coffee shop, but no such luck. Then one morning walking by the river, a runner approached. As he came closer I saw it was Ira. He nodded as he passed. I smiled.

So, he's a runner, I said to myself. God, I hate running. I noticed, however, how fit he looked for a man his age, guessing him to be in his mid-fifties.

Who is this guy? I thought, suddenly embarrassed by my lack of fitness.

One spring morning in 1993, I was jolted out of bed around 5:30 a.m. by the sound of a particularly loud semi-

truck on the freeway. Or so I thought. As the stillness returned, I closed my eyes, drifting back to sleep. Suddenly
the whole house shuddered and began rocking. I bounded to my feet. By the time I reached the kitchen it stopped.
My whole body trembled.

"An earthquake. An earthquake," I said, trying to calm
down. Slowly I walked to the radio and turned it on.

"That was quite an early morning wake-up call," the
DJ was saying, "Yes, Portland, we've just experienced an
earthquake."

I sat down, shaken. I've lived in Portland all my life,
and have never experienced a quake, although the year I
was born, my parents told me, an earthquake moved my
crib across the room.

"It's been confirmed, folks; the national earthquake
monitoring center has confirmed a 5.6 earthquake at 5:34
a.m. Not that we need any confirmation," the DJ chuckled. He cautioned that we should expect aftershocks for
the next few days.

Great, I thought, expect more shaking. I suddenly remembered Buddy outside. I opened the back door and
there he stood, tail wagging.

"Come on in and keep me company," I said as he
pushed past me.

Later that day Ginny, my realtor, called.

"Suzanne, you did know that was coming, didn't
you?" she asked accusingly.

"What do you mean?" I said, puzzled.

"Remember at escrow?"

I thought back to that day nearly a year ago, and then
laughed. Ginny had gone with me to sign and had read
and scoured the paperwork with me. When we got to the

list of closing costs she'd stopped abruptly at the home-owner's insurance line item.

"Why is your homeowner's insurance so high?" She asked, looking for a copy of my policy.

"Oh, here it is. Looks like you added earthquake insur-ance." She paused, removing her glasses. "Okay, I got to tell you, it concerns me when my psychic takes out earth-quake insurance. Is there something I should know?" She said this in all seriousness. I burst out laughing at her look.

"No, no," I said, shaking my head. "It's just such an old house, I want to protect my interests all the way around. I promise."

"Well, okay, if you're sure," she said warily as she re-turned the policy to its place among the stack of paper-work.

We laughed now as I maintained my innocence.

"So, any damage?" she asked.

"None that I can see, although I've not been down in the cellar yet," I told her.

As we hung up I thought about other friends through the years who'd accused me of knowing something just because it had come up somehow. It was hard knowing where the psychic ended and the person began. It made it difficult being casual with friends. I've tried hard through the years to only be psychic when I'm doing readings. From time to time, however, I'll respond to something I hear someone say, only to see that look on their face as they tell me they didn't say it...but they had thought it.

It's also hard for me as a friend knowing that people listen to me in that way. I guess in part, that is why I've always longed for peers in my field, or at least a mentor.

Now, of course, I realize our mentors are all around us. There's an old saying: "When the student is ready, the teacher appears." I think that's a bit misleading. It should say "When the student's awake, she sees the teacher everywhere." I say this, of course, because I was about to enter a whole new learning experience.

Thirty-three

Jeanne Boylan and I stayed in touch, occasionally meeting for lunch or dinner. A friendship of the sort we had both longed for was emerging. We understood each other's work in a way no one else possibly could. It was at one of these meetings that we learned we'd both worked on the same case once, a few years back. I was telling her how my work on the Lee Iseli case had been life-changing. As I made reference to "seeing the Pinto or Vega car with wood on the sides," she gasped.

"No way," she said, eyes wide with revelation. "No way."

The dialogue sped up as our mutual excitement increased.

"Remember the Neer brothers? The little boys who'd been found murdered in a Vancouver park?"

Of course I remembered. It happened a few weeks before Lee had disappeared. At the time, the police believed the two cases were not connected. Jeanne had been called in to work with an eyewitness from the park.

"The boy told me he saw the man get into a car and described it just the way you saw it in the Iseli case!"

We sat quietly a moment letting it sink in. We'd both worked on the same case, differently of course, but had gotten the same information.

"I wonder why the police said the two cases were not connected?" I mused.

"Who knows?" Jeanne replied. "The mysteries of law enforcement." She reached for her keys and purse. "Got a plane to catch," she said, smiling. As we said goodbye we concurred that we should really work together sometime.

Sadly, that time came only a few months later. In October 1993 a young girl had been brazenly snatched from her home during a slumber party. She lived in Petaluma, California. Her name was Polly Klaas. Two friends spending the night with Polly were the only eyewitnesses. The police had released a sketch.

As I watched the news coverage, I tried to "tune in" myself. According to Polly's friends, the man had walked in through the bedroom door, made them all lay face down on the floor, took Polly and warned them not to move or tell anyone. Polly's mother lay unaware, sleeping in her bedroom down the hall. He left with Polly. About 10 minutes lapsed, as the girls obeyed his orders not to move, before they got up and told Polly's mother.

As the days slipped by, the boldness and brashness of the abduction became more unbelievable, as did the young girls' story. Why hadn't they screamed for help? Why did they wait so long to tell Polly's mom? Speculation abounded as the media coverage continued. The girls clammed up and would no longer talk with police.

My heart broke for her parents, watching their tearful pleas. If only I could *see* something. How might I help? Would the police listen to yet one more psychic? My phone rang as I contemplated how and if I could help.

"Suzanne, have you been watching the news about the little girl missing in Petaluma?" Jeanne's soft, breathless voice sounded urgent.

"Yeah, it's horrible."

"I've just been called in on it. I'm packing as we speak."
She paused a moment. "How would you feel about joining me?"

I froze.

"Uh, why don't you call me when you get there?" I
suggested, feeling totally frightened at the prospect.

She didn't press. "Talk to you soon," she said.

After I hung up, my mind reeled. Fear gripped my
throat, a very old, very real fear. Exposure. A voice telling me not to tell anyone what I do. This was high-pro-
file media attention. What if I couldn't *see*? What if I was
wrong? What if I made a fool of myself? My ego had a
field day with this one. I could become famous after all.

Another psychic told me years ago, after she'd blun-
dered through a televised morning show where she *read*
the host, that in our field there was no such thing as bad
publicity. I found her offensive. Nevertheless, her words
ran through my brain as I struggled with the possibili-
ties.

By the time Jeanne phoned a day or two later, practi-
cality had settled the struggle. I simply could not afford
to take the time off. Her expenses had been paid; mine
would come out of my own pocket. Jeanne understood
and went on to fill me in on the investigation.

As she talked, I began to see pictures. I told her I saw
a man watching the girls. It felt like he'd followed them
home from a store or mall. Then I saw an open farm field,
a barn or silo, a farm house, a dirt or gravel road beside a
drainage ditch. The pictures stopped.

"How'd you do that?" Jeanne asked after I paused.

"I... I don't know. I just started seeing as you talked,"
I said hesitantly.

"So you can see over the phone?" she queried.

"I...I guess so," I answered, still uncertain.

"Well, I'll pass this on. The sheriff here is a great guy.
He seems real open." We went on to talk of other things.

Within days, Jeanne's amazing likeness of the man
who'd abducted Polly was all over the media. Flyers went
out to local communities. Days later Richard Allen Davis
was arrested. Someone recognized him from the drawing.
As the story of the investigation unfolded over the next
few weeks, a piece of it caught my attention. The night
Polly disappeared a woman who lived outside a neigh-
boring town called the police. She lived on a rural road
and from her farmhouse window could see car lights on
the road across the field. The lights hadn't moved for some
time. A patrol car was sent to investigate and found a man
whose car was stuck in a drainage ditch. They helped him
pull the car out and went on their way. Because of communication difficulties, this police department had not at
that point heard of the kidnapping. As the investigation
unfolded, it was learned that the driver of that car was
Davis. Tragically, Polly was still alive then, bound and
gagged and hidden from the car.

"A field, a farm, a rural road, a drainage ditch!" The
pictures I'd seen echoed.

What the hell good does it do to *see*, I lamented as I
tearfully dialed Jeanne's phone number.

"Yeah, I know," she said as I recounted my own words.
"I thought of you when I heard."

This event seemed to push me deep inside myself to wonder how it might have been different. The ability to *see* has been such an enigma in my life, a sort of nebulous landscape of my mind that I've learned to observe quietly, but not necessarily to act on or speak from. Its language is not always clear, not always easy to interpret. What good is seeing the pictures if no one knows how to use them? How might I do it differently in the future?

The police have enough on their plate without investigating the hundreds of calls from psychics and would-be psychics on high profile cases. They would need an interpreter or method of collating all the information from the psychic input, and isolating common denominators, perhaps by having one officer trained to work with psychics or hiring a civilian who knows how to listen to these nebulous clues.

Thirty-four

"Hey, what are you doing? I've been watching you. You stare much harder at that river, I'll have to jump in and save you!"

My contemplation was broken by a man's gruff voice. Buddy and I had walked to the river. It was early morning and an autumn mist lay heavy on the river's face. Startled, I turned to see Ira standing behind me in his running clothes. Hands on hips, he was a sight to behold.

"Hey," I said turning back once more to my rivergaze. I resented the intrusion, but his footsteps crunching in the cold morning grass told me he was coming closer. He spoke to Buddy. I ignored him and continued to stare across the water.

"So, somebody die?" he said with a chuckle. "You look like hell."

I was sitting on top of a picnic table on a small bluff above the boat ramp. I don't know how long I'd been there, but now realized I'd been crying. As I swung around to face him, he took a step back.

"Are you always this rude?" I asked.

"That's what they say," he said, again with a raspy chuckle.

"She's beautiful," he said, inclining his head toward the river. "Every morning a different face. Hey, I'm going for a run. Why don't you go home, wash your face, and meet me for coffee in an hour?" He asked as if we were old friends.

I looked at him a long moment. He grinned.

Finally I shrugged. "Fine!" I grumbled. Watching him run off, I smiled despite myself. Who is this guy? I thought again.

An hour later, I walked to the coffee shop. Ira was there, seated in his usual corner, cup in hand. He nodded as I stepped in. Marcia, ever-alert, noticed the nod.

Eyebrow raised in amusement, she smiled and said, "The usual?"

"Yeah," I said, my tone leaving no room for further comment. The last thing I wanted was to be the source of her entertainment or speculation.

"Thanks," I said as she handed me the extra-hot latte.

"Enjoy," she said with a smirk.

I sat down with Ira. He smiled. We sat in silence for a few moments. Then he spoke, leaning back a bit in his chair.

"So what's so awful in your life that you can't be pleasant? Can't be that bad, you're still walking; still know how to make change for your coffee," he said, slapping his hand on his leg, clearly amused at himself.

"You wouldn't understand," I said, looking out the window.

"Oh yeah?" he said with mock offense. "I understand a lot more than you know. Looks to me like you're pretty self-absorbed. Pretty puffed-up about your own self-importance." He spoke in nearly a whisper, leaning in toward me, a glint of fire in his eyes.

I was affronted. "What would you know? Who the hell are you to tell me anything?" I responded, aghast, wanting to flee, but stuck like glue.

Tilting back so his chair touched the wall, he spoke, this time barely audibly, drawing me in close to hear. Clearly, he was a man who relished control.

"I know a lot of things…." He cut himself off and we sat in silence again. Reaching for his cup, he said, "Let's exchange pleasantries," smiling a forced, fake smile.

I shifted uncomfortably and shrugged.

"So, do you work? I always see you out there walking your friend."

I smiled as he referred to Buddy as my friend.

"Yes, I work," I said sarcastically.

"Yeah, well, what do you do?"

I glanced at Marcia leaning on the counter in undisguised eavesdropping. She chuckled, shaking her head as she joined Evan in the kitchen.

"This ought to be good," I heard her say. I'd told her months before about my work.

"Cool," she'd said. Now it was obviously amusing her.

Ira followed my gaze. "What's the matter with her?" He jammed his thumb in her direction. "You a hooker or something?" he asked, amused at my discomfort.

"Oh, for god sakes. No! I'm not a hooker. So sorry to disappoint."

He had to lean in to hear me. I could play his game.

"Well?"

"I'm a psychic, if you must know," I blurted out, surprising even myself.

"That so?!" he said, sitting up straight. "Well, now I see why you're reluctant to say. That's almost as bad," he cackled, slapping his leg again. "So you got a crystal ball and a neon hand in your window? Your neighbors must love that," he chortled, laughing so hard he was wiping tears from his eyes.

I glared, both offended and amused by his brash comments. He was enjoying himself. That's enough, show's over, I thought, gathering my purse and jacket. I am out of here.

"Hey! Where you going?" he asked as I stood.

"I've had enough of your 'pleasantries.'"

"Oh, sit back down. Quit taking yourself so seriously," he said brusquely, but the tone of his voice was now quite sober.

I sat down, glancing again at Marcia who'd busied herself at the pastry counter. A pregnant silence began. Ira stared out the window as a wind lifted dry leaves into a mini whirl and scooted them across the road. I watched the tops of the tall firs bending deeply with the wind.

"Storm's coming," he said.

Seconds later a downpour hit, pelting the window with sideways rain.

"Aren't you glad you stayed?" he chided. "You'd be caught in this."

I grinned and for the first time wondered if he was married. He wore no wedding band.

As I opened my mouth to ask, he interrupted, "So you carry some medicine. Did you come in with it?"

"What do you mean?" I asked. "Are you Indian?"

He shook his head. "No, but I know some things. This psychic stuff, have you always had it?" he pressed.

"Yes," I said, wondering where this was going.

He smiled and looked down at his coffee. Silence again.

"So, this what's got you so down?" he asked.

I began to tell him about working with Jeanne on the Petaluma case.

"Who?" he asked when I mentioned Jeanne.

"The woman who sketched Polly Klaas's killer."

"Oh yeah," he said grinning. "She's pretty good-looking. Hey, how about introducing us?" he asked, leaning forward with a hungry smirk. That did it. I had enough.

"You are so…so disgusting! I'm not wasting any more of my time," I huffed, gathering up my things. The rain had stopped. Without looking back, I stormed out, kicking myself for wasting my time.

"To think I almost trusted that guy," I fumed, picking up my pace as the rain began again.

For the next few months I avoided weekday visits to the coffee shop. Buddy and I walked at different times, staying closer to home as winter rains increased. I did not want another encounter with Ira. Marcia said he'd asked about me a time or two.

"I'm pretty busy," I'd said in response. She nodded, knowingly.

Occasionally, I'd see him running on the road as I drove by. He never saw me. The truth was business had picked up. Between that and the holidays, my time was not my own. Even Buddy felt neglected, jogging expectantly up the driveway each time I went out to get in my car.

"Later," I'd say, patting him on the head.

During this time I received a call about two men who'd gone flying in an ultralight, and had not come home. The police had called off the search weeks before, but family and friends continued searching the Mt. Hood National Forest. One of these friends called me. It was the end of January 1994.

I met with the men's friends and family, describing what I saw from a perspective of being up in the ultralight looking down for landmarks. I observed a lumber mill, a river, something that looked like a storage yard for heavy equipment, a pyramid-shaped pile of dirt or sand. It felt like they would be looking for bodies. This is always hard reporting, and with families I always preface it with "...I could be wrong, but..." It's hard.

I've come to realize one of the other roles I play in a search is simply communication. For reasons which I'm sure make sense to the police, their protocol seems to leave families out of the communication loop. Families of missing persons want to talk, they need to talk, they cling to hope, even to speculation. They need to feel like they're doing something, even if it is just talking about it. Sitting and waiting is hell when your child or spouse is missing. We talk, we speculate. I remind them I will only be shown clues. How I wish I could see license plates, addresses, latitude and longitude, but I don't. I see clues.

In this case my clues seemed to point to a rural community on the mountain's hemline called Estacada, Oregon. The friend asked if I could recognize it from the air. I nodded.

"Great!" he said. "When can you go up? We can get a plane this weekend."

"Oh, no. No. I don't fly, especially in small planes. No, I really can't," I stammered. "I'd like to, really I would, but I was in a plane crash...." I went on to explain. The friend smiled.

"Well, there you go. Chances are you'll never be in another plane crash. The odds are with you!"

The silence that followed was like the weight of the world on my shoulders. All eyes turned to me. I noticed the young man's mother wiping tears away.

As my good sense told me no way, I heard myself say quietly, "Okay then. How about Sunday?"

It seemed so simple, so evident, seeing these *pictures* from the ground, but up in the air, flying over miles and miles of tall firs, it was not so clear. Hope grew, however, as we flew above the Clackamas River toward Estacada. Below us was the lumber mill and off to the south of it the storage yard for heavy equipment! The heavy equipment turned out to be sanding trucks and the pyramid-shaped pile was sand.

"We need to turn north and then east," I instructed.

Back and forth we zigzagged, eyes scanning the thick forest below. Fortunately, snow had not yet fallen. But what were we looking for at this late date? There's not much substance to an ultralight, especially after so much time in the weather. As the hours in the air passed, it became evident our search was futile. Our flight back to the airport was silent. Shaking hands with the men's parents that day I saw one final picture.

"The men will be found in the fall by a man wearing overalls and carrying a shotgun," I spoke.

"This is what you're seeing?" the father asked.

"Just now as I shook your hands."

With sorrowful eyes, the parents clung to each other as I took my leave.

Walking away from the airplane toward the car, a sigh escaped me. I knew that these bodies would not be found until it was time.

My work with missing persons has taught me to accept the oddity of the timing between when people go missing and when they are found. I have observed time and time again that a search would entail the precise location where the missing people would ultimately be found. I have witnessed the disbelief of search and rescue personnel when they found a missing body in exactly the place that they had searched so thoroughly months or years prior.

What is it that keeps some of the missing hidden from direct sight? Why provide me with visions that are of no direct use to anyone at the time? I receive validation when the body is later found, but of what use is that to a grieving family? It is truly one of the mysteries I work with. I can only keep the faith that the higher purpose is that searchers learn from the validations to be more accepting of true psychic visions and utilize them as intended, as clues, the same as any physical clues. They are signposts to suggest a look in that direction.

Months later, in October, I received a call from the friend of the missing ultralight pilots.

"Suzanne, you'll be hearing it on the news soon. They just found the ultralight, the men too. A farmer with a shotgun, out walking his property looking for hunters who might be trespassing, just like you saw," he said.

"Out by Estacada?" I asked.

"Yeah," he said. "We must have flown over it a half dozen times that day."

Thirty-five

One day in early May, the inevitable occurred. I'd begun walking Buddy again first thing in the morning and we stopped to watch the mist on the river. As I sat watching, a handful of geese skimmed the river's face. Today the river was as still as a pond.

A gruff voice behind me said, "Guess I haven't seen you in a while."

Rotating on my picnic table perch, I saw Ira smiling as he looked out over the river. I returned his smile despite myself.

"Where you been?" he asked, approaching slowly, closer.

"Busy," I said coolly.

"Yeah? You mean with your crystal gazing?" he said, chuckling.

"That's not...." I began, then stopped and shook my head. His smile disarmed me. He advanced a few more cautious steps.

"You been running?" I asked.

"No, not yet. Hey, you should come run with me."

"No thanks," I said. "I don't like to sweat."

He looked startled. "Well, you need to sweat," he muttered softly, more to himself than to me.

"I'm sorry, what?"

"Nothing."

In the silence that followed, the mist began its rise off

the river, the ripples shining like diamonds in the sun.

"I love the river when it sparkles like that. It reminds me of something… maybe a shiny sequined outfit I wore when I was a kid," I said, thinking of the costume I wore when I marched in a parade years before. Ira shook his head.

"No," he replied, "you're remembering something else, something from a very long time ago." The sound of his voice made me turn and look at him. His eyes were closed, face turned toward the sun; I was reminded of the smiling Cheshire cat.

"What do you mean?" I asked. A long silence followed. Thinking he didn't hear me, I cleared my throat to speak again.

But before I could say anything, he said quietly, "Do you know where you come from?"

"What? What do you mean? I come from here. From Portland."

He grinned. "Do you?" More of a challenge than an inquiry.

"Well, yes, of course," I began, but he cut me off with a wave of his hand.

Leaning toward me, dark eyes intense, he said, "I've been watching you. I see you. You can only be one thing." He paused mysteriously, lifting his eyebrows now.

He was making me nervous, uncomfortable. "I don't know what you're talking about," I said, trying to sound in control, but feeling a pressure in my stomach.

"Oh really," he replied. He was standing about two feet from me. Dangerously close, I thought. As he folded his arms across his chest he said, "Let me see if I can remind you. You're Celt aren't you?"

"What? What are you getting at?"

"Your heritage. What's your born name?"

"You mean my maiden name?" I asked.

He nodded.

"It's Murphy. But why…." He cut me off again.

"Celt," he said again speaking the word as if it were a prize, a treasure. He smiled broadly.

"Why? Are you Celt?" I asked, wondering where this conversation was going, but willing to play along.

He took a step back, sizing me up. After a moment he went on, ignoring my question as if it weren't worthy of an answer.

"The Celtic people carry the medicine of the world," he stated matter-of-factly.

I started to speak, but thought better of it. His words disturbed me. Was this man crazy? He seemed normal enough, a little eccentric, but normal. Maybe it was time to leave. But something held me tight.

"You've wandered and struggled, never knowing where you fit. Probably been married a few times, trying to make a normal life. Trying to look normal but feeling all along like you're bluffing, making pretend, not feeling real. Trying to fill up a hole, like some vital part of your soul is empty, flailing." He paused, seeing the hot tears on my face. "You feel like a damn aberration, a freak of nature."

"Stop! Stop!" I insisted, jumping up from the table. "Leave me alone," I spat, gathering myself up to leave.

Ira grinned. "Sit down," he said quietly. There was an unexpected gentleness in his voice.

I sat back down, heart pounding, ready to flee. He sat on the bench below me.

"That old man is right," he said enigmatically. "We have to walk the soil of our ancestors."

His silence continued to hold sway over me. I waited for him to continue. When he didn't I asked, "What old man?"

He sat quietly watching the river. A couple in a canoe paddled by, barely making a sound as they moved over her quiet face.

He turned to face me. "What do you know about your ancestors, your tribe?" he asked, ignoring my question.

"My *what*?"

He nodded, knowingly. "Ireland. The home of your ancestors, a fierce and mystical people."

"What has that got to do with anything now?" I dismissed him, giving Buddy a reassuring pat. He'd come to my side a few minutes earlier, wondering about my hysterics, no doubt.

Ira stood. He looked offended. "Don't be so disrespectful. Those people hold the secret to the pain that's been running your life."

Suddenly I felt scolded, superficial and insincere. What could this man possibly know about the pain in my life? Besides, I was taking care of that now, doing my therapy and my 12-step work. Still, there was something, something deep inside that was always reaching, always seeking. I wasn't about to share the intimate details of myself with him, but some part of me was listening eagerly, wanting to hear his words. What about this medicine he's talking about? I needed to know more.

"What do you know about Avalon, Glastonbury and the Druids?" he asked.

I shrugged. "Not much, except that they were brutal pagans."

He nodded, and then quietly said, "Just like the church taught you."

In the long silence that followed, I began feeling awkward. Nervously, I cleared my throat. "I read *Trinity* years ago." My voice sounded too loud against the quiet of the moment.

Ira's dark, penetrating eyes seemed to look through me.

Stupid! Stupid! I thought, feeling small again. I shifted uncomfortably under his stare. He was no longer looking at me, but some other place, some other time.

"Your people were the *Tuatha Dé Danann* and it has been told that the origins of the Murphy clan came from the sea." He paused and focused back on me. "It is said they were tall people, maybe even giants." He smiled, sizing up my nearly six foot frame. "The Celtic people knew about these Grandfathers," he went on, waving his arm towards the trees that stood nearby. "They knew about our Mother and lived with her in reverence."

I thought of how I'd fled to nature in my childhood, how the trees held me in their arms, bringing me comfort.

"To be who we are today we must know where we come from. We must honor the ancestors. We are all of our ancestors," Ira said, then adding something quietly to himself in another language.

He continued, "That old man says the old ways must return. He says the red dragon of our Celtic people has begun to stir. It is awakening once again and we'll begin seeing it in art and music."

I wanted to ask again about the old man, but instead blurted, "Are you a Druid?"

He stepped back from me, looking stunned or amused.

"Never mind about me," he said as if offended. He turned to leave.

"Wait Ira! Tell me more about the dragon," I asked.

A grin passed over his face as he sat down. For the next two or three hours I sat mystified as he spoke of ancient Ireland and Wales. He spoke masterfully, crafting his words like an art. I was beguiled and enchanted allowing his voice to carry me to another place and time.

When he finished the sun was directly overhead. I'd lost track of time. It took me a few moments to move, but when I finally stood to leave, Ira was gone.

What had just happened? I felt suspended between worlds: the world of then and the world of now. It was as if time had collapsed in on me. I needed something to hold on to, something to remind me where I was now. My eyes scanned the well-groomed lawns of the park, finally resting on a familiar face, a nose-face. Buddy lay about six feet away staring at me. When our eyes met he whined, tail thumping on the ground as if to say "Are we done yet?" His pleading look made me laugh, which brought him bounding over to me.

"What a good boy to wait all that time," I said, rubbing his back. "Let's go home."

I snapped his leash back on but as we turned to walk up the lane, things still weren't quite right. The trees were sparkling just like the river! It was as if they were more alive to me. I paused to reassess my situation. Over in the play area mothers had gathered with their children, laughing and playing on the swings and slides. In the ball field, a girls' softball team was warming up. I could hear ducks and geese by the river squabbling over bread crumbs someone was feeding them. It was still 1994 and just another day in the park. I looked back at the tree-lined lane. Indisputably, the trees sparkled. Every leaf on every tree was shimmering and sparkling.

"Okay, then," I said as we picked up our step again.

It felt as if the world had become a holy place, a cathedral, a real living being. This experience continued for some hours even after returning home. What had this man done to me? Or more accurately, what had he stirred up in me?

It was days before I saw Ira again. He was grabbing a coffee to go at Marcia and Evan's coffee shop. With him was a tall, dark-haired man whose hair was pulled back in a braid that hung almost to his waist.

"Hey, how you doin'?" he asked in his raspy voice.

"Great," I replied.

"Good. Good. Well, see ya later. We got work to do," he said, opening the door. They were gone.

"Wow," I said to no one as I stepped up to order.

"Yeah," grinned Marcia. "Want your usual?"

I nodded.

"So who's the guy with Ira?"

"The Indian? Oh, that's his friend Billy. He's Lakota," she answered. "Kinda cute, eh?"

"I guess," I said with a shrug. "What's Lakota?"

"You know, Sioux. Lakota Sioux."

"Hmmm," I said, nodding as if I understood.

Marcia handed me my latte, then leaned forward conspiratorially. She looked over my shoulder to make sure we were alone. I leaned in too.

"You know, Ira has a sweat lodge on his place." She spoke as if this news should be kept confidential.

"He does?" I asked sounding surprised but not understanding the significance.

She stood back up and nodded.

"Thanks," I said lifting my cup in departure.

As I left I wondered what in the hell a sweat lodge was and why a person would have one. I knew little about Native American culture and even less about its rituals. I'd heard some of my 12-step friends talk about drumming circles and smudging ceremonies, but it seemed odd to me that white people would take on Native people's customs; odd and even disrespectful. Who was this man who spoke of walking the soil of your ancestors and had a Native American sweat lodge? It was a warm June day, but as I considered these things, I felt a shiver. I needed to distance myself from this man and his strange beliefs.

Sitting in group later that week I shared some of my experience about Ira, the mystery man. As I spoke, I realized how silly it sounded. Trying to relate the experience with words only seemed to trivialize and diminish it. Caroline's comment was to remind me that I didn't know yet if he was married. I never spoke of him again.

I was starting to truly appreciate the natural flow and rhythm my life had taken on. Four years had passed since I'd first trudged up those stairs to meet Caroline. If anyone had told me then where I'd be in four years, I would not have believed them. I'd been in my own home for two years. My business was growing and taking care of me. To my delight and surprise, I had a life and it was working!

My old foes and companions, sadness and depression, had all but disappeared as well. I remember how startled I was when I realized they were missing. What really disturbed me was how attached I'd become to those feelings, how sometimes I'd find myself longing for the sadness to return, to wallow in a while.

Fortunately those feelings just didn't fit my life anymore. I rarely cried. The gratitude I felt for my recovery, Caroline and my group was sometimes overwhelming. Because of my commitment to myself, I had truly been reborn. I could finally hear and trust my own voice. I had a life!

This new life was affecting my work as well. More than once over the past four years, I'd had regular clients tell me how clear my pictures for them had become. I'd smile and thank them, knowing that my pictures were no longer encumbered with my own stuff. I was no longer projecting.

What I believe is that our natural gifts bring us to the door and set us on the path. It is how we walk the path that is important. It's very easy in our humanity to get stuck at the door, afraid to do the difficult required work, the personal work that makes our lives exceptional and faces us to our destinies.

Thirty-six

"You've got some medicine. How you walk with that medicine is all important. It is the only thing that should concern you. If you don't walk with it in a clean and honorable way, it will turn on you. It will destroy you." Ira's raspy voice was deep and troubling.

I'd bumped into him at the coffee shop. Weeks had passed since that intoxicating morning at the river, and now he sat at his corner table, legs crossed, one arm leaning on the small table as he whispered these words to me. Once again I wanted to flee this man, but again something held me captive.

"I don't know what you mean," I replied, taking a drink of water. My mouth had gone suddenly dry. He gave me a look of disgust and turned to stare out the window.

The bell on the shop door chimed heralding the arrival of a group of teenagers who were laughing and shoving each other. Ira watched them for a moment, then stood.

"Let's go for a walk," he said motioning with his head toward the door. Without waiting for my response, he left. I jumped up to follow, and caught Marcia's eye. She grinned. I smiled back, wondering what she thought she was seeing.

Outside I said, "Where to?"

"Got your car?" he asked, scanning the cars parked along the curb.

"Sure, but…."

"Good, you drive."

What was I getting myself into now? As I started the engine of my jeep, he climbed in on the passenger side.

"Where to?" I asked again, turning right onto the main road. Keeping his eyes focused on the road ahead he said, "Mary Young."

Mary S. Young State Park was a beautiful forested refuge along the Willamette River a few miles away. As I drove, I watched Ira out of the corner of my eye. He never moved and stayed focused on the road ahead. We rode in silence. I couldn't help thinking what a good-looking man he was for a man his age.

"This isn't about that," he said as I parked, noticing only two or three cars in the park's lot. He walked around the front of the car to join me as I locked my door.

"About what?" I asked nervously, wondering if he'd read my mind.

"You're pretty good to look at too," he said, stunning me with this direct confirmation of mind-reading. "That old man says to leave you alone. We've got work to do."

"The old man knows about me?" I responded, acting as if I was familiar with "the old man." "How could he…."

Ira cut me off with a quick glare. He walked briskly down toward the river. I had to nearly jog to keep up. We stopped at a fork in the trail.

He rounded on me. "Listen to me. You know nothing of the old man or me for that matter," he threatened, coal eyes flashing. From a hidden spot deep inside I felt a bolt of courage.

I spoke up. "Well, I do know you're married," I said almost shouting. Marcia mentioned a few weeks back that she'd met "Mrs. Ira."

A look that made me step back passed over his face.

"My marriage has nothing to do with this," he hissed. "It will never be mentioned again."

"Fine," I said, after a moment's pause. "But I have a right to know who the hell this 'old man' is you keep referring to and what he knows about me." My hands were on my hips, ready to be done with him once and for all.

To my surprise he chuckled and shook his head, muttering something as he turned to walk the trail which followed a small creek.

"Wait a minute!" I said grabbing his arm. He froze, staring at my hold. I pulled my hand back, feeling stupid once again. Slowly he turned to face me, looking at me with eyes that seemed to be assessing something in me. The way he stood, head cocked to one side, as if listening for something, made me think of a raven, or was it an eagle? I shivered.

Finally he spoke. "I'm going to tell you about that old man so maybe you'll be a little more respectful."

I waited, anticipation mounting. He looked around.

"But not here. Let's walk on up there," he said, gesturing to the ridge above us. I followed him as we walked in the now familiar Ira silence.

At the top of the ridge we veered off the trail into a beautiful grove of tall cedars. He sat down on a fallen log. The ferns growing from the log were damp with morning dew. He motioned me to sit. The park was still, with only the sounds of birds and the creek below. He looked up to the sky which was barely visible through the thick canopy. When he turned to speak he had the most serene look on his face.

"Twenty years ago I met a man who reached in and saved my life. God knows, it needing saving. He wasn't just any man. He was a Lakota medicine man. I guess my creator knew that's what it would take," he said wryly. "I've been all over the country with him, driving him here and there." Another long pause. Ira sat up straight and looked me in the eye.

"His name's Martin. Martin High Bear." His voice was warm with fondness and respect. A jay screeched past us. Its passage brought amusement to Ira.

"What has this got to do with me?"

"You?!" he said with surprise. He snorted. "Hasn't got a damn thing to do with you," he said. He squinted as he looked at me. "What's the matter with you? Does everything have to be about you? You asked me who the old man is, now I've told you."

After a few minutes, during which I questioned whether I'd fallen down the rabbit hole, Ira stood up.

"I'm gonna tell you something," he said, shoving his hands in his pockets. "That old man knows things. I don't know how. It's the medicine. But he knows things and when he says something, I listen. That's all. I pay attention."

As he spoke I stood up. We were now eye to eye. "You need to pay attention too. You, of all people," he said with a huff. "And show a little more respect," he added, walking back to the main trail.

The rest of our walk consisted of his pointing out plants and trees, sometimes describing their origins or medicinal value. I started to speak once or twice to ask questions, but thought better of it. It was becoming clear I was only along for the ride.

My wise, practical self should have questioned why an intelligent, increasingly independent woman would even acknowledge this irreverent, disturbing, jarring man.

But this was not a wise, practical journey. This was an intuitive, trusting journey of soul.

And so this strange tutelage continued throughout the summer and into fall. I would encounter Ira at the coffee shop or while out walking Buddy. We'd spend an hour or two talking. Sometimes he'd phone or stop by, always keeping a proper distance.

As time went on, I felt a real friendship growing. I mentioned this once as I was driving him on some errand. I'd become his chauffeur. He'd turned to look at me, surprise on his face.

"Friends?" he replied, shaking his head. "No, I am not your friend."

"Oh," I said quietly, hurt. We drove in silence. When I stopped the car in the parking lot of today's destination, Home Depot, he turned to me, placing his arm over the back of the seat.

"Now listen here," he spoke, not unkindly, "we got some things in common. We come from the same people. Those ancient tribes are scattered now, so when we find each other we need to stick together. Martin says the old ways must return. People need to remember their grandfathers, their roots, their ancient spiritual heart. That Roman church has desecrated the spiritual heart of every native land, robbing people of their natural heritage, weakening their very souls, creating fear, guilt and frustration. Look at the Ireland of today. And the church just gets wealthier and more corrupt. It has to stop. Our spiritual hearts must be restored to us and that can only come through remembering the old ways. We must remember who we are and where we come from."

I started to speak, but his glare silenced me.

"That doesn't mean white people should take on Native American ways or go learn from some isolated South American shaman," he continued with a smirk, "although they do love to see you blond-haired, white women coming!" he slapped his leg, clearly amused.

"Yeah, I know a white guy in the sweat lodge who claims to be Sitting Bull." His cackle suddenly became solemn. "We have been so spiritually deprived we're pathetic, pathetic. We are so spiritually impoverished, we go throwing ourselves at the feet of gurus and medicine people who in their pity and amusement will toss us a crumb or two, which our ego takes and runs with and we think we've found our heart. It makes us vulnerable to anyone with a new smoke and mirrors show."

We stared at each other. I didn't know what to say. My mind reeled from the assault on the foundation of my beliefs.

Ira went on. "Someone like you comes in, born with some things," he shrugged. "Maybe some medicine, and there's no one there for you. Certainly the church isn't there." He raised an eyebrow now. "They used to burn your kind at the stake. So you wander around, getting yourself in and out of trouble, not knowing where you fit, pretending. Maybe using drugs, alcohol, sex." He shrugged again. "It doesn't matter. No one sees you. No one understands you."

Tears began to well up in my eyes.

"It's the medicine." Ira spoke reverently in nearly a

whisper. "If you don't learn to walk with it, it will turn on you, maybe even kill you."

I was prompted to tell him my story, how I saved my life with therapy and recovery. Even as I thought about it, though, I became aware of a hollowness. He was right. Although the hard work I'd done on myself the last few years had taken me way beyond anything I'd imagined for myself, his words stirred in me a deep longing for something, somewhere inside of me, to hold onto.

I shifted in my seat. The steering wheel was intruding on my ability to sit comfortably. Finally I spoke. "So do… did all ancient people have 'the medicine?'"

He seemed to be pondering my question.

"How do you learn to walk with it today?" I asked, certain I'd interrupted his thoughts.

"You live a life of sobriety. By sober, I don't just mean drugs and alcohol. You clean yourself up. You sweat," he said emphatically. "All ancient people sweat in one form or another. That old man says that's why he lets white people sweat in his altar. Not so they can be Indian, but so they can call in their own ancestors, find their own way."

"Uh, no thank you," I said shaking my head. "I don't sweat."

He looked at me in stunned surprise. "You think you're special? I got news for you!" He reached for the door handle and stepped out. I hurried to fall in step beside him. He was half way to the door when I caught up.

"But wait. I…."

"This conversation is over." He dismissed me with a wave of his hand.

I felt horribly chastised. All the way home neither of us spoke. As we neared our exit he asked me to drop him off at his place.

Getting out of the jeep, he leaned back in giving me a curt "Goodbye and thanks" and a condescending smile. Perhaps he was right. Maybe we could not be friends.

I knew Ira was right about the desecration of our spiritual hearts by the church. I remember as a child sitting in church wondering how we could both love and be loved by God and yet must also fear Him. It never made sense to me. I had long ago abandoned hope of being accepted by the church, but like the abused child, I needed its acceptance. This was not about my relationship with God. That relationship had been wonderfully clear to me for as long as I could remember. I simply wanted the church's acceptance.

Thirty-seven

Through the years I'd become a fan of an author who had been a priest, but was excommunicated for his writings about the mystics and his belief that the Earth is our Mother. He wrote about the goddess. Rome didn't approve. He'd fought the good fight with those so-called Holy Powers. In the end he'd lost.

Fortunately another church welcomed him and offered a new home and pulpit. I'd followed his struggle through the years, feeling we had much in common. He was a hero. I'd once attended a workshop he held. As November approached I looked forward to seeing him again when he came to town to speak about his latest work.

I was relating this to Ira, who'd joined me at the river on a beautiful October morning. She was a mirror this morning, reflecting the reds and golds of the Grandfathers who lived on her shores. Ira seemed interested in what I'd been saying.

When I stopped talking, however, he turned abruptly and said, "Hey, let's go have coffee. See you there."

I watched as he ran up the hill, wondering if he'd heard anything I'd said. It didn't really matter. I'd learned by now to just go with the flow when we were together. To my relief, nothing more had been said about sweat lodge.

The day before the priest's presentation, Ira stopped by my place. "Let's go for a walk," he said. So we climbed into the jeep and headed for Mary S. Young State Park.

These walks had become opportunities for some of the most amazing discussions I'd ever been a part of. At times, one of Ira's Lakota friends would join us. I was happy to be just a listener then. I'd learned not only about sweat lodge, but vision quest and sundance. It seemed there was some division among the Sioux about white people sweating and dancing. Apparently Martin was responsible for opening both to white people, allowing men and women to sweat together as well.

It was during some of these walks I heard painful tales from these grown men about being taken from their homes as young boys and forced to live in government schools run by white people. Tales abounded of overwhelming pain inflicted by nuns if the children spoke their native language. They were forced to learn from someone who spoke a language they didn't understand and weren't allowed to grow up with their own families or culture.

I listened, mortified, more than once brushing tears from my face. I had read about these events, but now here I sat with these beautiful, gentle men, most my own age and witnessed firsthand their grief. I felt ashamed for being white even though I knew my own Irish ancestors had experienced their share of racial discrimination. It was no wonder that Native Americans might not want white people included in their ceremony and ritual. It also became clear how a wise man would know the value of such inclusion. With understanding comes peace. Although I had not met High Bear, I was beginning to appreciate his wisdom.

"Hey, what time's that talk tomorrow night?" Ira was looking at me as we walked. As usual he'd caught me off-guard.

"What?" I replied, confused by the sudden shift.

"That talk...the one you're going to downtown. The old man wants to go," Ira stated.

I paused, trying to sort out what he'd just said. I stared blankly.

"Cat's got her tongue...or maybe that crow up there," Ira cackled, nudging Billy, who'd joined us earlier. He nodded agreement.

"Why?" I continued, still confused. Ira leaned in.

"Do- you- know- what- time- that- talk- starts?" he asked as though addressing the village idiot.

"Sure, 7:00 p.m. But you won't get tickets at this late date," I added.

We'd now reached the car. Ira said something to Billy, who waved and smiled as he walked away.

"Ira, what's going on?" I asked, feeling a bit anxious. He just grinned as we drove the short distance home in silence.

"See you tomorrow night," he said, getting out at his driveway.

"We'll save you a seat," he added slyly.

All the way home my thoughts were racing. Was Ira pulling my leg? Why would Martin want to attend a church event? It didn't matter. They wouldn't get tickets anyway.

He must be playing me. But what if he wasn't? What if they really did show up? The real question was why I was so nervous about meeting Martin. After hearing so many stories about him, told with such reverence and respect, I realized I was afraid. Not scared, but afraid, like the fear and awe Dorothy felt knowing she was about to meet the great Wizard of Oz. I had never met a holy man or a medicine man. What if I really was the village idiot in his presence? I didn't want to make a fool of myself. Little did I know I wouldn't be the one who should be concerned.

It took a while to find a parking spot. The church's lot was full so I drove around the streets. Nothing. I began to panic. I didn't want to park blocks away. It was dark and I was alone. Then, something told me to go back to the church's parking lot. I argued with that thought, knowing the lot was full. It persisted.

"Fine," I said out loud, pulling back into the small lot. To my surprise there was an empty spot next to a long Cadillac.

"Huh, someone must have changed their mind," I spoke again feeling relieved and grateful.

By now I was late. Rushing up to the big red double doors of the sanctuary, I was surprised to see Billy standing just inside.

"Suzanne, hurry, we saved you a spot," he said, grabbing my hand. The church was packed, standing room only.

"You have seats?" I whispered, as he led me up to the front. He grinned, motioning with his head. Following his nod I looked and there sat Ira, enthroned in the front row!

In a wheelchair on the aisle next to Ira was a very old man. His long grey hair was pulled back in a tie. Both arms rested on the arms of the chair. He was bent, head resting almost on his chest. An oxygen tube ran from his nose to a tank behind him. He did not look up.

"Martin?" I whispered to Billy.

His grin said yes. I noticed several other Lakota sitting alongside us and Ira. Why would Lakota and their revered guide choose to hear an excommunicated priest speak to a crowd of white people in a church?

After a few announcements, a middle-aged woman introduced the man who had filled this venue on a chilly autumn night. As he spoke, I watched Martin out of the corner of my eye. His head still bent, he had not moved.

Soon I was immersed in the lecture. After perhaps 20 minutes, I noticed movement across the aisle. Ira was leaning, listening to something Martin was whispering. Ira nodded and looked over to me and Billy, who'd also noticed them. Ira motioned with his head toward the door. They were leaving.

"The old man wants to go," Billy said quietly. "C'mon."

My questioning look was answered with a nudge.

This could be embarrassing, I thought, panicked.

Ira gripped the handles behind Martin's chair. The speaker continued but was looking our way now. The other members of our group stood. As Billy rose, he took my arm.

"C'mon," he said again.

The nearest exit was to the left of the podium. We began filing out, following Ira as he moved Martin past the speaker. I stepped in behind Ira. By now the distraction had interrupted the talk.

The speaker stepped down and approached Martin's wheelchair.

To my horror he grabbed Martin's shoulder. Giving it

a condescending pat, he said, "Hey old man, thank you for coming. You're a long way from home tonight."

What was he thinking? Didn't he know who Martin was?

Martin, slumped in his chair, still hadn't looked up. But then, lifting his eyes slightly, he spoke quietly, "Am I?"

With that we continued to file out the side door. Outside I followed Ira and Martin to the parking lot. They stopped beside the long Cadillac.

"Is this Martin's car?" I asked, surprised. Ira gave me one of those exasperated looks.

"How about that! I'm parked right next to you," I blurted out.

"You're surprised?" Ira muttered, helping Martin from his wheelchair.

As he stood, I was amazed by how tall Martin was. Even though age had bent him, he was at least six feet tall. Ira quickly introduced us and before he could help Martin into the car, Martin turned back to me.

"You should come with us." He spoke slowly and quietly, motioning with his hand toward my car. His eyes smiled as they met mine. I agreed, despite Ira's disgruntled expression.

"Just follow us," Ira said gruffly.

"I know where Martin lives. I'll ride with you," Billy volunteered. Ira shot daggers, but Billy was unfazed.

We headed to Southeast Portland and were soon turning into a driveway that sloped down toward a small bluff. On the edge of the bluff was an old mobile home. It was dark, but I was certain down below were railroad tracks and Johnson Creek, both of which wandered from

Gresham to Southeast Portland. If that were true, in the daylight we'd be looking down on an industrial area of mills, quarries and warehouses.

A shiver went through me as I thought of this old medicine man's land. I stopped the car and turned off the lights. The Cadillac was already there.

"Let's go," Billy said.

"Wait. Wait a minute. I'm not sure."

"Sure of what?" he asked.

"This. I don't know. It's just that I don't...I don't know what to do," I whined haltingly. "I've never been around a real medicine man. What's the protocol?"

"The what?" replied Billy, amused and confused by my angst. "Man, just get out of the car." He opened my door and walked off.

I got out, took a deep breath, hurrying to join Billy who was nearly to the house.

"Wait," I said, grabbing his arm as he reached for the doorknob.

"Just pay attention," he whispered as he stepped into the modest home.

The door opened into the kitchen/living room. A woman greeted us. To my right, I could see two or three other women gathered in the living room. To my left, in another large space, a few men gathered around a table. Some sat on the floor, leaning against the wall. Billy said something to the woman and then turned to join the men, taking a seat on the floor. Ira sat at the table. I didn't see Martin.

I froze, not knowing if I was to join the women, none of whom I knew, or the men.

Ira stood up and stepped over to me. "The old man

wants to see you in there," he said, motioning to the back of the room.

The room was L-shaped. Since I couldn't see anything from where I stood, I assumed I'd find Martin around the corner.

"He wants to see me? Why?" I whispered nervously.

"Don't be so disrespectful," Ira said with disgust. "Just pay attention," he growled, returning to his place at the table.

Feeling awkward and misplaced, I walked through the room, past the men, all Lakota. They stared as I walked by; only Billy gave me a reassuring smile.

At the back of the room was a small alcove. A bed, shelves, a chest, a TV and a chair all fit into its very tight space. High Bear sat on the edge of the bed. I stepped forward. He turned his head and smiled, motioning me to sit in the chair. With his long arms stretched, his hands holding the edge of the bed, his head bent and eyes cast down, he sat quietly for what seemed to me an eternity.

In the silence I scanned the room nervously. I had been told to pay attention, but to what, I wondered now. My eyes came to rest on the chest closest to the bed. Stacked in two piles was every book tonight's lecturer had ever written. Their presence in this room was not unlike the awkward sight of a farm boy in last year's suit. I couldn't take my eyes off the books. It appeared, by the placement of a bookmark, that Martin had been reading one. The rest were unopened.

Martin's quiet voice broke the silence.

"Why do you read these?" he asked, bringing me back. "What does this man teach?" He raised his head slightly to look at me.

An old panic gripped my throat. In school I had been the student who prayed the teacher wouldn't call on me. I always felt exposed and vulnerable at those times. And now I had just been called on! A flush rose up in my face. My palms sweat.

"He teaches about our Mother the earth. He speaks of the goddess," I stammered. "I feel hopeful when I read his work. The church doesn't like him. They kicked him out for his teachings, but he wouldn't be silenced. I like him for that," I added, hoping that was sufficient.

High Bear nodded, returning his gaze to the floor.

Another long silence followed.

Feeling awkward in the silence, I blurted out, "The church has never liked me and what I do either."

Martin lifted his head again. Our eyes met. "That white man's church, they do what they have to do," he dismissed. Raising one arm, he pointed to the window. "Out there, there are your teachers. Those old Grandfathers who stand so tall. The four-legged. The winged ones. The ones who crawl and live in the earth and the seas." He paused, looking out at the night beyond the window.

After several moments he looked at me.

"Let's go in there," he said, motioning toward the men gathered around the table. I walked the few steps with him as Ira stood to pull a chair back for Martin. He sat down. I stood, not having a place to sit. Martin motioned to one of the men at the table, who quickly stood and offered me his chair, taking a seat on the floor with the others.

For the next several hours Martin spoke. He told about White Buffalo Calf Woman and how she brought the pipe to his people. He spoke of the prophecy that she would return one day. He talked about the pipe and the pipestone from which it was made. A white buffalo calf had been born on a farm in Wisconsin. Martin showed us pictures of the calf. He spoke of sweat lodge, the *inipi*, and the importance of the sweat. He talked of the ancestors.

By the end of the evening my life had been altered. For the second time since meeting Ira my world took on a new glow. Sometime after midnight the evening ended. I thanked Martin High Bear and bid him goodbye. I did not know then I would never see him again. Nor did I know what a far-reaching effect he was to have on my life.

Thirty-eight

It was December and the holidays loomed. For some reason I felt especially alone. Walking up the stairs to Caroline's office I thought about this group and how grateful I was for each and every one of us. A few weeks earlier, Caroline casually mentioned the group was approaching its fulfillment and perhaps we might consider it was nearing its end.

I smiled, sitting quietly in that padded room, pillows propped around me. I'd arrived early in hopes of some meditative time before the others arrived. I needed to get a grip on this loneliness.

Throughout the four years with Caroline and recovery I had not dated anyone. That in itself was a miracle and a real testament to my "sobriety." Maybe because I'd been hanging out with Ira and his male friends, this loneliness was staring me down. I'd heard it often said at meetings, "If you don't want to slip, stay out of slippery places." Was this a slippery place for me? I needed to check in with my group.

Speaking of my loneliness later, I shared with the group about my evening with High Bear.

"Why Suzy, that's wonderful," Caroline responded.

"I know," I agreed. "But they're all men."

"Oh, that," she said knowingly. "Well, do you want to date one of them? Are you having some feelings for someone?"

"Oh God, no, they're my friends," I quickly replied. "If anything I feel supported. They seem to really care about me." A lump formed in my throat. I swallowed hard.

"Has there ever been a man in your life who saw and accepted you just the way you are?" Caroline's voice, speaking softly now, urged me even deeper into myself. "A man whose interest in you was out of friendship and nothing more?"

By now tears were falling as I searched my mind. "You mean besides my dad?" I asked, sounding almost childish. "Only my gay friend, Steve, and my mentor, Bob Finnell," I said finally, with a laugh.

Wiping my tears now, I looked around the group.

"Well, then it sounds like you're having a new experience," Caroline said simply.

"So, I'm doing okay?" I asked, again sounding like a child.

"Suzy, I really trust that you know how to take care of yourself now. If things get uncomfortable, you know your way home," she said matter-of-factly.

As had happened so often, Caroline's words gave me courage.

"But what about the loneliness? It's like an ache in me," I said.

"Loneliness is never a good reason to seek relationships," Caroline cautioned. "I call it 'the warm-body syndrome.' The 'somebody- anybody' crap that gets us in big trouble." After a long pause, during which she seemed deep in thought, Caroline spoke again.

"Be careful here. This is part of your addiction to relationships. Try just being with the loneliness. I know a sort of panic sets in at the idea of just being in it," she said, reading my mind. "But I wonder if there isn't a gift in it too."

I nodded. I knew she was right. This was a big place in me. It felt like a bridge I had never quite been able to cross, a swinging rope bridge above a deep canyon.

Again, as if reading my mind, Caroline said, "Just don't look down."

Holidays are different when you're alone. Everyone is coupled. Or so it seems. Caroline's words to just "be with the loneliness" gave me a new view of the holiday frenzy.

Sharing coffee with Ira in mid-December, we were chuckling over all the holiday Hallmark moments when he blurted, "Hey, come run with me in the morning. You got running shoes?"

"Yes, but...."

"Good then, meet me at Mary Young," he said as he stood to leave. "Be there at 10:00 sharp," he ordered over his shoulder, as the door slammed behind him.

Marcia snickered as she wiped down the counter.

"Got a real way about him," she said.

"Yeah," I said rolling my eyes.

"Don't forget to stretch," she grinned.

Ira was at the park when I pulled up the next morning. He looked up from his stretching.

"Good to see you," he said, standing up. He sized me up for a moment, then said, "Let's go."

Though it was late December we hadn't had much rain so the park was mostly dry. We headed off down the paved trail toward the river. At the bottom of the hill we veered to follow a gravel path. Just before it ended at the river, Ira took off on a narrow dirt path that crossed a wooden foot bridge. Up to this point the run had been easy. We'd talked as we ran. After the bridge, however, the trail went straight up, rounding a corner and up again.

I watched as he scooted up the trail ahead of me. He's like a damn mountain goat, I thought, barely able to breathe. At the top Ira waited, continuing to run tauntingly in place.

"Come on, you can do it," he yelled down.

My legs were on fire. I was certain they had fallen off. They felt like dead weight. My chest hurt. Breathing hurt. Everything disappeared. It was just me, my legs, my breath and this hell of a hill. I cursed this man dancing like a leprechaun at the top. He was 13 years older than I! I couldn't quit. But I was sure I was dying.

I glanced up, wondering if I could trust him to carry my dead body back to the car and call 911. He seemed to be saying something.

His words broke through my fog of pain. "...I know you can. Come on, honey. You've almost got it now. You can do it. You're doing it. Damn, you're doing it!"

Suddenly, the most amazing thing happened. From somewhere deep inside I began to feel a new energy. It was like a power surge, starting in my legs and rising up to my breath. I could breathe again! I was nearing the top of the hill. Just a few more strides and I'd be there. What was going on? I could breathe! I could feel my legs.

Reaching the top, I flashed Ira a triumphant smile as he patted my back.

"You did it, honey. You did it!" he exclaimed.

I didn't stop at the top. I felt I could run forever. Ira moved on ahead, setting a new pace. As he moved around me, grinning, he said, "Now you're a runner. You got your second wind."

I'd heard runners talk about this second wind, but the few times I'd attempted running, I'd hit that God-awful wall and quit. No one told me to push through. I thought I just couldn't run.

The exhilaration I felt throughout the rest of that first run was euphoric, intoxicating. I was hooked.

Later, as we walked to cool off, Ira chuckled and said, "Hey, that's better than sex!"

"Yeah and safer too. When can we run again?"

Ira and I continued to run several times a week. Occasionally others would join us. Usually it was his Sioux friends who were preparing for vision quest or sundance. These times were especially moving. After our runs we'd meet for coffee and conversation. I felt like an outsider, privileged to sit in.

It was during one of these conversations that Billy spoke up. "So when are you setting up your sweat lodge again?" he casually asked Ira.

Ira looked at the floor.

"Sundance is just a few months away," added one of the others, hoping to give his friend a nudge.

Ira didn't respond. The moment felt awkward. Slowly he raised his head. Looking around the table at each of us he said with a slight smirk, "So when do we run again?"

Later Billy told me that High Bear had given Ira permission to use his altar for the sweat lodge. Over the last few years the lodge had been up and down several times.

"Do you think he'll put it back up?" I asked Billy.

He shrugged. "Who knows about Ira? He always has his reasons."

I sensed it might be a political issue. After all, Ira was still a white guy.

To my surprise I was soon running significant distances. At first it was a couple of miles, then I graduated to four to five. Frequently I would end my run by the river and walk the mile home. I realized that for the first time in nearly 30 years I was playing outside again. My hair smelled of the fresh outdoors, just like when I was a kid. My body had a new vitality. Friends commented on the glow in my face and the youthfulness in my step.

I mentioned this to Ira as we sat by the river after a five-mile run.

"Yeah, you're looking pretty good," he said. After a few minutes, though, he went on. "You know, that Great Spirit of ours created us athletic. We are natural athletes, just like the rest of creation."

As he spoke a young boy and his dog ran past, the boy laughing as the dog barked, chasing him.

"See there," Ira smiled. "But we became arrogant and lethargic. We believe we can think our way through life." Motioning with his eyes toward the boy, he went on, "Children sit in front of TVs and computers for hours. What do we think we're doing, allowing that? I'll tell you, what we're doing is unnatural. Soon the body will just quit and we'll become nothing but big heads," he said, making a comical gesture with hands and face.

I laughed.

He looked at me and then toward the Canadian geese easing down on the quiet river.

"It's a whole new form of insanity." His voice was so low I could barely hear him.

We sat quietly. These silences had become magical to

me, full of understanding and connection.

"Did you know that this spot where these two great rivers join, right here where we're sitting, was a summer camp for the native people who once lived here?" As he spoke, he stood up.

I smiled. I so appreciated this man who'd come into my life so unexpectedly. My smile, however, must have disarmed him.

He stepped back, hands on hips. "What's the matter with you?" His voice was gruff now.

I turned my smile to the geese squawking below.

"See ya later then," he said, stepping onto the road toward his home.

One morning, running alone past a deeply forested property, I spotted a deer grazing. Hearing me, she raised her head and struck a pose. Soon I was within a few feet of her. As I ran past, she took up a trot, pacing me for perhaps a tenth of a mile. We ran nearly side by side until she picked up her speed, darting in front of me and into the woods.

Running has given me an amazing connection with my community, and not just with the flora and fauna. Strangers wave. Some speak to me at the grocery store or coffee shop, saying they see me out there running.

The strangest encounter, however, happened on an eight-mile run. I was half way out. I'd just run under the freeway and into a long, open stretch. Grassy fields met the road here, where occasional rural mailboxes stood their posts.

Running past one of these boxes, I noticed an old woman on the opposite side of the street. She seemed out of place. Maybe picking up her mail, I thought. She stopped to watch me go by. She was disheveled, with stringy white, uncombed hair and an old blue shawl thrown haphazardly over her shoulders.

Suddenly, lifting her cane and pointing it at me, she screamed, "This is good for you! It's good that you run!"

"Nutty old woman," I thought, grateful that we were on opposite sides of the road. I took a few more strides then looked back at her. She was gone- completely vanished! I looped back to where she'd stood. There was nothing but open fields, nothing to duck into or hide behind. I continued my run, puzzled.

Later I shared this event with Ira. He listened thoughtfully until I finished my story.

"You need to sweat," he said brusquely.

This time I didn't object.

Thirty-nine

A few days later Ira phoned. "Grab an old dress and a towel. Come pick me up about 5:00. We'll go sweat."

"But I don't think I'm ready…."

"Good. See ya then." He hung up.

For the rest of the day I was distracted by fear. I'd heard so much about sweat lodge I was more than a little intimidated. When I got to Ira's, he was waiting on the back steps. He stood as I pulled in the driveway.

"Hey," he greeted me, getting in the car with a rolled-up towel in hand.

"Where are we going?" I asked.

He looked at me, exasperated that I continued to ask such inane questions.

"Turn right on the highway."

Except for sporadic directions, we rode in silence. Soon the suburbs were left behind. An occasional barn and farmhouse and fields fenced and cross-fenced became the pleasant backdrop for this anxious journey.

"Ira, I don't know what to do," I said nervously the further we drove. "You could at least tell me what to expect." I glanced over at his stoic presence.

"Turn here," he said suddenly. He pointed to a long dirt driveway that led past a large, decrepit white farmhouse. Near a shabby barn, cars had gathered.

"Park there," he ordered, pointing. I pulled in next to a blue van. Shutting off the car, I turned to face him.

"You've got to tell me what to expect," I demanded.

He sat still a moment, staring out the window. "Just pay attention," he finally said.

"But what if I get too hot?"

He turned to face me. "You pray."

"What?!"

"You pray."

"But what if I'm still too hot?" Panic took hold.

"Then you pray harder."

"But what if I nearly pass out?"

"You lie down and hug your Mother."

"I don't know what you mean."

"We're through talking. Get your things."

He waited for me as I, trembling, grabbed my towel and dress. We walked past the cars and barn. Down below at the foot of a small hill, a fire burned in an open pit. Twenty or so people were gathered around it. As we approached, several of them acknowledged Ira.

We sat behind the group on a log. To our right was a small hut-shaped tent.

"Is that...."

Ira nodded.

Now I was really nervous. No way would we all fit in that small lodge.

"Is that normal...."

Ira cut me off with a wave of his hand. He was looking beyond the fire at a small lean-to, where four or five men stood. One, an Indian wearing a cowboy hat, looked intently at Ira. Ira offered a curt smile. The Indian nodded, then turned and said something to the group of men. He appeared to be the leader. One of the men glanced our way.

"Who's that?" I whispered.

"He pours the water," Ira said, discreetly talking down toward the ground. Reaching out, he picked up a small stick at his feet.

"When do we go in?"

"Soon. You'll need to go change with the other women." His voice was kinder now.

I began to relax.

I looked back at the lean-to. The cowboy hat was watching us. Something about him scared me, but I brushed it off as part of my fear of the evening.

"Ira, I have to go to the bathroom," I whispered.

He stood up.

"C'mon. I'll walk you down there," he offered. A port-a-potty was set up at the end of the path. When I finished, to my surprise Ira was still waiting.

"We're leaving," he said gruffly.

"What?" I exclaimed in disbelief.

We drove home in silence. I tried to engage him in conversation once or twice, but he waved me off, staring out the window.

Finally, as we neared his house, he spoke. "Hey, thanks for the ride."

"Ira, why did we leave?"

"Some things aren't meant to happen. You pay attention and you learn. That place was dangerous for you tonight," he said protectively.

I swallowed hard. The man in the cowboy hat forced his way into my mind.

"Hey, why don't you come over about 10:00 or so and bring a couple of mochas?" Ira's voice on the other end of the line sounded unusually cheerful.

"Sure. What's up?" I asked, surprised by the call.

"See you then," he said as he hung up.

Ira's house was at the bottom of a steep hill by the river. He owned several acres of pasture, two or three old out-buildings, a well-kept garden and a modest but comfortable home. From the top of the hill, I could see him and Billy in the back pasture. It looked like they were cutting wood. I parked the jeep along the narrow road.

With the requested mochas in hand, I negotiated the heavy old pasture gate, following a rutted trail made by years of truck tires. Or in this case, maybe wagon wheels, I thought.

"Suzanne!" Billy called out.

I smiled, lifting a mocha-laden hand in response to his wave.

Ira looked up with a grin.

"Good to see you," he greeted slyly.

"What are you two up to?" I asked, scanning their work area.

"Ira's decided to put up the *inipi*," Billy grinned, using the Lakota word for sweat lodge.

"Oh," I replied, wishing I could sound as enthusiastic as Billy.

"Have a seat," Ira said, pointing to a bench made of log and stone.

"Thanks for the mochas," he said as I sat down. "How thoughtful of you."

For the next hour or so I watched as they prepared the skeleton of the lodge. Finally I had to go.

"I have to work, you guys," I said brushing myself off as I stood up. Ira, busy with the work, glanced at me.

"We'll sweat tonight. Come back about 3:00," he said, adding, "It's important that you're here."

"See you later," I said as I turned to walk back to my car. I had several clients to see over the next few hours. To my surprise, as the day went on, I found myself looking forward to the evening.

A few minutes past 3:00 p.m. I drove down the hill to Ira's. The winter sun was setting later, but still early. The evenings were cold. Smoke rose from his pasture. A few feet to the east of the fire sat a small igloo-shaped lodge. I parked again in the same spot. This time, however, walking the rutted trail toward the bench where I had sat earlier in the day, a different feeling rose up to meet me.

I was walking a sacred path. I felt older, wiser, closer to nature and Spirit. I felt my ancestors rising up in me, taking their place inside my present and accompanying me home.

Something had definitely changed.

Ira was tending the fire. He looked up and quietly acknowledged my approach. Between the fire pit and the lodge, an eagle feather and some red and yellow ties blew in the wind. They were attached to a long pole. I felt humbled. I was seeing Martin's altar.

Squeezing the beach towel and sweat dress I held in my hands as if grasping a lifeline, I sat down on the log bench.

Ira stirred the fire, sending sparks high into the air. Next to the fire pit was a pile of large river rocks. A quiet reverence permeated. Sparks crackled and flew again as Ira threw more wood on the fire, and then came to sit beside me. We spoke quietly for a few minutes and then he stood up.

"I have to go in the house for a while," he said.

I watched him walk away and then returned my gaze to the fire. The sun had given way to evening. A February chill hung in the air. I looked at the hills surrounding our little community; lights twinkled in the upscale suburban homes that had spilled over the hillsides in recent years. I imagined families arriving home to their TVs, computers and microwave dinners. As my eyes scanned the hills, a movement caught my attention. The feather was blowing with the wind again.

I realized the irony in the contrast of these two sights. Here I sat in the midst of modern suburbia, alongside a primitive sweat lodge, a pole signifying a medicine man's altar and a fire set to warm the stones. In that powerful moment of awareness, the disparity and collision of worlds, modern and ancient, overwhelmed me. I smiled, grateful for this time and place and feeling a bit covert about this ancient ceremony.

A twig snap behind me interrupting my musings. I turned to see Billy and another man approaching.

"Hey Suzanne," Billy greeted me warmly. "This is my brother, Ron."

Ron nodded, taking a seat on an old stump to my left. Billy took up his place next to me. No one spoke as the fire quietly drew us back into it.

Soon Ira returned and began arranging the stones into the deep coals of the fire's belly. Billy reached for the bag he'd placed next to him, removing a few items and his drum. He moved to a spot near the altar, removing the tie that held his long hair in place. Kneeling, he began drumming.

Ira sat next to me and in a hushed tone suggested I change my clothes. He motioned to a spot beyond some tall firs. In the twilight I could see the silhouette of an old cow shed beyond the trees. I nodded, gathering up my bundle. It was time.

In the shed, I quickly slipped on my old dress. As Ira had instructed, I also removed anything that would get hot such as earrings, rings and metal clasps. Fear made me fumble. When I returned to the fire the men were wearing towels and swimming trunks. Billy began to sing.

Resuming my seat, I soon found myself mesmerized by the drumming and song. Illuminated by the fire's glow, long hair flowing over his dark shoulders, Billy was a picture out of the past. Time had collapsed. I was drifting.

"Hey!" Ira whispered.

Startled, I looked up. He motioned for me to stand. He held a small bundle of what looked like twigs. With a stick he reached into the fire. The stick flamed to life and he used it to light the bundle. He blew on the bundle, encouraging the sparks and creating smoke.

"What's that?" I asked.

"Smudge," he replied. "Raise your arms."

With the smudge in one hand, he began fanning the smoke it created with a feather held in his other hand. He continued fanning the smudge smoke up and down my body, motioning me to turn. When he was done, he turned to Ron and did the same. He continued on with Billy, who, in turn, did the same for Ira.

"It cleans you off," Ira said, extinguishing it now.

He then turned to the altar, saying something I couldn't hear, and began walking slowly around the lodge clockwise. The other two followed. I stepped in behind. Slowly we halted before the altar at the entrance of the *inipi*. Ira turned solemnly to the four directions, stopping to quietly salute each one. Then he saluted up and down, bending low as he entered the lodge. I watched nervously as Billy and Ron did the same. Following their gestures, I bent low and crawled into the lodge.

In the darkness, I could see a large pit in the center. Crawling to the space left for me, I took my seat in the south, crossing my legs and placing my towel beside me. Ira, who was seated at the entrance, crawled back out. Using two large sticks as tongs he began bringing in the hot stones, placing them gently in the pit. In all, he brought in seven stones.

Returning to his place at the entrance, he pulled the door flap closed behind him and began speaking. It was pitch black inside the lodge now.

"These are the stone people," he said softly. "We come into this lodge to pray. We invite the ancestors in to help us. We come to pray and to be cleaned off. *Ho, mitákuye oyás'n.*"

It was so dark I couldn't see Billy who was sitting beside me a few feet away. He began drumming softly. Then I heard water being ladled from a bucket. The next sound was the water hitting the stones, followed by a loud hissing. More water, more hissing and then a wave of steam washing over me. I was taken off-guard by the hissing and the steam. My heart pounded furiously. I began to pray.

Please God, don't let me die here, I thought.

More drumming, more water, more hissing. After about 20 minutes, it all stopped. The door of the lodge opened and Ira crawled out. The steam escorted him out.

I could breathe again. Billy and Ron looked across at me. That wasn't so bad, I thought.

"The steam carries our prayers to Eagle, who carries them to the Great Spirit," Billy explained. Then Ira returned, bringing in more stones.

"Seven more stones," Billy said. "We do four rounds, seven stones each round."

"Doesn't it get really hot?" I asked anxiously.

He grinned. "Yeah," he said. "That's what your towel is for. You put it over your head so you can breathe. And," he said, "you pray."

Ira placed the last stone and closed the entrance again. Blackness followed.

"This round we sing and welcome the ancestors who join us," Ira instructed.

Again the sound of water hitting stones, the hissing, the wave of hot steam. The heat increased. I prayed.

Before I knew it, Ira was opening the door again. Out went the steam.

"Our prayers," I thought watching it sweep out into the open night.

Seven more stones were brought in. The door flap closed. Darkness. Water. Hissing. Steam.

I was surprised to find myself enjoying the experience. This third round was the prayer round. Ira explained we would take turns praying, either out loud or to ourselves. As I sat listening to each one pray, I quietly gave thanks for my years of 12-step meetings and group.

At the end of our prayer we said *Ho, mitákuye oyás'n* to signify we were done so the next person could pray. This translates to "all my ancestors," which could be said instead.

At the end of the prayer round, water was passed around. It could either be drunk or thrown back to the stone people. The door flap was opened again. I felt grateful for the cool night air rushing in as the steam edged out.

"Our prayers," I thought again, watching it curl up and into the night. Seven more stone people were brought in.

By now the air inside the sweat lodge was hot and thick. I groaned as Ira closed the entrance flap. The prayer round had, however, created such a feeling of sacredness that I was willing to endure one last round.

"This is 'the going home' round. We drum and sing thanks," Ira said with reverence.

Again, the water, the hissing, the waves of steam. I could barely breathe. The towel over my head helped for a while, but I could still feel the heat permeate my face and skin. I prayed.

What had Ira said? "You lie down and hug your Mother." Now I understood. We were seated on carpet remnants on the lodge's dirt floor. Pulling the carpet back, I laid down, placing my face on the cool earth. The cool dampness of our Mother soothed me.

Earth, air, water and spirit. It is what we are. It is all we ever really have in our lives, I thought as I lay there, truly humbled in this awareness. As is the nature of true revelation, words cannot really describe the experience, but in that moment something in me seemed to connect with something very old and very powerful.

"Suzanne," Billy whispered, "it's time to go."

In my earth embrace, I had not noticed the drumming

stop, the door open. I sat up and crawled out of the lodge. The cold night air was like a fresh blanket on my face and shoulders. It was hard to stand straight after sitting for so long.

"Come," Billy said, taking my hand. He led me a short distance, motioning to a spot in the tall, thick grass.

"Lie down. Let our mother care for you," he spoke softly and kindly.

As I lay down he walked back to the fire pit which now burned low, joining the other two who stood speaking in quiet voices. I lay on my back looking at the stars and the nearly full moon. Wispy clouds hurried past the moon's face, remnants of an early morning rain. The ground was damp and soft. Billy was right. Her soothing touch gave tender comfort after the heat of the sweat lodge. I could feel myself drifting up to the stars on old childhood memories of sleep-outs with friends. Drifting....

"Hey!"

My star journey was aborted by Ira's rough voice. He loomed over me. Our eyes met and I saw a slight smile.

"You need to join us. We're not done yet," he said, then walked back the few feet to the fire.

"Thanks for the hand," I muttered, pushing up with unsteady arms.

The men gathered around the altar. I stepped in to the circle where Ira was holding a pipe, tamping the bowl and preparing to light it.

The pipe...High Bear had told of White Buffalo Calf woman and the pipe. I felt the grip of anxiety.

"I don't smoke," I blurted.

Ira's glare silenced me.

"This is Martin High Bear's altar. We smoke the pipe

outside the lodge," he explained, ignoring my comment.

Lighting the pipe, he took a few smokes and then ceremoniously passed it to Billy. Reverence entered our small circle. Once again my eyes absorbed the twinkling lights of the suburbs. If they could see me now, I thought randomly the lines of the song Shirley MacLaine sang in her movie *Out on a Limb* going through my mind.

I took the pipe from Ron, took a quick puff and passed it back to Ira. We were done. My first sweat lodge experience had come to an end.

We sat by the fire afterwards. Billy explained about the pipe, or *chanupa,* being smoked outside the lodge instead of inside. I apologized for speaking out inappropriately. The fire was nearly gone and I shivered. The cold night air meeting my steam-soaked sweat dress brought a chill to my bones. I stood up, pulling the towel over my shoulders.

"Time for me to go," I announced. "Thank you so much for letting me be here with you and for putting up with me." I turned to Ira who was now also standing.

"Good that you could come," he grinned. "We'll sweat every week, probably on Tuesdays. I'll let you know." He paused, adding, "You'll see the fire."

He was right. Smoke from the fire had been visible from the main road.

"We'll see," I responded noncommittally.

"You'll be here," he commanded.

Tucking my clothes under my arm, I said good-bye to the other two.

Who does that guy think he is telling me what to do? I thought as I drove the short distance home.

Ira was right, of course. As the week passed, I eagerly

looked forward to the next sweat. Soon word got out and each week a few more people would show up for sweat lodge. I and five or six others, always men, were the constants. Occasionally another woman or two would come. I asked Ira why more women didn't attend. He shrugged. This was not a social event.

Sitting around the fire, I'd watch as others arrived, quietly nodded and took a seat. Occasionally after the pipe, folks would linger and chat. I usually left right away, not wanting to break the feeling by visiting.

By April, sundancers began to join us. Ira, in his vague way, had described Sundance to me. Dancers prepare for a year or two before they dance.

"They clean themselves up," Ira explained. "They do sweat lodge and vision quest. They eat right and stay sober. They prepare. We sweat in Martin's altar. They'll join us."

One evening 14 of us sat at the fire. I felt awkward being the only woman. Of the 14, 10 were sundancers, the scars on their chests and backs telling the tales of past dances.

Ira came and sat beside me.

"I feel out of place. Maybe I should leave," I said quietly, leaning in close to him so no one else would hear. His gaze never left the fire. When he didn't respond I thought he hadn't heard me. He was, most conveniently at times, deaf in one ear. As I tried to recall which ear, he spoke, still staring at the fire.

"You'll stay. This is your lodge too."

Okay then, I thought, taking my place to circle the *inipi*.

Two men remained by the fire. One was the designated fire-keeper who brought the stone people in between rounds. The other was a very old, blind man in a wheelchair.

Tonight felt special. After the stones were brought in and the door flap closed, the men began drumming. There were 10 drums in all.

I appreciated the darkness inside the *inipi* because the smile on my face was sheer bliss; the drumming and song carried me to a vast unknown place of deep serenity. In short, I was blown away. To my surprise more stones than usual were brought in between rounds, nine stone people each round, totaling 36 stones. I was able to remain upright through the prayer round which lasted longer than usual.

Just before my turn to pray the most remarkable thing occurred. I'd been told fascinating stories about metaphysical events taking place in the *inipi*. I'd also been told, more times than I could count, to pay attention, especially during sweat lodge.

To my amazement and bewilderment, during one man's prayer, Eagle flew through the lodge. Quite literally. I both felt and heard the flapping of wings. It came so near my face I instinctively jerked my head back. It seemed to circle, starting in the east.

My mind sought a rational explanation, but there was no explanation. It was physically impossible for any of us to perform such a feat. Seating in the lodge was close and tight. The pit with the stone people took up the entire center of the lodge leaving only a narrow space to sit between the pit and the walls. There was no room to walk or move around. The eagle had to fly over the pit. It was impossible. I was awestruck.

I began praying quietly, so absorbed in the event I didn't hear my cue to pray aloud.

"*Ho, mitákuye oyás'n,*" the Sundancer next to me repeated. I kept my prayer brief, praying for my young cousin who'd recently died.

Soon the door flap opened, ushering in the cool night air, carrying our prayers to Eagle. The fire's glow offered some light into the *inipi*. I looked around, hoping to see a feather fan, anything, that might explain what just happened. There was nothing. Only the hot and silent faces of each man holding his own sacred space.

Nine more stones joined us. The flap closed. This would be the last and hottest round. As the drums and singing began, I placed the towel over my head for respite from the heat. Soon I had to lie down. With each pour of the water, the heat became unbearable.

Please stop, I thought with each new hiss of the water on stones. The coolness of our Mother's face brought small relief tonight. I prayed harder. Finally the flap opened.

Following the others, I crawled out, and unable to stand, kept crawling a few feet away to collapse in the cool dampness of the field. I was not alone. Several others lay nearby soothed by our Mother's embrace. After a while I heard them rise and slowly walk back to the altar. It was time for the pipe. I stood carefully, my legs unsure. Standing in the circle watching Ira prepare the pipe, my mind still reeled from the eagle experience.

I heard one man whisper softly to another, "Did you feel Eagle fly through?"

The other nodded.

I was bursting inside. Oh, my God. They felt it too! I was barely able to be still. The pipe was passed, the ceremony was concluded. Eager to talk to Ira, I lingered by the fire. Everyone else remained as well.

Oh well, it can wait, I thought, feeling the night chill settle around my shoulders. I gathered my things, not wanting to disturb Ira who was talking with two of the sundancers.

"Hey," he said, seeing me walk away. "See you later."

I waved in response and kept walking.

The next morning Ira showed up at Marcia's for coffee. We sat in our usual corner by the window. I didn't wait for morning pleasantries.

"Ira, you won't believe what happened to me in sweat lodge last night," I burst out.

He sat back, like my words had hit him.

"Ahhh," he said, with an understanding nod. "Now, you listen here," he said, leaning in and tapping his finger on the table for emphasis, "what happens to you in there is for you. I don't want to hear about it." He waved a dismissive hand and turned to stare out the window.

We continued to sweat through the summer. From time to time something amazing would happen, which I would keep to myself.

Ira said, "It's our damn ego that wants to talk about these things...to chew them up and spit them out. But things that happen in the *inipi*...they are meant for the soul. We don't talk about that stuff. It's damn personal. It's between us and that Great Spirit. The ego would send us out with these stories to tell how great or special we must be. We're not special. We're pathetic in our spiritual greed and neediness. What happens in there, stays in there."

In midsummer, I experienced another magical moment of sweat lodge that was shared by another. A friend's 18-year-old daughter, Sasha, had heard me talk about going to sweat, and asked if she might go. After clearing it with Ira, I told her to meet me at my place and I'd take her along. She arrived punctually, towel and dress in hand.

"Hi," Sasha grinned as I met her at the door. "I'm kinda nervous."

I smiled back. "Yeah, I know." I thought back to that day in February. It seemed like years instead of months earlier.

"Get in," I said, motioning to the jeep. "I'll explain a few things as we drive."

She was most concerned about getting too hot. I told her what Ira told me, adding, "If you really feel scared or near death, just say 'All my ancestors.' Ira will open the door and let you out."

I'd only seen this happen once. A woman with claustrophobia panicked about 10 minutes into the sweat. Ira had kindly taken her out, talked with her a few minutes and let her sit by the fire. When the door opened for the second round she rejoined us, remaining for the entire sweat.

"'All my ancestors?'" Sasha asked. "Why that?"

"Huh? Well you could say *'Ho, mitákuye oyás'n* instead," I laughed.

She rolled her eyes. "Yeah, right."

I thought about the significance of inviting in the ancestors. I'd become aware not only of their presence but the fact that I am all of my ancestors. They line up with me in sweat lodge and I am all of them extending from the past into the present and reaching on into the future. The knowledge is not only powerful but reassuring. My lineage extends through me, like it or not. Until sweat lodge I'd never considered this. In the *inipi* they come to be present with us and pray. They teach as well as learn from that invitation. We honor them. In return we receive our grounding roots, our history.

Smiling at this thought, I parked the car.

"What?" Sasha asked. "You're smiling."

"Yeah, let's go," I replied, stepping out of the car. That night was a group of 10 or 12 people. I was grateful there were no more. The day had been warm. The lodge would be hot. I could feel Sasha's excitement as we crawled into the *inipi*.

For the most part the night's sweat was like all the others. There were a few sundancers and even a couple of other women.

Toward the end of the third round, Sasha lay down. In the fire's glow when the door flap opened, I could see she was fine.

The stone people were brought in, the door closed and the heat quickly rose. I lay down. Within minutes after resting my face on our Mother's cool skin, I heard something, faint at first and becoming louder. I could hear the soft, rhythmic pounding of a heart. Thinking it might be the pulsing of my own heart in my ears, I lifted my head off the ground. I could still hear it. It was coming from deep inside the earth.

Our mother's heartbeat, I thought in disbelief. My God, she has a heartbeat. She is alive.

I lay there afraid to move, afraid it would stop. Too soon the round was over. We crawled out and I motioned Sasha to follow me. We lay side by side in the cool field grass looking up at the stars. I didn't want to speak. Sasha broke the silence.

"Suzanne," she whispered, "I heard the earth's heartbeat in there, when I was lying down."

"I know," I whispered back.

We rode home in silence. At the house Sasha hugged me. "Thank you, Suzanne. It was awesome," she said sincerely.

"No, thank you," I replied, knowing that I'd been given the gift of validation tonight.

Forty

"Hi, Suzanne. It's Jeanne."

Jeanne's voice on the other end of the line was always a welcome relief. It usually meant fun, mischief and sometimes even a road trip. We'd become great friends through the last few years.

She'd also frequently call about cases she was working. One fall it had been about Susan Smith, a woman who claimed someone had stolen her car and kidnapped her children. She had tearfully pleaded on TV for their safe return. As I watched her on the news, I *saw* the image of Diane Downs; this Oregon woman had made the same plea years earlier and was later arrested for the murder of one of her children and the attempted murder of her other two children, crimes committed because her boyfriend wanted her but not her children.

"Oh no, it can't be," Jeanne groaned, catching the implied parallel when I'd told her what I had *seen*.

Days later Susan Smith confessed, leading police to the lake which held the car and her little boys' bodies still snugly fastened in their child seats.

"This job really sucks," we commiserated later yet still thankful for friendship it had provided us.

"So, what's up?" I asked.

"How would you like to join me for a few days? I'm moving soon and could sure use some help. Besides, we need a girls' weekend before I go," she said enthusiastically.

"Yeah, I know," I responded, with less enthusiasm. I hated to see her move. Though she lived in the desert a few hours from Portland, we got together frequently. It would be harder with a plane trip between us.

"Okay, when?" I asked, checking my calendar. We arranged a three-day weekend for the following week.

"I love the desert smells," I thought, sitting on Jeanne's deck. The day's heat mingled with the soft desert breeze brought the scent of the earth and pine to our evening repose. Wind chimes sounded gently. From the living room, Sheryl Crow sang about her "and Billy and the car wash."

"All I want to do is have some fun," I sang along with her.

A tap on the sliding glass door interrupted my performance.

"Hors d'oeuvres, anyone?" Jeanne asked, smiling. I opened the door. There was always a lot to say, stories to be told and much laughter when we got together. By the end of the evening, tears of laughter streaming, I grabbed my face.

"Stop. Stop. My face hurts," I lamented, which only brought more laughter.

"Okay Tiffany," Jeanne said, her words making me bend double. It was a nickname I'd earned on a trip to Colorado, where we'd argued over the lyrics to "Hotel California." The woman at the doorway's mind was "definitely twisted," according to Jeanne. I, however, heard the lyrics as her "name was Tiffany Twisted." Overcome with laughter, barely able to speak, I got the words out, "but-it-IS-Tiffany-Twisted" and the old hilarious argument was on again.

Finally able to catch my breath, I shook my head and smiled across at her.

"I'm going to miss you," I said.

"Me too," Jeanne agreed. Standing abruptly, she began clearing the table. "You gotta look at it this way… At least it will get you on an airplane." She smiled, taking a jab at my fear of flying.

The next morning we busied ourselves with boxes and clean up.

"Let's run down to my storage locker. I have some things to sort through," Jeanne said as she tethered her long hair back into a pony tail.

We took the short drive to the locker.

As she opened it, I asked, "What do you want me to do?"

"Just help me keep things sorted," Jeanne replied. "God, I hate moving."

For the next 20 minutes we busied ourselves. Then she handed me a large, gold-framed picture.

"I'm not sure what to do with this."

I took it, stepping back so I had room to turn it around. I stopped and caught my breath.

"What?" Jeanne queried.

"It's you," I said quietly.

"Yeah, that would be me," she replied with a shrug.

I was standing spellbound in front of a portrait of a woman in the window of Sorenson's Photography in the John's Landing area of Portland. I was to meet my sister at Billy Bang's for dinner. She had something important to tell me. But I was now late, mesmerized by the portrait of this stunning woman, who seemed so familiar. "She's beautiful," my sister had said when she came looking for me. "But there's something else. I know her," I said, beguiled. I felt my sister tugging at my arm....

"Suzanne?" Jeanne repeated, tugging at my arm, concern in her voice.

"Walter Cronkite" was all I could say.

Jeanne stepped back, hands on her hips.

"Now, I know you're Tiffany," she exclaimed. "What's wrong? Where are you?"

"Did this picture ever hang next to one of Walter Cronkite in John's Landing?" I asked.

"Yes, years ago. But why?"

After a moment I said, "It's the most amazing thing. I'll tell you later."

"Good," she said, "you had me worried there for a minute. No one's ever accused me of looking like Walter Conkite before!"

Driving home the next day over Mt. Hood, my mind drifted with the twists and turns of the mountain road. I loved this drive among the tall firs. It had been hard telling Jeanne goodbye, but as she'd said, "Distance can't separate good friends." Besides I'd promised to visit her in a few months.

"You know your way home." Caroline's words again echoed as I thought of my little house waiting for me on the other side of this mountain.

"Look at what you've done," I said out loud, thinking of my home and business and the friendships that had come through my work. None of it would have happened had I remained in my old life. If ever I needed proof of a Higher Power, this life was proof enough.

And the perfection of it all, I mused, thinking of the portrait I'd stood before 20 years ago. When I'd held it in my hands yesterday, I felt the hand of God on my shoulder, reassuring me of a plan, a plan for my life. And all I had to do was listen to myself, honor my feelings and show up for it. I shook my head at the simplicity and complexity of it all.

"Trust the perfection," I spoke out loud, hoping to imprint this moment of awareness on my soul.

Later that week in group I eagerly shared this story. As the women laughed and shared in my amazement, I turned to Caroline. "It was as if something had come full circle in my life."

After a few moments of silence she spoke. "It is time for us to think about doing closure with this group." Caroline's solemn words fell hard.

We sat in silence. No one wanted to be the first to speak. To my astonishment, what she said felt right. I looked at the others, wondering how we would fare without each other.

One of the women said with resignation, "When?"

It was nearly the end of summer. "How about the 31st?" Caroline suggested, looking at her calendar.

"August 31st," she said looking up at each of us.

"You mean in two weeks?" someone asked.

I began to feel panic. A date had been set. We spent the rest of our time talking about how we all felt. In spite of the fear, we all agreed it was time.

Forty-one

It was 6:00 a.m. From the fog of sleep, I heard a phone ring.

"Hello," I answered in the dream. It kept ringing. Confused, I held the receiver in my hand. It rang again. I sat upright. It rang again; this time I answered.

"Hello," I said again, my heart pounding. No one calls at 6:00 a.m. unless it's a crisis.

"Mom." My son's voice sent an alarm through my entire being. He had been hired by the sheriff's office, and was now in a patrol car on his own. Being a novice, he'd been assigned a rural area no one else wanted, an area known for its marijuana grows and redneck survival mentality.

"Mom," he repeated with urgency.

"My God, are you okay?" I answered.

"Yeah, yeah," he reassured me. "Quick. Is there a woman and is she dead?"

"What?!"

My son the pragmatist usually pooh-poohed what he called "that psychic stuff."

"You're kidding," I said sourly.

"No. Quick. C'mon. What do you *see*?" he insisted.

I took a deep breath to regain myself.

"Well?" he pushed.

I closed my eyes until images appeared.

"Yes, there's a woman. She's hiding. She's scared. There are drugs and a knife," I reported.

"Where's she hiding?"

"In the woods. She's crouched down. Pulled branches or leaves down around her." I stopped *seeing* and demanded, "What's this about? You don't believe in this stuff. Why are you calling me?" I was irritated by the rude awakening.

"I know," he admitted, "but my buddy does."

He explained he'd been called to a rural convenience store. Around 3:00 a.m. a man had pulled up in a small pickup truck camper. After the man bought cigarettes, the clerk noticed he was pacing in the parking lot. After a lengthy time the clerk alerted the police. My son arrived and questioned the man, who seemed extremely anxious. My son looked through the windows of the truck. He saw a woman's clothing and a woman's shoe. The man denied having a woman with him. Knowing there was a nearby riverside park where people often went to drink or do drugs, my son called for back-up from the local police. His shift was nearly over and he wanted to hand the call to the locals.

As it turned out, the buddy he referred to was the local cop who'd lamented, "What we need is a psychic." My son just happened to know one.

"I'll pass this information on to John. He really believes in this stuff. Thanks, Mom. See you later."

Later that day John called.

"Excuse me, ma'am," he began.

I listened, wondering why cops always say 'ma'am.'

"I just wanted to give you some feedback on what you told your son this morning," he said respectfully. He went on to say they had dragged the river hoping to find a body.

"But because of what you'd *seen* we also did a grid

search. We found her hiding in the bushes, just like you *saw*. There were needle marks on her arms. She thought we were him. He told her he was going to get a knife and come back to kill her. She was strung out and scared."

He paused and then repeated, "Thank you, ma'am. I do appreciate the work you do. When I was a kid, my mom always went to psychics."

His enthusiasm and rare appreciation made me smile.

Forty-two

I'd just finished a long morning run and was walking back from the river to cool off. I was running alone more often, meeting up with Ira only occasionally. It never ceased to amaze me that I could run long distances. I thought about my first few runs with Ira. That first mile was always the most difficult.

I'd whine about how it was killing me and he'd say in his gruff way, "The first mile's just a warm-up. Quit whining." Now, running alone, I so appreciated I'd had a partner those first few months. I never would have done it alone.

"God, I've come a long way."

As I reached for the back door handle, I heard the phone ring. As I hurried in to catch it, Buddy hurried out, nearly knocking me over. He was getting too old to run the distances with me.

"Damn," I said, tripping on his hind legs. "Sorry, Buddy," I apologized as I lifted the receiver.

"Sorry, what?" Ira's voice asked.

"Hey, what's up? I didn't see you out there on the road today."

"Listen, I just called to tell you that the old man's not doing so good. They took him to the hospital a few days ago."

"Oh," I said, pulling up a chair. "That's not good."

"No, no, it's not good. They've been doing pipe-ceremony for him. It's not good."

"Where is he?" I asked. "Where is the pipe-ceremony?"

"He's at Providence Hospital. They do ceremony right outside his window. Hey, I gotta go," he ended abruptly.

"Thanks."

But he'd already hung up.

The week before at sweat lodge someone said Martin wasn't doing well. He had lung problems, maybe emphysema. Sitting quietly then, I whispered a prayer for him.

It was August 29. In two days we'd be doing closure at group. Letting out a heavy sigh, I stood to stretch.

"God, I should have stayed out on the road longer," I said quietly.

I parked in front of Caroline's office and stared up at the large brown house that had witnessed and embraced me the last five years. August 31 had arrived too soon. Slowly I got out of my jeep and climbed the steps to the large front porch. Well-tended roses bloomed robustly. How many seasons had I passed them, absorbed in my personal angst? I paused, appreciating their beauty, breathing in their fragrance.

Oh, c'mon now. You're not saying goodbye forever, I told myself, my misplaced nostalgia irritating me.

Caroline had been clear that we could continue to see her individually.

I made my way to our pillow room. Two of the other women were already there, sitting quietly, waiting. I took my place, the same place I'd taken the last four years, the unspoken assigned seating.

We could hear muffled voices from the other room, what we called the furniture room.

Assuming it might be a new client with Caroline, I said, "Wonder if they know about the padded room?"

We all laughed.

"Probably not or they wouldn't still be here! Caroline's got to ease them in slowly," one of the other women said.

We laughed again, and then quietly slipped back into our own silences.

I looked around at the padded walls, the large over-stuffed pillows, the little lamp on the floor in the corner, the boxes of tissues. Tears formed as I said, "It's like a womb." Through the years these walls and these women had given birth to me. We had birthed each other. How could we say good bye?

"Hi girls." Caroline's cheerful, confident voice warmed the glumness that had settled on the room. As she took her seat, quick footsteps on the stairs announced the last member of our group. She quietly joined us. She'd been crying.

After a few minutes, Caroline spoke, "What I'd like to do is go around to each of you and say a few things. And then, if you want, you can each have a say."

As she spoke to each of us, her remarks were candid, poignant and sometimes hilarious.

Then she got to me.

"And you, Suzanne, you are completely unrecognizable today. I remember our first meeting, watching you trudge up the stairs, head down, afraid to speak. You were so scared, so weary. Your life was like a weight on your shoulders. Look at you now!" she exclaimed. "I am so proud of you. I have never seen anyone take to their own recovery like you. I'd merely suggest something and you'd have it done the next day." Pride truly reflected in her eyes.

I thought my heart would burst. No one in my 46 years had ever looked at me that way. My tears turned to sobs.

"You are amazing," she said, smiling with pride and fondness.

In turn we each responded to her, speaking both to her and to the group. I have no memory of what I said. There were more tears and hugs. Then we were gone.

Across the street, I started the jeep. My tears had stopped but I still felt dazed. Caroline was right. It was time for us to move on. We'd become redundant. Sentimentality was no reason to stay.

I began my turn out of the parking lot onto the street.

Don't turn right. Turn left, a voice coaxed in my head.

Why left? I argued. Left would take me past Providence Hospital and into the city. I wanted to go home, not to the city.

"Providence," I said out loud, suddenly remembering that was where Martin High Bear had been taken.

I drove the few blocks to the hospital, not knowing what to expect. As I pulled into the parking lot, I saw Ira getting out of his car. I parked next to him. He glanced my way but kept walking.

"Hey," I said, scrambling to catch up with him.

He stopped, turning to face me. "What are you doing here?" he asked gruffly.

"I...I came to honor Martin. To see pipe-ceremony," I answered awkwardly, not knowing for sure why I was there.

He glared for a moment and then said, "I'm going up to his room. I won't be long. Wait here."

I nodded and returned to my jeep. Shortly, he returned.

I jumped out of my car to greet him. "How's Martin?"

Ira looked at me like I was stupid. "He's dying," he replied through tight lips.

We walked through the parking lot, following a sidewalk past the hospital's east wing. At the emergency entrance we stepped onto the lawn, continuing toward the main entrance. As we rounded the west wing, I heard the drumming, softly at first, then louder as we neared a grassy knoll next to the building. Fifteen or 20 Lakota men drummed and sang, all turned toward the building, heads and voices lifted toward a third floor window.

"Martin's room," Ira said softly.

The men honoring their medicine man in their ancient tradition in this urban setting was a powerful sight. I was moved to the core of my being.

I said softly through my tears, "They're singing him home."

I could imagine High Bear lying in his third floor room hearing the familiar songs and voices of his people. It must have brought great peace and comfort.

Soon the drumming stopped.

"Come this way," Ira said, moving toward a circle of about 30 people seated on the lawn. He sat next to a man with a pipe, motioning me to sit next to him. Seven men with pipes sat to Ira's right. After a few more songs, silence fell as the pipes were lit. They were passed to Ira, then to me, then on around the circle. Ira held one pipe tenderly like he was cradling a baby in his arms.

He smoked, then passing it to me he whispered, "Martin's pipe."

It was the pipe he used when High Bear put him on

the hill for vision quest the first time. Martin's pipe. I held it with reverence and awe. As I smoked it, I prayed for High Bear, thanking him for allowing me to sweat in his altar. Then I passed it on. After pipe-ceremony we walked in silence back to our cars.

"See you later," I said to Ira. He waved, not looking back.

I retraced my earlier route and headed home. What a night, I thought, so overcome with feelings from this day of closure and transition that I'd grown numb. My life had come to this amazing convergence: saying good-bye to group and Martin High Bear in virtually the same moment.

Two days later, September 2, 1995, Ira called. "Martin died."

"Thank you," I said to the dial tone.

I sat still for a moment, and then decided to go for a run. I ran down past the woods where the deer had joined me one morning and back up the hill that follows the river. I ran through town past Marcia and Evan's coffee shop. She waved as I ran by. I ran past the grade school and up to the hill overlooking Ira's place, the hill where rising smoke had signaled "sweat tonight" for the last nine months. Running down the hill past the lodge, I saw Martin High Bear's altar lying down in the field; the sweat lodge lay crumpled beside it.

I gasped, nearly falling to my knees. I ran on, down to the boat landing, past the picnic table where months ago I'd been enchanted by stories of Avalon. I ran past children playing in the park. I heard the Canadian geese squawking in the morning sun. I kept running. By now sweat poured from my brow and down my face.

Just like in sweat lodge, I thought. I thought of all my ancestors. I thought of my own grandchildren yet to come.

I run for them. I invite them to sweat with me, here on this road. I smiled now.

"*Ho, mitákuye oyás'n!*" I yelled to the world.

At last I knew my way home.

Acknowledgments

From the first draft to the final edited copy, much like raising a child, it takes a village. I would like to thank my literary village, without whom this book could never have matured.

First and foremost, I would like to thank my re-write coach and publisher, Alina Blankenship. The moment she read the original manuscript she became its champion. Her wit, commitment and enthusiasm kept the project alive and on course.

Liz Halley, for her optimism as she transcribed my long-hand original draft to computer disc.

Lisa Dale Norton and her book *Shimmering Images - A Handy Little Guide to Writing Memoir*.

Randall Fitzgerald, for taking time from his busy editorial work to read and encourage when the doubts crept in.

The art of Steve Hanks. His painting "Like Diamonds in the Sun" became my muse. Many thanks for allowing her to grace the cover of this book.

Laura Foster, for her dedicated copy-edit. She kept the pages flowing.

Kathleen Krushas, whose confidence and connections carried these pages over the top and into print.

My grandson Conner, for his critical voice and good descriptive words.

Dee Togikawa, Jill Spitznass, Judith Vaught, Linda Mraz, Nancy Fox, Christine Miles, Leah Campbell, Sandi Serling, Jeanette Heinz, Tom and Marci Tsohonis, Sally Mercer, Will Goldstein and all the other advance readers.

Finally, my most beloved thanks to Jerry, whose encouragement, patience and understanding lifted these pages through doubts and darkness. He believed when I did not.

Thank you.